Public and
Performance
in the
Greek Theatre

Public and Performance in the Greek Theatre

PETER D. ARNOTT

Routledge
London and New York

First published in 1989
by Routledge
11 New Fetter Lane, London EC4P 4EE
29 West 35th Street, New York, NY 10001

© 1989 Peter D. Arnott

Photoset and printed in Great Britain
by Redwood Burn Limited, Trowbridge, Wiltshire

British Library Cataloguing in Publication Data
Arnott, Peter D., *1931–*
Public and performance in the Greek theatre
1. Ancient Greece. Theatre.
I. Title
792′.0938

ISBN 0–415–02914–7

Library of Congress Cataloging in Publication Data
Arnott, Peter D.
Public and performance in the Greek theatre.
Bibliography: p.
Includes index.
1. Theater—Greece—History. 2. Theater audiences—
Greece—History. 3. Greek drama—History and criticism.
I. Title
PA3201.A77 1989 792′.0938 88–32156

CONTENTS

A NOTE ON SOURCES

This book is intended for the generalist, not for the classical specialist; it is intended, particularly, for those who have an interest in Greek plays as works for performance, rather than as purely literary texts. I have assumed, therefore, no knowledge of ancient Greek, and no familiarity with the traditional apparatus of classical scholarship.

This assumption raises problems of its own. Even the titles of the plays present difficulties. As long as Latin was the primary language of scholarship, it was customary to refer to Greek plays by Latin titles. Some of these have stuck: we still talk easily of *Oedipus Rex* and *Iphigeneia in Tauris*. Hellenic sensibilities, however, have often preferred to give the plays their Greek names; and, more recently, with increasing numbers knowing the works only in translation, English titles have become common. Thus, depending on which source you read, you may find the same play listed as *Hercules Furens*, *Herakles Mainomenos*, or *The Madness of Heracles*. To use one system consistently invites incomprehension. I have therefore tried to use the most familiar form in each case.

The same is true of spelling. Traditional scholarship gave Latin forms to Greek names; modern fashion prefers the Hellenic originals. But although the layman may easily recognize Aischylos as Aeschylus, he may have trouble identifying Aias as Ajax. I have therefore, once again, tried to find the more popular form, at the cost of enormous inconsistency. In practice, this means that characters in plays are normally given in the Latin form which has been perpetuated in most translations, while other names are cited in the Greek form.

Translations themselves present another problem. They proliferate on both sides of the Atlantic; they address different kinds of readership; and they differ in great and small ways. For purposes of reference, therefore, quotations cited in this book (which are in the author's own translations) have line references to the generally accepted numbering of the Greek texts, to which all translations more or less adhere.

It will be obvious that the footnotes and bibliography in no way attempt to reflect the full range of scholarly opinion on any topic. Rather, they indicate merely those works and passages which have influenced my own vision of the Greek theatre as a working playhouse: a vision which, I am happy to say, I have been able to support with forty years of directing and performing Greek plays for English-speaking audiences. In almost every instance, scholarship stops far short of certainty. It remains for the practitioner to suggest what, in theatrical terms, seems most likely. The present volume attempts to make just such an accommodation between the study and the stage.

One brief section has appeared in print before: in 'Some costume conventions in Greek tragedy', *Essays in Theatre* 2, 1 (November 1983).

INTRODUCTION

Plays are conditioned by their environment. Every age produces its handful of closet dramatists, who elect to write in dramatic form as a literary convenience, with no expectation of production; and there are always a few who write for some visionary theatre of the future, asking more than the state of the art can give. But practising playwrights work from a basis of practical stagecraft. They write for the kind of playhouse they know; for actors whose skills and training they are familiar with; and for an audience whose preconceptions are known, and whose responses are predictable. The design of the theatre building, the nature of the space available, the possibility of adapting and decorating this space: all these factors help to shape the play. We would have a very different *Hamlet* had it been written for a picture-frame stage rather than for an open platform. The same factors work upon the actor. The grammar of his art – the way in which he communicates with his audience – may be influenced by tradition or societal patterns, but is controlled in large part by the space in which he works. An actor in a large theatre works differently from an actor in a small one. Indoor and outdoor acting pose different problems, and invite different solutions.

In purpose-built structures, performance style and theatre architecture are often mutually influential. An actor accepts certain constraints upon his art because of the nature of the space available, or the quality of the acoustics; conversely, new buildings may be designed to capitalize on certain skills, or allow the actors to explore new dimensions of their art. In earlier dramatic cultures, however, the space comes first, and imposes its own rules on the performance. The art of the theatre did not spring fully born into the world. In all the manifestations that we know, drama emerged as a by-product of

1

some other activity, usually some magico-religious activity. The first actors were priests, shamans, or sacred dancers, and the emergent dramas were first performed in spaces that had been designed for other purposes. Only after some time does drama establish itself as a separate and independent activity, and only then are buildings constructed specifically for the performance of plays. Almost invariably, these purpose-built theatres are influenced by the temporary spaces available before, to which the performers have now become accustomed. Plays, in other words, come before theatres; and when the theatres begin to appear, they illustrate the factors that brought the drama to birth.

The small group of plays, survivors of a vastly larger number, that we know collectively and rather misleadingly as Greek drama, were written for theatres of a unique and distinctive shape whose like has never been seen again. This shape was dictated by the cultural patterns of Greek society and by the nature of the Greek terrain. Its general features are well known from ancient evidence and surviving examples, a number of them still in use. Scholars argue endlessly, and ultimately unprofitably, about the details. Many features of the theatres remain obscure to us for lack of information. We have no contemporary description of the structures that Aeschylus and Sophocles wrote for and acted in. Probably none was ever written. Why bother to describe something so familiar to everyone? The earliest written accounts date from centuries later, when much had changed and it was already too late. Surviving structures, still amply visible throughout Greece and the adjacent countries, are architectural palimpsests, obscured or obliterated by the successive rebuildings of subsequent generations. We know considerably less about them than we know about Shakespeare's Globe, in spite of the fact that the stonework is still there for us to see.

The general principles, however, are reasonably clear. In the Greek theatre complex the central and characteristic feature was the orchestra or dancing floor, a circle of flattened earth (later paved with stone), on which the chorus performed. In the theatre of Athens the orchestra is large enough to give ample room for a large chorus and complex dance patterns. The Greeks themselves traced the origin of drama from local festivals of song and dance, and the design of the theatre seems to bear this out. It is tempting to think that the earliest orchestras were the stone threshing floors still to be seen throughout the Greek countryside. These floors – in most places the only flat open space available – would lend themselves naturally to the rustic performances. When, in the course of time, a special orchestra was built for larger ceremonies, it would retain the shape of these remembered associations.

Round most of the orchestra, tiers of seats were built into the convenient hillside, so that spectators could look down on the performance. Such a structure, like a vast bowl set into the land, was a logical answer to the constraints of the Greek terrain. In a country where flat land is at a premium, the theatre grew organically out of its environment, opening the performance to the maximum number of spectators. On the far side of the circle stood the actors' place. This was the *skene*, literally hut or tent. In the early days of the theatre this was probably all it was: a rudimentary, temporary structure serving as a dressing room, a place from which the actors could make their entrances and, perhaps, a sounding board for their voices. An alternative theory suggests that the first *skene*, in Athens at least, was the façade of the Temple of Dionysus which abutted onto the orchestra. Even when, like the rest of the theatre, it became a structure of solid stone, the *skene* still retained its original name. On either side of the *skene* a processional entrance-way, the *parodos*, led into the orchestra.

This is all we can be sure of. Everything else is conjecture. Was there a raised stage for the actors, to give them prominence by elevating them above the chorus level? A case can be made for and against. We know that the fifth-century theatre had some machinery. Where exactly was it located, how did it work, and what was it supposed to do? We have tantalizingly brief descriptions, mostly late and sometimes contradictory.

On one aspect of the productions, however, there is fairly general agreement. Although the Greek *skene* gives us, by way of Latin, the English word 'scenery', the fifth-century theatre seems to have had nothing like scenery in our sense of the word: no backdrops, no realistic stage pictures, no scenic illusion. The only background was the façade of the *skene* building, decorated perhaps in architectural perspective but ubiquitous and unchanging. Our first evidence for movable panels to create different sets comes from a century later. The orchestra was a blank surface against which the audience could watch the choral evolutions. Sufficient setting was provided – as in Shakespeare's theatre – by the audience's imagination, prompted by the language of the playwright. Song, dance, and the spoken word provided an ambiance for the play as well as carrying forward the action.

If we have such difficulty in picturing the theatre, how can we hope to reconstruct the actor's, necessarily transitory, performance? Once again, many details elude us. But, equally, certain dominant principles become clear, and we may assume certain imperatives from the nature of the space involved. The following chapters, by focusing on the nature of the Greek actors' art, will endeavour to show how closely intertwined the actions of author, actor, and theatre were, and illuminate some characteristic features of Greek playwriting that seem alien to us only because our conception of stage space and the actor's relationship to it has radically changed.

1

THE AUDIENCE
AND THE CHORUS

Periodically during the late winter and early spring the Athenians assembled to celebrate their festivals of drama. The dates were associated with religious celebrations that had been in existence long before plays were invented. But one practical reason for holding them so early in the year may have been protection for the performers: Greek acting, which involved strenuous physical and vocal effort in mask and costume, was hot work at the best of times. It helped, too, that in the Theatre of Dionysus where the plays were given, the auditorium was south-facing, while the actors had some benefit from the shade. But in the early months the weather was past the worst of winter, and not yet oppressive; though some festivals, we know, were virtually closed events, because the seas were not yet navigable and outsiders could not travel.

There are many things we do not know about the Athenian audience. It is still not certain, for example, whether or not women were admitted (though it is a reasonable surmise that they were). There are important things we do know, however, or about which we can make logical assumptions. The audience was massive in size; the consequences of this, for both playwright and actor, will be considered in a later chapter. It was talkative and unruly. Although drama, for the Greeks, was part of a religious festival, we should not make the mistake of equating this with our own church-going, or the Greek audience with a modern religious congregation, or Sophocles, as H. D. F. Kitto once said, with 'an enlightened bishop'. For us, religious worship tends to be passive. For the Greeks it was participatory, and took many forms. The gods were honoured by human achievement: by athletic meets and boxing matches, by singing songs and acting plays.

We have ample testimony that the Greek audience was hardly a church-going congregation, in our sense of the word. In the early days of the theatre, when the seats were still of wood and not yet of stone, a favourite way of showing disapproval was for the audience to drum their heels against the benches. The effect of this, in a theatre with a huge audience and excellent acoustics, can be imagined. There are numerous stories of audiences disrupting performances by shouting, jeering, throwing fruit, and worse. Aeschylus was once in danger of his life because of some offence he had unwittingly committed; Euripides' tragedy *Ixion* was halted by a crowd outraged by its blasphemy, until the poet had explained that, if the audience was patient, it would see the protagonist's transgressions punished in the end.

The temperament and habits of the audience helped to shape the plays. This is most obvious in comedy, where it is clear that Aristophanes had to work hard, and carefully, to catch his public's attention. Part of the problem arises from the use of an open, naturally illuminated playing area. In a modern theatre we are given ample warning that a play is starting. We are plunged into darkness, the curtain rises, and our attention is focused on one small, brightly lit space. Aristophanes has only his performers to work with. They must enter, small dots in a huge theatre, and secure attention by their own unaided efforts.

In modern open-air theatres, it is possible to quiet the audience with a fanfare or announcement. Whether this happened in Athens we do not know. It is doubtful whether it would have been enough. We see Greek plays in isolation, out of their festival context. For the Athenians the plays were simply one element, though an important one, in a mixed programme. The festival day must have been full of fanfares and announcements. For special attention Aristophanes needs other devices.

Obviously a strong beginning is indicated. Equally obviously it is as well not to proceed too quickly with the main theme of the play, or important exposition may be lost while the audience is settling down. It is safe to assume that the audience for comedy would be more relaxed and jocular than for tragedy. In the Aristophanic prologues a pattern is discernible which appears to be dictated by these factors.

The openings take two main forms. Several of the comedies begin with broad horseplay, fast and noisy to catch the audience's attention. Thus *The Knights* opens with two slaves – caricatures of well-known contemporary generals – running on, complaining that they have

6

been beaten, and weeping loudly together. This familiar low-comedy motif (Aristophanes complained when other playwrights used it, but did so happily himself) offers slapstick opportunities to which the audience would readily respond. *Peace* opens with a similar scene, in which slaves run back and forth with shovels of dung to feed the giant beetle on which Trygaios plans to ride to heaven. Lavatory humour amused the Greeks no less than it does the mass modern audience. *The Birds* opens with two old men staggering over the rocks, tripping, tumbling, and misled by their bird guides.

Alternatively, the comedy begins with a string of topical references and irrelevant jokes. *The Acharnians* opens in such a way. Dikaiopolis, alone, soliloquizes on the miseries of his life. We have jokes about the mob-orator Kleon, feuding with Aristophanes at the time – as the audience would have been well aware – and that 'cold fish' the tragedian Theognis, the composers Moschos and Dexitheos, and the flute-player Chaeris. All this is gossip-column stuff, and has nothing to do with the play. We do not get an inkling of the plot until line forty.

The Wasps opens in the same manner. Again we have two slaves, Xanthias and Sosias. They talk about their dreams, which happen to be about well-known people: Kleon again, the notorious coward Kleonymus, Theoros, one of Kleon's political lackeys, and Alcibiades, the golden boy of fifth-century Athens. All this is funny but irrelevant. When it is over, the play proceeds. In *The Frogs* Dionysus and his slave Xanthias perform what is virtually a vaudeville dialogue, full of familiar patter, vulgarity, and innuendo.

The function of these openings is obvious. They serve to quiet a restless audience, to focus attention on the stage, and to establish a happy actor–spectator relationship. Modern comedians would call them a 'warm-up'. It does not matter if the jokes are not properly heard. All the essential information comes later. Mazon aptly compares these introductions to a barker's patter at a sideshow in a fair.[1] They attract attention, and give a hint of the entertainment to come.

Tragic prologues are more immediately informative. We may surmise, perhaps, that the audience for this portion of the festival was better mannered, and more receptive. Some things, however, may still have been lost. When Aristophanes makes Euripides, in *The Frogs*, complain of Aeschylus' habit of 'raving haphazardly, and rushing into the thick of things',[2] he may have touched upon a genuine flaw in the senior dramatist's method.

There are other generalizations we may make about this audience. Once again, the evidence comes principally from comedy. Athens, by modern standards, was a small town, and the small-town mentality was in many ways no different from what we are familiar with today. In such enclosed communities privacy is limited, difference is suspect, and tastes become parochial. Aristophanes makes many jokes about contemporary individuals. The notables of the state are satirized, as we would expect. Men of the stature of Kleon in the world of politics, Socrates in philosophy, and Euripides in the arts, are developed into major characters. In addition, there are the lesser figures who would still, by modern standards, be considered newsworthy – the personnel of the tragic theatre, for example, actors and playwrights alike, the politicians of the second rank, and even Orestes, the highwayman.

But this by no means exhausts the list. The little men are represented also, and the jokes about them tend to be of the same kind. A man is a fit subject for humour if he is in any way unusual. The smallest departure from the norm is potentially risible. A man may be mocked because he is too fat (Kleonymos) or because he is too thin (Kinesias, Kleocritos); because he tells tall stories (Proxenides, Theagenes) or because of his unpleasant sexual habits (Kallias, Kleisthenes, Lysistratos); for his lack of self-control (Patrocleides) or for his haircut (Kratinos); because he grows his beard (Agyrrhios) or because he has difficulty with his hatplume on parade (Pantakles). The fact that these apparently trivial characters and incidents are considered fit material for humour tells us much about the nature of Athenian society and the popular mode in comedy. It is evident that, at least so far as these personal references are concerned, we are dealing with a limited society whose tastes are essentially parochial. As in small-town humour of all countries and of all ages, any departure from the norm is funny. Most significant of all are the various allusions to foreigners and to resident aliens, such are Exekestides, Sakas, and Spintharos; Aristophanes derides them and expects his audience to do the same. To this group we may add the various personages, sometimes real, sometimes fictitious, who are mocked because they are unable to speak Greek – Kleophon, the Persian ambassador, the Triballian, and others. The comic foreigner of Aristophanic comedy is the comic Frenchman of English farce, and the comic Swede or Italian of American vaudeville. This type of joke is the surest index of middle-class tastes, and of an audience which dislikes, or distrusts, the unfamiliar.

8

Tragedy lacks this kind of topical reference, but the xenophobia remains. It appears in the subject matter of tragedy, which tends to take its stories from the lurid mythic and legendary past of other cities – principally Thebes and Argos, both long-standing rivals of Athens. It is in those places that men marry their mothers, and wives murder their husbands; it is there that incest and cannibalism thrive. Out of the whole surviving canon of Greek tragedy, there is really only one play which shows Athenian worthies in an unflattering light: Euripides' *Hippolytus*, where Theseus, King of Athens, misled by false evidence, curses his own son in a fit of savage rage, and destroys him.

This exception is all the more conspicuous because Theseus is normally the shining hero of Athenian tragedy, as he was of Athenian legend. In Sophocles' *Oedipus at Colonus*, when the old, blind, and beggared Oedipus seeks sanctuary from his oppressors, it is Theseus who takes him in. In Euripides' *The Madness of Heracles*, when the hero cannot face life amid the consequences of his own insanity, it is Theseus who comforts him, reasons with him and persuades him to rejoin the living world. In *Medea*, when the heroine, deprived of home and husband, seeks a refuge, it is Aigeus, father of Theseus, who offers one.

Appeals to Athenian chauvinism resound within the plays. Sometimes they have only the barest connection to the plot. *Medea*, besides the character of Aigeus, offers a striking example of this. The Corinthian women of the chorus try to dissuade Medea from murdering her children, because such behaviour will be unacceptable to the city that has offered her shelter:

> Happy of old were the sons of Erechtheus,
> Sprung from the blessed gods, and dwelling
> In Athens' holy and untroubled land.
> Their food is glorious wisdom, they walk
> With springing step in the balmy air.
> Here, so they say, golden Harmony first
> Saw the light, the child of the Muses nine.
>
> And here, too, they say, Aphrodite drank
> Of Kephisos' fair-running streams, with garlands
> Of scented roses entwined in her hair
> And gave Love a seat on the throne of Wisdom
> To work all manner of arts together.

How will this city of sacred waters,
This guide and protector of friends, take you
Your childrens' slayer, whose touch will pollute
All others you meet?[3]

This tribute to the city of the playwright and his audience is all the more poignant because, a few months later, the Peloponnesian War broke out; the glory of Athens was tarnished, and its image would never be the same again.

If Athenian heroes are the champions of the oppressed, Spartan characters – particularly during the war years – are portrayed as weak or villainous. Menelaus, in Sophocles' *Ajax*, argues that the hero has no right to burial; in Euripides' *The Trojan Women*, he enters to accuse his errant wife, and leaves the stage once more Helen's willing prisoner. Such xenophobia is even more evident in the case of those who are not even Greek. Particularly hideous crimes in Greek tragedy tend to be committed by foreigners. Phaedra, who lusts after her stepson and contrives his death, is Cretan, sprung from an alien race, exotic and decadent. Hecuba, who blinds her enemy and murders his defenceless children, is a Trojan – non-Greek, in Greek eyes, though ethnologists now believe both races to have descended from the same stock. Medea, who murders her own children, is from a land on the fringes of civilization, Colchis, in what is now Georgia in the USSR. At the close of the tragedy, when Jason mourns the death of his loved ones, he points a moral that would have been dear to the prejudices of Euripides' audience:

There is no woman throughout Greece would dare
Do such a thing. And these I overlooked
To marry you, my ruin and my curse.[4]

The Greek theatre was what we are now accustomed to call an arena theatre: that is, an acting area largely surrounded by its audience. This spatial arrangement always imparts a distinctive quality to the actor–audience relationship. For the Greeks, the intimacy of this relationship was emphasized by the fact that playing area and auditorium were spatially continuous, and by the absence of any barrier of structure or illumination separating the players from the public. The twentieth century has rediscovered the arena stage, and produced some notable examples. The Chichester Festival Theatre in England, the Olivier in London's National Theatre complex, the Guthrie in the

United States, the Stratford Festival Theatre in Canada: all of these have sought, by abolishing the proscenium arch, to bring the spectator into a closer relationship with the performance. Advocates of 'theatre in the round' find a precedent in the Greeks, and claim to be restoring the actor–audience contact which characterized the Theatre of Dionysus in the fifth century BC.

The comparison, however, fails on one point. When modern directors revert to the older concept of the open stage, they almost invariably, either from necessity or from choice, retain the demarcation between performance and spectator which modern lighting technology provides, and to which we have become accustomed on the proscenium stage. The acting area is illuminated, the audience is not. The pretence is still kept up that the audience is not physically present; that it is a magical observer, an eavesdropper on the action. This illumination is hazardous, for it can never be completely selective. The front row of the audience on each side comes into the spill of the lights, and their presence is a distraction for the spectators opposite – a distraction, be it noticed, only because the use of lighting creates the presumption that the audience is not to be seen, so that when it is seen its presence is doubly noticeable.

In the Greek theatre there was no such convention. The players could see the audience, the audience could see the players, and – just as important – the audience could see one another. Thus we see operating in the theatre the same factors that operated in the conduct of public worship, or in the assembly, and these factors produce a pattern of performance that is not the modern pattern. We tend, often unwittingly, to foist our own preconceptions onto the Greeks and their affairs. But their theatre was not our theatre, any more than their worship is our worship. The Greeks had no conception of an act of worship involving an active priest preaching to a passive multitude, or of the process of democratic government as the handing down of edicts from the rulers to the ruled. Nor did their theatrical concept envisage a passive audience. In all three spheres, which were in any case less distant from each other than in our world, the public was an active partner, free to comment, to be commented upon, to assist, or to intervene. The playwright, no less than the orator, could turn this to account.

This is most obvious in the uninhibited world of Greek comedy, where the presence of the audience could be readily acknowledged and easily used. The scripts of Aristophanes bristle with examples.

Actors can make physical assaults upon their audience: Aristophanes lists, as one of the familiar features of comedy, the showering of the audience with nuts and fruit. Characters address the audience collectively or individually, by name. In *The Frogs* the terror-stricken travesty Dionysus on stage calls out to the Priest of Dionysus, the real-life representative of the actual god, 'My priest, protect me and we'll dine together!'[5] The priest was sitting in the centre of the front row of the auditorium, a spot still marked by its special throne in the ruins of the theatre. Other victims must have been less easily spotted: one can imagine the buzz that would have arisen from the Greek audience when such a joke was made, and the craning of necks that would have followed as the audience attempted to identify the target. In this context also we may perhaps place the much disputed reference to Socrates' rising at the performance of *The Clouds*, when his caricature appeared on the stage, to reveal himself to the audience.[6] This self-identification has been attributed to pique, or bravado; perhaps we might also attribute it to friendliness, and suggest that he stood up so that surmises as to his whereabouts could stop and the performance proceed.

Such references serve constantly to remind us that we are in the theatre, and that actor and audience, conscious of each other's presence, are participating in the same act of enjoyment. There is constant acknowledgement and awareness of the audience's visibility, and particularly of the presence of the judges on whom the playwright depends for a favourable verdict. In *The Birds* the chorus threatens that, if the play is not awarded first prize, the birds will cover them with droppings;[7] in *The Clouds* the chorus alternately wheedles and menaces:

> And now we're anxious to inform our judges
> What they'll get if they treat our chorus right.
> First, when the season comes to turn the soil
> We'll water yours first and keep the others waiting.
> What's more, we'll oversee your fields and vineyards
> To keep off press of drought, and cloudburst too.
> But if any mortal slights us, who are goddesses,
> Let him beware, we'll give him lots of trouble.[8]

This habit of addressing the audience reaches its most conspicuous extent in the *parabasis*, one of the regular formal components of Aristophanic comedy. *Parabasis* means literally a turning around – of the chorus, in this case, from the action of the play to talk directly to the audience. Most of the surviving comedies contain examples. These digressions may be spoken in or out of character; they may be relevant to the author and his play, or address some other issue entirely. In *The Clouds* there are two, deriving from different versions of the comedy. In one the chorus, still as clouds, discuss the vagaries of calendar reform and the folly of departing from the lunar month (an issue of topical interest to the audience); in the other, the chorus, dropping out of character completely and speaking for the playwright, accuse the audience of poor taste in not appreciating Aristophanes' new and more sophisticated style of comedy. In *The Birds* the chorus, still as birds, recite a mock genealogy in which the gods, and men, are made to rank below birds; in *The Frogs*, though characterized as celebrants of the Eleusinian Mysteries, the chorus discusses the urgent issue of the revision of the voter registration lists, which has nothing to do with the plot of the comedy.

Such violent and apparently random departures from the plot have suggested to some critics that the *parabasis* derives from earlier, nondramatic sources, and represents a fossilized remnant of primitive ritual which has remained embedded in the plays. This was the explanation offered by F. M. Cornford, whose *The Origin of Attic Comedy*, first published in 1914, suggested that the *parabasis* and other recurrent elements of comedy were explicable in terms of a ritual pattern that had preceded the evolution of a drama proper, but whose influence had been so pervasive that the ritual was still remembered in the plays. Thus he argued that the *parabasis* – in which the chorus urges a case – derived from a ritual choral conflict, in which two groups argued against each other; what survives in the comedies, he suggests, is one half of this.

Some support for this view may be found, indeed, in Aristophanes himself. *Lysistrata* shows precisely such a divided chorus, old men against old women; before the play's end, they are reconciled. But, given the freedom of actor–audience communication in the Greek theatre, it is doubtful whether we need resort to such extra-dramatic explanations. The *parabasis* is perfectly explicable in terms of common theatre practice; it represents simply a momentary heightening of a tendency always present.

In comedy, clearly, this involvement may go further. The audience may be drawn into the action, virtually as participants. Once again, this is made easy by propinquity of place. In *The Acharnians*, *what's this mean*

Aristophanes' earliest extant play, the action opens with a meeting of the *ekklesia*, the body of Athenian voters. During Dikaiopolis' opening monologue the stage is supposed to be deserted, and therefore the audience, by implication, is assumed not to be present; but from the moment when the 'assembly' proper begins, the spectators are identified with the voters in the *ekklesia*. There is no need to assume a stage crowd here. Given the conditions of the Greek theatre, the audience is pressed into service as the stage crowd. When Dikaiopolis spies the reluctant citizens coming into the assembly 'dodging the red paint', he probably swings round to acknowledge the audience at large. This recognition of their presence, combined with their memory of their own apathy on similar occasions, would produce a good-humoured laugh. The identification of the audience with the voting body is facilitated by the fact that the two groups were, in any case, largely synonymous. By the same token the Pnyx, where the assembly met, is only a short walk from the Theatre of Dionysos. The places were also similar in structure. In the Pnyx the relation of the public to the *bema*, or orator's platform, was approximately that of the audience to the *skene* in the theatre. It demands no great leap of the imagination to make one stand for the other.

In *The Knights*, the atmosphere of the *ekklesia* colours the whole play, and the identification of theatre with Pnyx is almost total. The action is explicitly located in the Pnyx from at least v. 754 (the location is made clear in 751), but in fact we might as well be in the Pnyx for the whole duration of the action. This comedy, with its tiny cast and action which is simply a prolonged debate, is constructed along the lines of a public meeting. Of the five characters only two, the Sausage-Seller and the Paphlagonian, are of real importance, and the argument, with its balanced rhetorical structure, is designed to eliminate in the audience's mind the distinction between fiction and actuality. The Paphlagonian and the Sausage-Seller are rival politicians playing on the feelings, and competing for the attention of, the crowd: stage is *bema* and *bema* stage. Once again, this sort of identification is made easier by the attested similarity between acting and rhetoric. Both were carefully studied and well rehearsed performances, employing the same gestures, and, we may surmise, substantially the same type of delivery.

In *Thesmophoriazusae* a partial identification is made with another type of gathering. The play's setting is the women's festival, with its attendant rituals and speeches, and the presence of the audience reinforces the impression of a large and important concourse: when the lady herald makes her proclamation (vv. 295ff.), she is surely speaking to the theatre at large, and not merely to the chorus. Once again we must remember to put the play into its festival context: such announcements and proclamations must have been a regular part of the day's activities, both in the plays and outside them. The dramatic and the non-dramatic merge to a point where they are virtually indistinguishable. It is the Pnyx again that is in question here; and when the women hear that there is a man among them, they announce (vv. 656ff.): 'We must ... look to see if any other man has slipped through; we must overrun the Pnyx and hunt through all the tents and alleys [*tas skenas kai tas diodous*].' While *skenas* and *diodous* are intelligible here in their non-theatrical use, as referring to the tents which the women may be presumed to have erected for the festival, it is difficult to escape the association of words. It seems likely that when the chorus said *skenas* the audience was reminded of the *skene*, the building which stood in the background of the theatre, and associated the *diodoi* with the gangways in the auditorium. And surely we can imagine the chorus, at this point, as turning on the audience and threatening to search them. This play on technical and non-technical usage serves to remind the audience that they are in a theatre, watching a play, and to bring the action more closely home to their immediate situation. The same play on words seems to occur in tragedy. In *Oedipus the King* the chorus sings of the decline of religious observance, and of the apparent triumph of the unjust life. When such things are held in honour, they ask, why should we celebrate the gods 'in our choruses?'[9] Although the word can be taken simply enough in its non-technical sense – of the old men of Thebes singing about their own religious celebrations – surely the theatrical usage of the word is meaningful also. The audience is reminded that it is in a theatre, watching a dramatic chorus perform; and the chorus is in effect saying 'If there is indeed no religion, this performance may as well stop here and now'.

Finally, the comedy may be temporarily identified with the very festival in which the audience is presently participating, and in the context of which the play is given – Dionysia or Lenaea. The frequent proclamations and announcements made in the comedies attest to this. In *The Birds*, the bird chorus addresses the audience directly (vv. 1,071ff.):

15

> Now here's our special announcement for today.
> One talent reward for anyone who kills
> Diagoras of Melos. And for anyone
> Who kills one of the tyrants (long deceased)
> One talent reward. And now we wish to announce
> The following. If anybody kills
> Philocrates, who sells the birds,
> One talent reward. Five talents if he brings him
> Back alive.

The language here, and the form of direct address, are what the audience would have been accustomed to in the non-dramatic parts of the festival, and Aristophanes draws on them and uses them freely.

Even when the presence of the audience could not be so pertinently employed, they could still be drawn into the action in various ways. For example, in *The Clouds* Strepsiades has, as he thinks, had his son successfully educated in the sophistic school. All will go well with him now; he has a home-grown advocate, and an answer for anything. He defies his creditors, and the world at large. When he reaches the height of his dementia he offers to take on all comers (vv. 1,201ff.):

> Oh you poor stupid devils, sitting there
> Like stones, just waiting for us clever boys
> To work you over, ciphers, sheep, you heap
> Of empty vessels!

Here he is surely strutting round the orchestra, speaking directly to the audience, and offering to take on any man in the house. By embracing the whole theatre in his challenge he demonstrates the immensity of his conceit. In *The Frogs* the audience is identified, briefly and hilariously, with the denizens of the Underworld. Dionysus, having made the perilous crossing of the Styx, is quivering with fear. Xanthias asks him if he sees any of the criminals he has heard about: the ones who beat their fathers, or broke their sworn word. 'Why, yes!' cries Dionysus, pointing at the audience. 'I see them now!'

Such examples are easy to accept in comedy. They show a free-and-easy give-and-take which belongs to burlesque and music hall no less than to Aristophanes. It is not so easy to envisage them in tragedy. Nevertheless, they still exist, although we may have to look a little harder to find them. This sense of the common involvement of actor and audience, and of the theatre as a place of corporate action, manifests itself in the more serious form no less. The conditions of the theatre are the same; the audience is visible; its physical presence can be utilized. Once again the playwright, through his players, can call upon the spectators to assist in the situations that he is presenting, and to allow themselves to be physically implicated in the action.

Aeschylus' *The Eumenides* is the outstanding tragic example of such involvement. In this play audience participation is progressive, cumulative, and, by the end of the play, total. The action opens in front of the temple of Apollo at Delphi, and the prologue is spoken by the Pythia, the old woman who serves as priestess of the god and his interpreter to man. This prologue has two functions. One is a familiar device of Aeschylean dramaturgy: to offer a forecast and abridgement of the play's theme. The priestess traces the history of the oracle from the most primitive and fundamental deities – 'First in my prayers I honour Earth' – to Apollo, from Titans to Olympians. This transition anticipates a similar transition in the play. The Furies, cruel embodiments of primeval justice, change their natures and enter the service of the Olympians, dedicating their powers henceforth to the furthering of a more humane and civilized code of duty and responsibility.

At the same time, the prologue's second, more mundane, end is served. As soon as the Priestess begins her recital of Delphic deities, the audience is presented with a clear identification of place. As she continues to invoke the gods connected by association with the shrine, and their places of residence, Aeschylus reminds the audience of sites which many of them would have visited, and with which they would have been familiar:

> And in my invocation she that lodges
> In the forecourt of our shrine, Athena, has high place;
> And with her I must rank the nymphs in honour,
> Who have their homes in Korykos, the cave
> Where birds find welcome, and the spirits walk
> And Bacchus too – for I am not unmindful –
> Has made his home among us, from the time
> When he came godly with his legion of mad women
> To harry Pentheus like a hare to death.

By these means, by the subtle reminders of place and association, the spectators are drawn within the Delphic orbit. By the end of the speech the identification of place is total, and the spectators may safely be identified with visitors to the shrine. When the Pythia concludes

> If there are Greeks here, let them now draw lots
> And enter, according to the custom; and I
> Shall give them counsel as the god inspires me

there is surely no need to imagine a stage crowd here. She is speaking, simply and directly, to the actual crowd, the audience, which is clearly seen, and whose visible presence surrounds her. The spectators have acquired a dramatic utility. They have been drawn within the compass of the play, and may be used almost as characters.

When the action moves from Delphi to Athens the presence of the audience takes on a new significance. Orestes comes before Athena to be cleared of the charge of matricide. Athena announces that even she is incapable of resolving so momentous an issue; she will, however, create a court of law before which the case may be judged.

> But since the judgement of this case has fallen
> On Athens, I shall delegate a court
> To sit upon this murder under oath, and give it
> Jurisdiction for all time to come.
> And you must call your proof and testimony
> To give your arguments sworn warranty. I shall return
> When I have made election of my citizens,
> Which is most fit to serve, and to decide the case
> Impartially. They shall be sworn to keep
> An open mind, and judge it on its merits.[10]

The court eventually assembles. We learn that it is the Court of the Areopagos, Athens' oldest judicial body. Every Athenian was familiar with it, for it still met on the hill from which it took its name. Here again, propinquity of place is important. The Areopagos was little more than a stone's throw from the theatre, on the road to the Acropolis. In 462 BC, shortly before the *Oresteia* was performed, its most important functions had been transferred to the popular courts. Nevertheless it was still alive and venerated. Its origins were lost in the mists of history. Aeschylus, in his trilogy, gives it divine sanction, identifying its beginnings with the *cause célèbre* of mythology.

The audience, then, are watching a fictional representation of a body familiar from their own experience. They are addressed by a character surely costumed to resemble the statue of Athena that looked down on the theatre from the Acropolis, their own patroness deity. We are reminded of the woman dressed as Athena who, in Herodotus' account, led the tyrant Peisistratos back to his own city, giving dramatic colour to a political coup. Athena orders the trial to begin:

> Herald, make proclamation, call the host to order.
> Let man give to the Etruscan clarion
> Its complement of breath, and send its call
> Incisive into the assembly,
> For as they take their place, on the seats
> Of counsel, we may use this silent time
> To tell my citizens in convocation
> Of the ordinance I have established for eternity,
> And these too, so their case may have fair trial.[11]

Seduced by the close association of place, reminded of familiar ceremonies by the mechanism of trumpet and proclamation, the audience must once more identify itself with the play. The plot assumes the presence of the Athenian people, summoned to watch a trial conducted by their goddess. Actuality places the Athenian people in the audience. Thus, when Athena delivers her address, the distinction between fact and fiction, allegory and actuality, becomes almost imperceptible.

So far in *The Eumenides*, then, the audience has been identified successively as Greeks in general, and then as Athenians observing a trial set in their remote mythic history. It remains for the concept to become timeless, for past and present to merge as fact and fiction have already merged; and this is accomplished, at the play's conclusion, by the simplest technical means.

The human element, which has become progressively less important as the action proceeds, is now almost eliminated. Orestes, acquitted, has returned to Argos. If the jurors still remain (the text gives no indication) they must by now be totally identified with the Athenian audience. The Furies, implacable, threaten to destroy Athens in revenge; but Athena persuades them to mollify their anger, to become benevolent spirits, and to take up residence in her city's soil. They are welcomed by the women of Athens – a subsidiary chorus, presumably – who dress the Furies, now truly the Eumenides, the Kindly Ones, in new robes. Here Aeschylus once again leans on ceremonial patterns already familiar to his audience.

The procession of women bearing robes, and the accompanying language, invoke the best-known festival of Athens, the quadrennial Panathenaia. In this, the women carried to the Acropolis a robe woven by their own hands, and draped it on the statue of Athena. *The Eumenides* concludes in the same spirit. Dramatic time is forgotten; the present is paramount; and the audience sees itself performing one of its familiar actions. Drama has become identified with the public will. Herbert Blau has summed up the mood: 'Who wouldn't want the theater that is implied in the Panathenaic procession at the end of the Oresteia, where the life of the drama flows right into the life of the community, clarifying its laws, and the audience were to go home to carry it on.'[12]

And, incidentally, the playwright fulfils the basic and most prosaic requirement of his theatre: he ends clearly and requests applause. The double procession files out with grandeur:

> Go on your homeward way
> In reverence exalted,
> Children of Night grown old,
> Jocund in processional,
>
> Let all around keep dignity of silence.
>
> To a dwelling old as time
> In the earth's enfoldment,
> In honours proud
> In sacrifices and fair fortunes.
>
> Let all around keep dignity of silence.
>
> Visit our land, grave powers,
> With grace and loving kindness.
> Let fire feed on the torches
> And make glad your coming
>
> Now to our song make acclamation.
>
> There shall be peace for ever
> For Athena's people.
> So has destiny agreed
> And Zeus all-provident
>
> Now to our song make acclamation.

The final refrain is deliberately ambiguous. The song referred to is both the women's song that ends the play and the poet's song that is• the play. The fictional Athenian public is asked for its approbation, the actual Athenian public for its applause; and the two are now one. No playwright in his senses would have reversed these invocations, and brought in the appeal for silence last.

This device is used elsewhere in Aeschylus. It seems probable, for instance, that it appears at the beginning of *Seven Against Thebes*. Eteocles enters, and makes his opening address to his people. It cannot be the chorus to whom he speaks, for they have not yet entered; and in any case, it is clearly men whom he is addressing. Unless we wish to suppose a silent stage crowd here, it seems more than likely that the audience is addressed directly, and stand at this point in the trilogy for the citizens of Thebes. It is also possible that the audience has another use in this play: to represent the enemy. The locale represents the Theban citadel; the action involves the Theban warriors surrounded by a mighty army. It is not unlikely that the physical layout of the theatre, in which a small group of performers is surrounded by a mass of spectators, could be used at least to hint at this encirclement.

It has recently been argued that such a use of the audience as participant occurs in Sophocles also, in the opening sequences of *Oedipus the King*. Here, as the play has been traditionally interpreted, we have a situation unique in Greek tragedy: the entrance of a silent crowd, before the prologue begins. Oedipus enters from his palace, and addresses them referring to their plight and asking why they have come. A Priest replies, telling of the suffering of the people and apparently indicating specific elements of the crowd (vv. 14–19):

> Why, Oedipus, my country's lord and master,
> You see us, of all ages, sitting here
> Before your altars – some too young to fly
> Far from the nest, and others bent with age,
> Priests – I of Zeus – and these, who represent
> Our youth.

Editors and stage directors have almost unanimously assumed that a stage crowd is present here. The crowd is not synonymous with the chorus, although this identification is sometimes mistakenly made. It is clear from v. 144 that the two groups are distinct. It is assumed that the crowd enters when the play commences, and takes up position in front of the *skene*; that it remains in position through the scene with Creon; and that it departs on the priest's cue, vv. 147–8:

> Let us arise, my sons. He promises
> The favours that we first came here to ask.

In modern production this can undeniably make a moving scene, as in Laurence Olivier's production of 1945, when the silent scurrying figures created a mood of dread and foreboding before a word had been spoken. Perhaps the stage effectiveness of such a device, and the fact that such crowd scenes are commonplace in modern stage practice, have prevented us from questioning its employment by Sophocles. For it is, by Greek standards, very unusual indeed, particularly in the hands of a tragedian who seems to have gone out of his way to avoid the spectacular effects that both Aeschylus and Euripides in their various ways employed. The argument of William Calder, therefore, has much to commend it.[13] He suggests that there is no stage crowd here, and that the Priest, by indication, uses the audience to stand for the crowd. Certainly this would be possible in terms of the theatre structure, and could be reinforced by the positioning of the Priest; he could be given a variety of positions and still be seen by most of the audience, with a sea of faces behind him, one figure speaking for this multitude and serving as the focal point of their fear and anguish. This identification would be doubly meaningful if, as is usually suggested, the description of the plague is coloured by the horrors through which the Athenian people had recently passed. If the play truly belongs to 429 BC, it was seen by the survivors of the great plague of Athens which opened the Peloponnesian War. In *Ajax* there is, perhaps, another example: when the protagonist is about to die, he bids farewell to a range of figures – his father, his mother, his home in Salamis, and, a trifle oddly, the city of Athens. This is both a tragic hero's farewell to the living world, and an actor's adieu to his audience.

Apart from these specific examples, there is a function of the audience that we have already noted, that of serving as 'jury' in the conduct of the agon. When Medea accuses Jason, or Theseus Hippolytus, they are ostensibly addressing their antagonists, but in reality the audience, the jury; the speeches are forensic orations designed with a public in mind, and intended to influence public opinion. It is interesting that the same feeling has been sensed in the neo-classical

French drama, both by a notable playwright and by his no less notable interpreter. Louis Jouvet writes:

> Giraudoux once stated that the Frenchman 'believes in the spoken word and not the decor' .... Combat, assassination, or rape, which are often seen on German stages, are replaced in France by lengthy speeches, sometimes almost similar to a barrister's pleading. The audience, therefore, is not merely a passive witness, but on the contrary, an active juror.

In the disposition of the Greek theatre, the audience was closely related to the chorus. It almost entirely surrounded them, and the auditorium was an extension of the orchestra circle. This architectural contiguity, however, merely symbolized a deeper relationship. Audience and chorus were different aspects of the Athenian public.

The chorus was drawn from the public at large. Each year, a substantial body of citizens was selected – we do not know how – to participate in the coming festivals. Plays were probably in rehearsal for the best part of a year. The chorus members were unpaid volunteers, who undertook this service as part of their civic duty. They were trained and costumed at state expense through the person of the *choregos*, a wealthy citizen who chose this way of paying his taxes. More often than not, rehearsals were conducted by the playwrights themselves. The earliest generation of dramatists taught their own choruses and devised appropriate choreography. Both Phrynichus and Aeschylus were famous for this. We must assume, for lack of evidence to the contrary, that both Sophocles and Euripides did the same. Aristophanes was the first to separate the functions of author and director. In the *parabasis* of *The Knights*, he states that staging a comedy is the most difficult thing in the world; that many try, but few succeed; and that it is better to start at the bottom, and have experience in all branches of theatre work before attempting a production. We thus find several of his plays brought out under other names, surely not as aliases, but representing specialists who were making their own contribution to the dramatic event.

It is safe to assume that choruses would not rehearse in the open-air theatres where they would eventually perform. Such rehearsals would attract curious spectators, and the festivals would lose half their attraction if the plays could be seen and discussed beforehand. We would expect, therefore, private rehearsals in an enclosed environment, and this in fact seems to have been what happened. The chorus master of a boys' choir for the Thargelia (a non-dramatic festival) described his arrangements as follows: 'I began by fitting out a training room in the most suitable part of my house, the same that I had used when *choregus* at the Dionysia'.[14] We have other references to rehearsal rooms of this type, and a note from an ancient lexicographer informs us that the chorus worked to chalk lines on the floor.

This close involvement between playwright and chorus had two results. First, it created an informed audience. We cannot calculate exactly how many choristers would have been involved at each festival, but the number must have been considerable; and over the years an increasing proportion of the audience must at some time have taken part in the festivals they were now watching. Audience and chorus were united in spirit, as well as in space; most of the audience could call upon their own experience when evaluating a new production.

Secondly, the level of public co-operation ensured that the theatre flourished, no less than the Athenian navy and the Athenian law courts, as a function of the democracy. In the history of Athens choral drama and participatory democracy are coexistent: when one declines, so does the other. After the shattering defeat of the Peloponnesian War, an increasingly apathetic public removed itself from the decision-making process, and with the ascent of Macedon a centralized government imposed itself upon the city-states. A parallel manifestation occurs in the theatre. Aristophanes' *Ekklesiazusae* (*The Congresswomen*, or *The Parliament of Women*) is a comedy about voter apathy. It shows an Athens where the legislative and executive procedures have broken down; where the male population has grown so lethargic that it must be bribed into attendance at the Assembly; and where women find it easy to take over. In its dramatic structure, it also marks the virtual death-knell of the chorus. Although there is still a chorus in this play, its appearances are spasmodic and perfunctory. The action, as in politics, is left to the principals. But, at its best, the Greek dramatic chorus bore the distinctive features of its place and time, an index of a public mentality that recognized arduous and time-consuming service to the state as a necessary component of the well-rounded life.

We have equated the chorus with the audience; the Greeks equated it, no less, with the play itself. For them, the two words were virtually synonymous. In Greek tradition, the chorus was the source from which the drama sprang, by the addition first of one actor, then of more, to create increasingly complex possibilities of dramatic action. The shape of early choral drama can still be detected in surviving plays. Aeschylus' *The Suppliant Women*, now known to be a later work, was for centuries believed to be our earliest surviving Greek tragedy, because of the predominance of the chorus. Here, the chorus begins the play, and carries the burden of the dramatic action; the actors' speeches are, for the most part, solo arias interpolated into the primarily choral pattern; and dialogue between the actors is minimal. Aeschylus seems to be reverting, for reasons of his own or from the necessity of this particular story-line, to an earlier kind of tragedy, before actors had been fully assimulated into the tragic scheme: a predominantly lyric tragedy which worked through pageantry and mass spectacle, through choral song and dance.

In another work of Aeschylus, although the role of the actors is increased, the chorus still opens the play, and takes a major part in it. This is *The Persians*, performed at the festival of 472 BC and now recognized as the earliest tragedy we have; the largely static action is bracketed between a massive choral opening and a no less impressive finale with chorus and principals joining in a lament for the Persian dead. But even when the chorus entrance was delayed, as in the other plays of Aeschylus and in all the other tragedies we have, it was still recognized as the official beginning of the play. Anything that came before was prologue: whether an explanatory monologue, in the Euripidean style, or a complex acted scene, as Sophocles preferred. To this extent, even when the importance of the chorus had diminished, play and chorus were still recognized as one.

The chorus entrance was the *parodos*. This word had two meanings. In theatre architecture, it referred to the aisles leading into the orchestra on each side of the *skene*; it was used also for the song the chorus delivered as it made its entrance. Surviving plays suggest that this entrance was processional and stately, although there were some obvious exceptions. Aeschylus seems to have experimented with different ways of bringing the chorus on. In *Prometheus Bound* the chorus is characterized as Oceanides, winged water-nymphs, daughters of the sea-god Oceanus; they seem to make their first entrance on an upper level of the *skene*, probably in a dance, illustrative of flight, and only afterwards to take their more accustomed position in the orchestra. In *The Eumenides* the chorus represent the Furies, black-winged, red-eyed horrors, with writhing snakes for hair. An ancient commentator tells us that they came on in twos and threes accompanied by a hideous wailing and groaning off stage. According to a famous story, their appearance was so frightening that women in the audience miscarried on the spot. (True or false, the tale suggests at least that the audience was not composed exclusively of males, as some historians insist.)

Just as the chorus entrance marks the formal beginning of the play, its exit (*exodos*) marks the ending. In almost all the plays we have, the chorus remains in the orchestra throughout the action. Where it does not, its temporary absence may serve to indicate an important change of scene. In Aeschylus' *The Eumenides* the action begins at Apollo's prophetic shrine at Delphi. Orestes is sent by Apollo to find sanctuary and judgement of Athens. After a brief altercation with the god, the Furies follow in pursuit. The orchestra is temporarily empty. When Orestes returns, his address to Athena's statue indicates that the action has now moved to Athens. Hard on his heels come the Furies, complaining of their long and weary chase. Similarly, in Sophocles' *Ajax*, the action opens in front of the hero's tent. Humiliated in his colleagues' eyes, Ajax determines on suicide, and goes to find a lonely place to kill himself. The chorus follows. When Ajax reappears, it is clear that we are now supposed to be somewhere on the seashore, away from the Greek encampment. He speaks his dying words, and falls upon his sword; the chorus then re-enters, on the hunt for him.

Sometimes the chorus leaves the orchestra in mid-play through dramatic necessity. In Euripides' *Alcestis* the heroine dies early in the play; her body is removed indoors, and dressed for burial; it comes out once again, borne on a bier; and Admetus, the bereaved husband, leads the chorus out in solemn procession to inter the body. Their exit leaves the stage clear for Heracles to discover, from a servant, the cause of Admetus' troubles. Heracles leaves on his self-appointed rescue mission, and the mourning chorus returns. A similar movement occurs in Euripides' *Helen*.

These, however, are exceptions. Once on, the chorus normally remains on to the end, and serves the play in a variety of functions.

The chorus gives the play its musical component. What this meant to the original performances we can only guess, for all the music has been lost to us. The texts show us, however, that the music was extensive. Although the actors broke out periodically into song, the choral lyrics shaped and divided the play. We know enough about Greek music, too, to be aware of the subtle range of moods and feelings that such choral music could induce. Plato, in uttering his strictures on traditional music in *The Republic*, associated the principal modes with specific emotions in a way that our own musical sensibility can scarcely grasp. This loss is perhaps the most important that we have to face in our dealings with Greek drama. Its unique combination of music, dance, and the spoken word remains beyond our powers of reconstruction; it is as if we had the libretti of Wagner's operas, but not the music that he wrote for them. And we have to remind ourselves here that for the Greeks the connection was an intimate one, with the poet serving as his own composer, and his own choreographer too. In Aristophanes' comedy *The Frogs*, when Aeschylus and Euripides debate their merits in the Underworld, they criticize not only each other's plots and language, but each other's music also.

Given our lack of knowledge, we are left with puzzles. Given that a large part of the play was choral lyric, how much of the sung language could be heard? Was the music such that it offered no obstruction to the meaning? Were the ears of the audience more acute than ours? (Other considerations suggest that this might have been so.) Or did the Greek audience hear a chorus perhaps as we hear an unfamiliar Verdi opera, catching two or three words out of every five? This suggestion may be near the truth. It is noticeable that the playwrights do not rely upon the choral lyrics to give information essential to the plot; or, if the lyrics do contain such information, it is repeated elsewhere. The chorus may enlarge upon information already received; it may reflect on it, and colour it. But it does not originate it.

It is noticeable, too, that when the chorus in comedy addresses its collective harangue (*parabasis*) to the audience, it shifts into metres closer to the pattern of ordinary speech; and when the chorus, both in tragedy and comedy, engages in conversation with the actors, it falls into the actors' common speech pattern of iambic trimeter. The presumption here – though it is unverifiable – is that in such cases a single voice, that of the *koryphaios* or chorus leader, engaged in the dialogue, for the sake of clarity. Sometimes – though again this is unverifiable – the chorus seems to break down into single voices, debating amongst themselves. This almost certainly happens, for example, in *Agamemnon*, when the chorus responds individually to the off-stage cries announcing their king's death:

> It was the king who cried, the thing is done
> Let us think, there may be a way –

Hear what I propose; send criers out
And rouse the people to defend the house

No, let us force our way within
And catch the murderers with sword in hand.

I say so too. Let us do something,
This is the time to act, and quickly.[15]

To what extent did movement supplement language in conveying meaning? Did the patterns of the dance translate into visual images the metaphors contained within the verse? Or, more concretely, did the chorus depict in action the subject of their song? Once again, we have no means of knowing, though modern directors have played productively with the idea. Andrei Serban, in his New York production of *Agamemnon*, illustrated the choral description of the sacrifice of Iphigeneia by a balletic re-enactment of the event. Members of the chorus took the roles of Agamemnon and his attendant priests, and at each performance a new 'victim' was selected from the audience.

Although we know so little of the details, it is clear that the vocal contribution of the chorus was both rich and varied. It could punctuate the action with bursts of song and dance which both enlarged upon the immediate dramatic moment and provided a relief from tension. One critic has suggested, perceptively, that the Greek audience refreshed itself periodically with music as a modern audience refreshes itself in the theatre bar: there were no intermissions in Greek drama. The chorus could also communicate with the audience on one side, and the actors on the other, in a more conversational manner if the occasion demanded.

The relationship of the chorus to the action was similarly flexible; it could vary according to the immediate needs of the play. The chorus role shifts as the action shifts, and the chorus had not one function, but several. Some critics have attempted to define the chorus as 'the ideal spectator', reacting to the dramatic events as though each one were fresh and new, possessed of no knowledge but what the play itself had afforded them so far. But this generalization clearly does not hold true. There are, certainly, occasions when the chorus knows much less than the audience. We have one such example in Aeschylus' *The Libation Bearers*. Orestes has committed the revenge-murder of his mother Clytemnestra and her paramour Aegisthus. The chorus assumes that the sorrows of the palace are now over, and the slate has been wiped clean:

> Even for these I can find tears, and for
> Their coupled death. But since Orestes has been bold
> To top this long and bloody history
> We find it better that the light within
> The house not be extinguished utterly.
>
>   . . .
>
> Cry joy now for the mansions of our lords,
> The end of pain, the end of rich things wasted
> By two in infamy, the dark days gone.[16]

The chorus, of course, could not be more wrong. As the audience is well aware, the deaths have settled nothing. There is more to come. Orestes, standing triumphantly over the dead bodies, proceeds to go mad before our eyes. He makes his exit, haunted by the avenging Furies; the drama has another phase to go.

In *Oedipus the King* we find the chorus making a similar mistake. Acting on the information brought by the messenger from Corinth, Oedipus proclaims himself 'the child of luck', a foundling miraculously preserved to enjoy a royal destiny. He awaits the herdsman, the remaining witness who will solve the riddle of his identity. Jocasta, who knows by this time all too well who Oedipus is, has left the stage in an agony of grief and remorse. At this point the chorus sings, with an air of almost desperate gaiety:

> Which of the nymphs, the long-lived ones,
> Lay with the mountain-wanderer Pan
> To bring you to birth? Or was it Loxias?
> He is a god who loves the upland pastures.
> Or was it Cyllene's lord, or the god
> Of the Bacchanals, dwelling
> High in the hilltops, who received you,
> A new-born treasure, from the arms of a nymph
> Of Helicon, the favourite
> Companions of his pleasure?[17]

Once again, the chorus could not be more misguided; their optimistic speculations have come nowhere near the truth.

But this is not true in every play. The fact is that, like so many things in Greek drama, the chorus does not admit of simple definition. Basically, its functions are two; and these functions tend to interweave throughout the play, often in defiance of logic and dramatic probability.

The first function of the chorus is as narrator. It tells stories; it dispenses information. This seems to be a function inherited from the chorus' early, pre-dramatic days. If the Greek tradition of their own dramatic origins was correct, we may assume – as surviving literature tends to support – a body of choral song describing the lineage and adventures of the gods, and in particular their relationship with the community performing the festival.

With the introduction of the first actor, attributed by tradition to Thespis but certainly the product of a much longer and more complex period of development, another function was added. The advent of the actor transformed narration into impersonation; but once the actor took a role, the chorus could assume a role also. If the actor played the god, the chorus could play his worshippers; if the actor played a king, his subjects. But the addition of a new function did not supersede the old one. Although the chorus was now characterized, it could still work in its old role of narrator.

This duality of function remains implicit in literary tragedy. The chorus can be in the play, or out of it. It can work within the limits of the action as character, knowing no more than such characters would know, responding to what the principals say and do; or it can stand outside the action as an impartial commentator, objective and omniscient, and illuminate factors in the action of which the principals themselves are not aware.

To study these intertwining functions, we may look at Aeschylus' *Agamemnon*, a play which offers a good balance between principals and chorus, and in which the shifting nature of the choral role can be seen almost from the beginning. *Agamemnon* opens with a prologue spoken by the Watchman on the roof of the palace at Argos. He tells of his long vigil, waiting for the beacon that announces the end of the Trojan War, and hints of the troubles brooding in the house. Then comes the formal opening of the play, the *parodos*. The chorus enters to an anapaestic rhythm, one regularly associated with such processional entries. It begins with what is virtually a proclamation, establishing the time and historical context of the action:

Ten years since high summons came to Priam
From Menelaus in his majesty
And Agamemnon, by the gods' appointment
Twin-throned, twin-sceptred, but as one
In harness, sturdy sons of Atreus
Sea-questing with an Argive fleet
To arm their cause, ten thousand strong
Wrathful, and trumpet-tongued for war[18]

The chorus speaks impartially, objectively, as a voice set high above the action, forecasting the war's outcome:

And for a woman's wantoning many
A lance will shiver, many will fight
Till they knee the dust, their strength wrung dry
Before the consummation. Such the will of Zeus
For Greek and for Trojan. Things stand now
As they are; as it has been appointed
So will it come to pass.[19]

Suddenly, they switch into another metre, and another mode of being. They characterize themselves as old men of Argos, useless in the conflict, crippled by their age and infirmity:

But we were bone-tired, bankrupt of years,
Passed over when the summons came for more,
We wait at home with stripling's strength
On old man's crutches. Youth
And age are alike; at the sap's green rising
There is no place for Ares; so
In the fall of life when the leaves wither
We walk three-legged, weak as children,
Dreams that wander abroad by daylight.[20]

As old men of Argos, they assume a position of ignorance. Gone is the Olympian stance of their opening announcement. As characters, they now crave guidance and illumination:

Daughter of Tyndareus, our queen
Clytemnestra, what now, what news?
What have you heard? What messenger
Moves you to send about the city
Making ready for sacrifice?[21]

Following this, another shift; the chorus assumes the function of narrator again:

> It is given to me to sing the portentous
> Marching of the host, the kings and proud young men
> For heaven breathes this benison upon me
> Still, the spell of song.[22]

So we hear of the aborted expedition. We learn the details of the fleet's long stay at Aulis, held in harbour by contrary winds; of the decision to sacrifice Iphigeneia, and the manner of her dying:

> She called her father, prayed to him;
> So young was she, a virgin still;
> But of this the bloody captains made no mind.
> Her father offered up a prayer, and ordered
> The acolytes to hold her fast, for she
> Was struggling to clasp his vestments close
> And lift her like a kid above the altar,
> Checking her soft lips, so no sound might fall
> To bring the house bad fortune.[23]

This narrative defies logic. It is a vivid, eyewitness account of an incident witnessed by the whole Greek army. But as the chorus have already informed us, they were at home throughout the war. They were never in the army in the first place. This shifting viewpoint of the chorus does not respond to any logic of characterization. It merely answers the requirements of dramatic necessity.

So, later in the play, this freedom allows them to see the abandoned palace at Sparta through the eyes of Menelaus, or the impact of Helen on the city of Troy; but when the action calls for it their vision is restricted, and they are old men of limited understanding. Cassandra warns them, and they do not comprehend. The king's cries ring out from the palace, and they bicker aimlessly in ignorance and fear. But in the *kommos*, the great dirge that follows Agamemnon's death, they shed their fallible personae and leap unerringly to the heart of the mystery:

> Great the demon battening on
> Our house, and terrible his wrath,
> Whose name you sing – an evil song
> Insatiate of sorrow.

> And oh, it was by will of Zeus,
> The one cause, the all-mover;
> For what is brought about for men
> Without his will approves it?
> Nothing of this had been, save he
> Had shown himself herein.[24]

Throughout this dirge, in fact, the chorus weaves back and forth between its two positions, singing alternately as moral commentator and as a body of loyal but aged and helpless subjects mourning their dead king.

Agamemnon demonstrates how the chorus could, at the author's will, revert to its earlier, purely narrative function and say things which its members could not, as characters, say, and know things that, as characters, they could not know. As usual, the pattern is more obvious in comedy, because of the looser structure of the plot. Aristophanes' choruses move into character or out of it depending on the needs of the immediate moment. There is no pretence of logic or consistency.

In tragedy, choruses regularly transcend the limits of their characterization in another way: by linking the immediate action to a larger body of stories, or placing the present in a wider context, to demonstrate that what the audience is watching is no mere isolated event, but illustrative of a general principle. In Aeschylus' *Prometheus Bound* the immediate action concerns a suffering Titan pinioned on a rock; it consists of little more than a series of conversations between Prometheus and his visitors, some of whom have come to sympathize and some to gloat. To demonstrate the cosmic implications of Prometheus' punishment, Aeschylus employs his protagonist's prophetic foresight to project the issue into future time, and the chorus to give it geographical expansion. The tragedy is nominally located on a mountain peak somewhere on the fringes of the world, but through the choral lyrics it becomes part of the whole human experience:

> And now upon the earth's face
> Comes a cry of mourning,
> Lament for the greatness
> And glory past, the grace
> Of you and your kin.
> All mortals that inhabit
> The homes of holy Asia
> Grieving and sorrowing

Partake of your labours.
And the maiden dwellers in the land
Of Colchis, terrible in battle,
And the Scythians mustered
At earth's end, the fringe
Of Lake Maiotis

And the flower of Araby, who hold
Their mountain fortress in the country
Close by Caucasus, savage
In battle, who whoop
As spears fly round them[25]

By nature, composition, and placement the chorus belongs both in the world of the play and in the world of the audience. It serves, therefore, as an intermediary in universalizing the story, and in relating the tragic action to the audience's present. As in so many ways, the structure of the theatre serves here as an architectural metaphor for the function of drama in this society. The auditorium follows the contours of the orchestra, rising tier by tier into the community; the play's impact is transmitted through the chorus to the greater public, like ripples spreading out in ever-widening circles from a stone cast into a pool.

Similarly, the chorus may invoke a body of comparable legend to sharpen perceptions of the immediate situation. Thus as Antigone, in Sophocles' play, is conducted to her living death, the chorus reflects on mythic heroes and heroines entrapped in similar predicaments:

So Danae in her beauty endured the change
From the bright sky to the brazen cell
And there she was hidden, lost to the living world
Yet she was of proud birth too, my daughter,
And the seed of Zeus was trusted to her keeping
That fell in golden rain. . . .

And the king of the Edonians, the fiery-tempered
Son of Dryas, was held in bondage
For his savage taunts, at Dionysus' will,
Clapped in a rocky cell; and so the full
Flowering of his madness passed from him gradually
And he came to recognize
The god he had insulted in his frenzy.[26]

34

Sometimes the chorus introduces stories designed to mislead the audience and suggest an outcome which does not in fact materialize. In Euripides' *Medea*, the protagonist has killed her children to avenge herself upon her faithless husband. The chorus immediately compares her to another familiar figure from mythology:

> One woman, one woman only
> I have heard of before this time
> Who laid hands on her darling children –
> The heaven-demented Ino
> Whom Hera made mad, and drove abroad.
> And because of her children's dying
> The wretched mother drowned,
> Leaping from cliff to water
> To join her two sons in death.[27]

The implication is obvious: Medea must clearly commit suicide also, there can be no escape for her now. But in the event she does not die. Suddenly, miraculously, she appears in mid-air, borne aloft by her magic powers and

> the chariot my father's father,
> The Sun, gave me to keep away my enemies.

This rapport between the chorus and the audience is one of its most characteristic and useful functions; it keeps this contact almost to the end of its existence. Nevertheless, as the century goes on, we see this contact increasingly restricted and the focus of the theatre shifting. In Aeschylus, as we have seen, the centre of the orchestra still tends to be the focus of dramatic interest. From this centre the implications of the play radiate through the audience. In *The Suppliant Women* the chorus is still the principal character, initiating action. In *The Eumenides*, although the role of the principals is increased, the chorus is still vital as a collective character, and serves as Orestes' prosecutor in the trial that takes up most of the play. At the processional conclusion, when the chorus has changed its nature and is dressed in ceremony by the women of Athens, the chorus is absorbed, almost literally, into the citizen body. In this play the social function of the chorus could hardly be more clearly demonstrated.

Increase in the number of actors, however, not merely reduced the proportion of the play devoted to choral lyric, but drew the focus towards the *skene*, where the actors were, rather than the orchestra, where the chorus was. In Sophocles, although the chorus may still command its old objectivity, and address the audience directly with its moral pronouncements, it is increasingly assumed to be within the immediate world of the dramatic action. In *Antigone*, the chorus of elders begins on Creon's side:

> Such is your pleasure, Creon, son of Menoeceus,
> Concerning our city's friend and enemy,
> And you have the power to order as you wish,
> Not only the dead, but the living too.[28]

By mid-play, in the Creon-Haemon debate, it has shifted to an intermediate position:

> My lord, if he speaks to the point you ought to listen,
> And Haemon, you to him. There is sense on both sides.[29]

By the time Antigone is led out to her death, it has swung firmly over to her side:

> It is my turn now; at a sight like this
> The voice of the laws cannot hold me back
> Or stop the tears from pouring down my cheeks.
> Here comes Antigone, on her way
> To the bridal-chamber where all must go to rest.[30]

Similarly, in *Oedipus the King*, although the chorus may at times display an Aeschylean omniscience which permits it to transcend the action, for most of the play it represents a group of Theban citizens limited in their understanding, torn between their respect for Oedipus and their loyalty to those who accuse him, and representative of all-too-fallible mortality in not knowing who or what to believe:

> The wise man with his birds and omens
> Leaves me troubled and afraid,
> Unable to believe or disbelieve.
> What can I say? I fly from hope to fear.
> Dark is the present, dark the days to come[31]

As in *Antigone* they sway from one side to another, and our concern is not so much with them as with those who sway them.

Euripides, as in so many other ways, intensifies the changes that we see beginning in Sophocles. For him, clearly, the chorus was often an obstruction and intrusion. He would probably have preferred to do without it, and there are tantalizing hints that he may sometimes have done so; there are indications that some of his works were offered first in private performance, out of the festival context, with a minimal chorus or perhaps none at all. Equally clearly, the conditions of the festival made a chorus obligatory.

The playwright, then, was often in an impasse. Euripides' evident desire to remove tragedy from the realm of myth, and locate it in the context of common human experience, demanded a more realistic handling of his materials. The chorus, however, is not a realistic device. Euripides attempted to reconcile these divergencies by one of two expedients. One was to reduce the chorus to a nullity; to deprive its lyrics of substance and to make it virtually a crowd scene, a provider of background music. This is what happens in *Hippolytus*, for instance, where the chorus are virtually ciphers, hovering on the periphery of the main action without contributing; the same is true of *Iphigeneia in Aulis*, of which at least one modern revival has been offered with the chorus omitted entirely.

Euripides' other, contrary device was to tie his chorus so closely to the main action that they became participants in it; thus he hoped to justify the presence of the chorus in purely realistic terms. In *Medea* the protagonist appeals to the chorus, as woman to women, not to reveal any plan of revenge she may devise against her husband. The chorus promises, and is thereafter bound as her unwilling accomplice. Medea may, without incongruity, expound her plans before the women of Corinth. Though they may disapprove, they may not tell. In *Hecuba* the women of the chorus, fellow prisoners in the Greek encampment, actively assist the former queen of Troy in her revenge. In *Ion* the chorus, having promised, as in *Medea*, to keep silence, breaks its word, thus causing a new twist in the plot.

In either case the impact on the play's dynamics is the same. Our attention is drawn to the principals throughout, and the chorus exists in their shadow. Although the chorus is still physically present the orchestra is no longer the focus of the action. That role has been transferred to the *skene*. The orchestra is now a void, looking forward to the time, not far distant, when the chorus has only a vestigial presence; when the orchestra circle, impinged upon on one side by the enlarged stage area and the other by seats of honour for the dignitaries in the audience, has been reduced to half its original extent; and what was once the centre of the action has become a gulf, with the spectators on one side and the performers on the other. Euripides paradoxically, by attempting to bring tragedy closer to the everyday experience of the public, distanced it. Instead of participating in a dramatic communion, his audience observed, at a distance, a picture as realistic as Euripides could contrive with the means currently available to him. Presentational theatre had become almost representational. Although the proscenium arch had still to be invented, its presence already made itself felt on Euripidean tragedy, asking the spectator to consider the plays as real actions, involving real people, at a known point in time and space. In such a world the chorus, as the Greeks originally conceived it, could have little part.

In his last play, however, Euripides astonishes us by restoring the chorus to its primacy of position. *The Bacchae* in many ways seems to reverse Euripides' habitual stances; the handling of the chorus is one of them. The *parodos* recalls the shock effect of *The Eumenides*, half a century before. It is urgent, strident, a frenzied dance accompanied by exotic music, establishing the theme of a settled community about to be torn apart by a blind, irrational force. Throughout the play the chorus is a brooding presence, waiting to pounce. Its dance conjures up the earthquake which destroys Pentheus' palace; its songs anticipate the off-stage destruction of the king and the triumph of the god. There are in fact two choruses in this play: the visible chorus of the Asian worshippers of Dionysus, and the unseen chorus of Theban women, the maddened Bacchantes, whose psychic presence is so powerfully evoked by the chorus that we see. The on-stage group sings of what the off-stage group is doing.

Just as the *parodos* marks the formal beginning of the play, the *exodos* concludes it. When the chorus leaves the orchestra, the play is over. In Aeschylus' *Agamemnon*, the principals have the final word, perhaps because this is the first play of a trilogy and there is more to follow; the same is true of *Prometheus Bound*. But normally the last words that the audience hears are choral. In tragedy the *exodos* tends to be brief, even perfunctory. Euripides is the most perfunctory of all, sometimes not even bothering to write new material. He uses one *exodos*, with only token changes, for three plays at different points in his career:

> Many things are wrought by Zeus in Olympus
> And heaven works much beyond human imagining
> The looked-for result will fail to materialize
> While heaven finds ways to achieve the unexpected.
> So has it happened in this our story.

This closes *Alcestis* (438), *Medea* (431), and, with one line-variant, *The Bacchae* (406). Another stock *exodos*, a blatant appeal for the verdict of the judges, closes two of the extant plays. But Euripides' plays tend to tail off anyway; the action is often finished about fifty lines before the text ends, petering out in a string of prophecies and allusions to rites and places with which the audience is still familiar. These may have been designed to further the author's realistic intentions, by linking the action to the world of the spectator's experience. One suspects also, however, that Euripides may have been wary of a festival audience prone to make for the exits when a play was obviously drawing to its close, and cushioned the ends of his plays just as Aristophanes' works – the only evidence we have for comedy – commonly conclude with a revel (*komos*) or feast, in which the principals and chorus join. Thus, *The Acharnians* ends with a banquet celebrating the triumph of peace over war. Dikaiopolis, drunk, is entertained by a pair of prostitutes. In *The Knights* a regenerated and joyous Demos invites the population to a feast, and the same theme of regeneration and celebration concludes *The Wasps*. In *Peace* and *Lysistrata* the company celebrate their release from hardship, given particular emphasis in the latter play by the joyous reunion of husbands and wives. *The Congresswomen* ends with a banquet, and *The Frogs* with a triumphant chorus celebrating Aeschylus' return to the living.

This almost universal comic ending has a strong sexual content: *The Birds* in fact ends with a celebration, and *Lysistrata* with a re-celebration, of marriage. This has suggested to some critics that this obligatory *komos* derives from something external to the plays; in fact, from some remote fertility rite which employs obscenity to call down a blessing on the crops. This theory is most fully stated by F. M. Cornford, whose view of the *parabasis* has been discussed earlier in this chapter. He argues that the ancient *komos* was the nucleus of comedy; that the dramatic form began when a religious rite acquired an elementary plot; and that comedy, by still including a celebration of fertility, remembers its distant origins. Cornford additionally argues that, in the plays, the *komos* is not organic to the story; it often gives the impression of something which has been grafted on, out of deference to tradition, rather than evolving naturally from the dramatic action.

Evidence for a pre-dramatic *komos* is certainly impressive, and the etymological relationship (*komodia*, comedy = *komos* + *odē*, song) is clear. That there was some type of early fertility ritual in which a chorus of revellers wore animal costumes and engaged in rough, obscene jesting is beyond doubt. Thus the identification of *komos* and comedy, and the attribution of the endings to the origins of the form, is now often cited as received truth. It is still worth enquiring, however, to what extent the revel-endings of comedies may be attributed to other causes.

It is now generally accepted that, in selecting the ancient *komos* as his dominant factor, Cornford was overstating his case. He argues that the endings of the plays often seem to be arbitrarily applied, and not to arise naturally out of the plot. In fact this is only true of one comedy, *The Birds*. Here, for most of the play, the sole issue has been the attempt by Pisthetairus, at the head of the bird-army, to depose Zeus as ruler of the world. At the last minute a new factor is introduced. Prometheus, an exile from Olympus, tells Pisthetairus that he must ask for the hand of Zeus' daughter. Sovereignty is treated off-handedly, and Aristophanes gives her no lines to speak. In this case the *komos* does indeed appear to be an arbitrary addition. If all the plays ended in this way it would be harder to refute Cornford's argument. It would seem likely indeed that the *komos* finale, with its sexual motif, was a ritual feature that, by custom and tradition, had to be appended to the plays, whether it was dramatically appropriate or not. In fact, however, this is not the case. The other comedies, except one, end with a revel that derives naturally from the content.

The single exception is *The Clouds*, from whose ending the notion of revel is conspicuously absent. Here the old countryman, Strepsiades, turns against the teacher, Socrates, who has so misled him. In revenge, he turns on Socrates' academy. As the philosopher and his disciples run screaming from the stage, Strepsiades beats and abuses them. Though this does not fit into any *komos* theory, it does suggest another reason for the endings of these comedies.

Once again, we must remind ourselves that Aristophanes and his contemporaries were writing for an open-air theatre in which the acting area could never be concealed from the audience. Performances were given in full daylight. Perhaps by the time the comedy concluded, the light had waned sufficiently to give torchlight processions, such as those which conclude *The Wasps* and *The Frogs*, some additional spectacular value; but this must remain uncertain, and even if it were true, there was no possibility of using artificial lighting for focus or blackouts for sudden concealment. Aristophanes is writing for the same conditions that governed his Roman successors

Plautus and Terence, and the open-air public playhouse of Shakespeare. In such circumstances, the writer has a fundamental technical problem, for which there is only a limited number of possible solutions.

The problem is, simply, how can the writer show his audience that the play is over? This is not such an easy matter as might at first appear. The ancient playwright could not, like his modern counterpart, signify the ending of his piece by dropping a curtain, which would both cut off the actors from view and serve as a recognized signal for applause. Nor could he use the alternative and equally valid modern method of darkening the acting area and bringing light up in the auditorium. He has to work with the only means at his disposal, the actors, and use them to contrive an obvious finale. The necessity for a strong and obvious closure to the play is particularly relevant in ancient comedy, where the logical connection between one scene and the next tends to be tenuous, and there is often no particular reason why the action should cease at the particular point that it does. A weak ending would leave the audience hesitant, wondering whether there was more to come, and even if a trumpet were blown or a flag run down to signify that the play was over, the effect would still be one of anticlimax. The action of *The Frogs*, for example, really concludes with Dionysus' awarding of the prize to Aeschylus. A modern playwright could bring down his curtain at this point, or fade his stage lights on a tableau, and still end his play on a high note. For Aristophanes such an ending was impossible. The case is the same in Roman comedy. The *Menaechmi* of Plautus closes with a recognition scene, the rewarding of the slave Messenio, and his announcement of the forthcoming auction. Although the play is obviously coming to its end, there is no definite indication, until the final words, of where that end will be. There is still the possibility, for example, of another scene with the wife of Menaechmus of Epidamnus. The *Mostellaria* ends so abruptly and implausibly that it would be hard to believe it has ended at all were it not for the final appeal to the audience.

Audience inattention is a complicating factor. In a closed and darkened theatre, audiences are easily controlled. They are kept captive by enclosure and darkness; their attention is focused on a lighted stage, and they are given clear signals when they may talk and when they may not, when they should stay and when they must leave. Restlessness and early departures are rare; it is normally only the strong-willed few who disapprove violently of what they are seeing, or the critics rushing to write their reviews, who brave the disapproval of their fellows and break the spell upon the place by leaving early. In open-air theatres, the opposite is true. There is every opportunity for distraction. The audience feels, and is, less confined, and more free to exercise its prerogative of leaving the theatre at any moment. One may observe this restlessness, even today, in the classical revivals given in the ancient Greek theatres. When the audience senses, or knows, that the play is almost over, they will rise to leave. In audiences so large, there is a natural desire to reach the gangways first, and not be kept waiting at the end of a long queue. A dramatist faced with these problems must give his audience clear signs. If he wishes to hold their attention for the whole of his message, he must indicate beyond doubt when the play has ended, or when the end is imminent, to forestall any false surmises on their part.

Euripides' answer to the problem has already been suggested; the true ending of the play comes early, and it does not matter if the audience fails to hear the final lines. In comedy, where the story is not known or the end so easily predictable, there is all the more need for a clean and definite finish. Plautus and Terence solved their problem in the simplest way, by the effective device of a formal announcement. One of the characters, or a supernumerary, steps forward and requests applause. At a later period of theatre history, Elizabethan playwrights were to employ the same formula. In Marlowe's *Doctor Faustus*, the chorus, who has opened the play with a formal introduction, closes it and rounds it off neatly with a formal epilogue. Ben Jonson ends his *Volpone* with a brief epilogue spoken by the leading character:

> The seasoning of a play is its applause.
> Although the Fox be punished by the laws
> He yet doth hope there is no suffering due
> For any fact he has incurred 'gainst you.
> If there be, censure him, for here he doubtful stands;
> If not, fare jovially, and clap your hands.

Another device, and one which the Elizabethans use frequently, with or without a formal epilogue, is to end with a spectacular scene, often accompanied by dancing, and involving a processional exit. We may think here of Hamlet's body borne off by four captains to the sound of cannon fire; of Malcolm standing triumphant among the cheering soldiers; of the Prince addressing the assembled Montagues and

Capulets over the bodies of Romeo and Juliet; of Theseus and Hippolyta escorted by their court to their nuptial chamber, and followed by the dancing fairies; of the revelry that closes *As You Like It*. For Aristophanes, who already has a chorus at his disposal (and the added difficulty of removing them) this type of finale, with its attendant spectacle, is the simple and obvious solution. If he can contrive to end his play with an elaborate song and dance, or at least a procession of some sort; if he can include as many of his main characters in this rout as possible; and, finally, if he can empty his stage with a grand processional exit: then his play will end strongly, the audience will be left in no doubt, and the applause may commence. If, to secure this effect, he must wrench his plot a little, and sometimes, as at the end of *The Birds*, append a revel that has not evolved logically from the preceding action, the structure of Greek comedy is flexible enough to stand such treatment, and the audience will not object. It seems that, quite apart from any question of ritual origins, the practical reason for this technique, in terms of pure stagecraft, are overwhelmingly strong, and are sufficient to explain the practice without going any further afield.

Once we admit the technical necessity for such a finale, there is no longer any need to exclude *The Clouds*, which Cornford can fit into his scheme only with difficulty. The play ends in something which is conspicuously not a revel. Strepsiades, indignant at the treatment he has received from Socrates and from his own son, avenges himself by burning down the Phrontisterion with Socrates and his pupils inside. The philosophers escape, and caper madly over the roof; Strepsiades pursues them, and they are expelled from the stage. Cornford explains this action in ritual terms as 'the riddance or expulsion of the evil', and thus as the equivalent in value to a *komos*. But in practical terms such an explanation is unnecessary. The effect is the same as in the other plays. A sudden burst of physical activity sweeps the acting area clean of principals and chorus together.

2

THE ACTOR SEEN

About the selection and training of Greek actors we know little. They were almost certainly not full-time professionals. Although actors were paid for their festival appearances, opportunities for performance were limited. In Athens, the major dramatic festivals occupied only three weeks of the year, and although smaller, local festivals existed, in which actors from urban centres could be invited to participate – the Greek theatre, too, had its straw-hat circuit – we may assume that for part of the year they had to turn to other things. Several of them are known to have taught public speaking, one of the major components of Greek education, and a discipline that had important connections with the theatre.

We can assume, too, that they were fairly limited in number. According to the tradition which has come down to us through Aristotle, tragedy began as monodrama, with one actor separating himself from the chorus and assuming an individual role. This step was identified with the legendary Thespis, who does appear to have possessed a historical identity, but who was elevated by the Greeks to the role of the sole founder of the theatre. Aeschylus added a second actor, and Sophocles a third.

The extant plays support this notion of a restricted personnel. Aeschylus' *The Suppliant Women*, though no longer considered to be the earliest surviving play, is written largely in terms of one actor and a chorus. Dialogue is minimal. In Aeschylus' other work, the two-actor pattern predominates. *Seven Against Thebes* is composed for two solo voices and a chorus. Although Aeschylus adopted the third actor in his later work – for example, for the roles of Cassandra in *Agamemnon*, the Pylades in *The Libation Bearers* – he reserved this innovation for special effects, and never fully integrated it into his dramatic scheme.

44

For Sophocles, however, the third actor was assumed from the beginning. His key scenes are all triangular scenes: *Philoctetes* depends on the interplay of three principals, the debate over the hero's body in *Ajax* demands a proponent, an opponent, and a mediator, and in the most famous example of all the Messenger from Corinth, in *Oedipus the King*, tells a story to Oedipus and Jocasta which has vastly different meanings for each of them.

The three-actor limitation did not, of course, mean that the author was limited to three characters. Cast lists of Greek tragedy are often long. But it did mean that no more than three characters could ever appear together. Each actor could take a number of roles in the same play. This process was facilitated by the use of mask and formal robes, which could be changed in a few seconds to allow the actor to appear as someone else. Some consequences of this tradition, and the relation which it implies between the actor and his role, will be explored in a later chapter. Non-speaking characters could be introduced as needed. At the end of *Oedipus the King* Sophocles introduces, with powerful effect, Oedipus' two small daughters, who are wept over by their blinded father but who never speak. Euripides does the same thing in *Medea*: the two children are seen repeatedly during the play, but their voices are only heard off-stage. A number of plays have silent attendants, soldiers and the like, and dramatists vary in their use of these. Sophocles is conspicuously economical in his casting, rarely using a character who is not dramatically important: his plays are virtually devoid of extras. Euripides, on the other hand, loves crowd scenes, pageantry, and processions.

This restriction on actors seems strange to us, conditioned as we are to take larger casts and the principle of one actor for each role for granted. Modern actors, too, find it difficult to imagine playing a series of interlinking parts in the same play. There are several possible reasons for the Greek procedure.

First, the three-actor limitation may derive from the origins of the drama. If we accept, as the Greeks did, that drama came from the chorus, then we may suspect that the first question was not how many actors were needed to turn this form into a play, but how few. We take our viewpoint from the other end of a long and continuously developing tradition. Given the primacy of the chorus, a minimal number of actors may well have been thought sufficient.

Secondly, we must consider the effect of tradition among the Greeks themselves. The modern theatre changes fast, because there is so much of it. Any new theory is rapidly diffused; any technological advance is immediately imitated; new productions are mutually influential. By contrast, the Greek theatrical output was scanty. With so few performances each year, there can have been little demand for change and innovation, and few inducements to depart from a system already established. There were, of course, changes in the Greek theatre, but limited in number and hotly argued over. But the theatre for which Euripides wrote at the end of the fifth century differs remarkably little, in its practical aspects, from that for which Aeschylus wrote near its beginning. A similar time span in the modern theatre would cover the years between *The Importance of Being Earnest* and *Hair*. Perhaps, if the Greek theatre had been allowed to develop unimpeded, the slow increase in the number of actors might have continued. But the end of the century saw not only the end of the Peloponnesian War, with all the disruption that this entailed, but also the end of the great age of tragedy. With Sophocles and Euripides both dead, and leaving no successors, the fourth-century theatre contented itself with revivals.

Thirdly, the restriction may have been encouraged by competition. Greek plays were offered in a contest; there were prizes for the winners; and in any contest one must have rules, so that all may start square. Financial necessity may have played a part in this. The festivals, though state funded, were still expensive, and we know that the number of extras, at least, depended on the resources of the citizens whose taxes supported the theatre.

All in all, however, the chief motivation was probably aesthetic. In this, as in other respects, the Greeks seem to have decided that less was more, and that there were great dramatic virtues in economy. This is borne out by the fact that, even when three actors were available, they were not always used. Euripides' *Alcestis* is a two-actor play: though Alcestis, Heracles, and Admetus are seen together at the end, Alcestis, just resurrected from the dead, is conspicuously silent:

ADMETUS But she just stands there. Why does she not speak?
HERACLES She must contain her tongue in silence still
　　Until three days have passed, and she has made
　　Fitting offerings to the gods below.[1]

Alcestis at this moment is presumably played by a *persona muta*, a non-speaking extra. By the same token Euripides' *Medea* – apart from some off-stage lines which could be spoken by anybody – can be played by two actors.

Alcestis presents another apparent anomaly which can be easily resolved. When Alcestis dies, she, her husband, and her two children are all on stage. The chorus notes the moment of her passing:

> Now she is dead. Alcestis is no more.[2]

Her small son immediately sings a lyrical lament over her body. This in itself is unusual, for children are normally silent in Greek tragedy, probably because a young voice could not rise to the enormous vocal demands of the art. Oedipus' children are seen but not heard; the boy who guides Teiresias has no words to say; Astyanax, in *The Trojan Women*, never responds to the laments of his mother; and Medea's children are only heard off-stage, when their lines may presumably be spoken by an adult actor. Only in *Alcestis* and *Andromache* do we see children delivering a complex lyric monody. The case of *Alcestis* has been convincingly explained as follows: Alcestis 'dies'; the comment of the chorus makes it clear that this is so; and the child playing her son, standing before his mother's body, mimes the monody. The voice is actually provided by the actor who has just played Alcestis, lying still behind his mask. The audience would automatically associate the voice, though coming from the adult actor, with the character who was moving, the child. Thus a third actor is not necessary.

The extant tragedies, then, can be performed with a maximum of three actors, and often with less. At least in the early theatre, it was common for the playwright to act in his own work. Aeschylus regularly took the leading roles in his own productions. Sophocles did not; the ancient *Life* says that he was the first to divorce the functions of actor and poet, because of his own weak voice. He did not, however, cease to act entirely. The *Life* goes on to say that he played the harp in his *Thamyras*, and may possibly have been painted in the Stoa Poikile, in the Agora, in this role. Other sources suggest that he played Nausicaa in the lost *Plyntriai* (*The Women Washing Linen*). According to the *Life* again, it was by overstraining his voice while reciting *Antigone* that he died, an indication of the great vocal demands made by Greek tragedy. Euripides seems not to have acted, but to have confined himself to writing the plays and, occasionally, directing them.

The limited cadre of actors, and the involvement of the authors in their own productions, may explain one great gap in our information about Greek acting. No one, in the fifth century, seems to have written about the art. It is not merely that no manuals of acting have come down to us. None were written in the first place. Sophocles is known to have written a treatise *On the Chorus*. Given that the Greeks regularly equated 'chorus' with 'play', it has been surmised that this work dealt with production as well as literary composition, and may have included notes on acting. Aristotle, however, flatly contradicts this. Writing a century later, he states that no such treatise has been composed before his time. The art of *hypokrisis*, acting, though of the greatest importance, has been ignored 'because it came late to tragedy and recitation. The first tragic actors were the poets themselves'.[3]

No such works were composed because, presumably, they were not necessary. The dramatist originally selected his own assistants, and a master–disciple relationship appears to have prevailed. In the early theatre, indeed, the actor seems to have functioned merely as an additional mouthpiece for the poet, with no opportunity to make an original contribution. Aristotle illustrates the difference between epic and tragedy by comparing them to the old and new schools of acting respectively. The old, he says, made its effect by voice only, without the lavish use of gesture which characterizes the new. But by the time he wrote, gesture had become so necessary to acting that he could advise the poet, as an aid to composition, to act out the story with the very gestures of his characters.

This development from a simple, declamatory style to one more vivid and expressive parallels the literary development of dramatic writing and the changes in theatre architecture and mechanics over the fifth century. Aristotle illustrates his point by quoting the censure of Mynniskos, who acted for Aeschylus, on Callipides, an actor of the younger generation, for excessive gesture; later on, he notes that the women Callipides acted were no ladies, which meant, in Greek terms, that they moved about too much.[4]

Aristotle clearly disapproved of excessive gesture, and thought the later actors inferior to their predecessors. Elsewhere he complains that the theatre which had once belonged to the poets by his time belonged to the actors.[5] He applies the same criticism to the professional reciter of epic, Sostratos, and to the singer Mnesitheus. Tragedy may produce its effect without movement or action, like epic; the fault lies with the interpreters, not the poet.[6]

Aristotle is clearly venting his own prejudice. He dislikes what he considers to be the flashy histrionics of the contemporary theatre, and longs for the greater simplicity of the past. At the same time, however, he is recording a process. Initially, acting as a distinct art scarcely existed. Thus no manuals were necessary. Eventually, the actor achieved recognition as an independent artist, making his own contribution to the performance over and above what the author had provided. We may see this recognized, perhaps, by the institution in 449 BC of prizes for actors at the festival, as well as for authors. But even then, there was probably no need for information and training beyond what could be communicated verbally or by practical experience. An oral tradition, however, leaves problems for those who would reconstruct the art, and we are compelled to rely on other sources.

First among these are the plays themselves. Here, however, we are faced with another enormous gap. We are accustomed to look for information on movement and business to stage directions. For all practical purposes, Greek drama had none. Readers of tragedy should be reminded more often than they are that in almost every case the stage directions are the translator's, not the author's. The Greek texts give us five examples in tragedy – all from Aeschylus' *Eumenides* – and two from satyr plays, Sophocles' *The Searching Satyrs* and Euripides' *Cyclops*. All of these directions refer to off-stage noises. From Aristophanes we have seven more. Five, again, refer to noises off. Only two indicate stage business. They come from *The Acharnians*, and instruct the Persian ambassador to shake and nod his head. Though these directions all seem to be authentic (in the sense that they were part of the texts from the beginning) they offer little help in reconstructing state action.

Why this paucity? As with actor's manuals, the answer seems to be that there were no stage directions because none were needed. The actor took direction, in most cases, directly from the poet; and there are indications that he never even possessed a written script. Rather, he learned his roles from hearing them recited. Sometimes the poet himself performed this function. Plutarch gives a story of Euripides singing a lyric to his chorus, which may reflect this practice.[7] Sometimes the work was done by a subordinate, the *hypoboleus* – a word usually translated 'prompter', which will serve as long as we remember that he was more active in rehearsal than in performance. This technique of learning through listening is still familiar in the Greek and Italian theatre. Tape recorders have given it a new lease of life elsewhere.

Though there are no stage directions as such, the plays contain numerous indications of movement and business written as part of the text. Greek tragedy is show and tell; the characters tend to describe what they are doing, at the same time as they do it. Thus, for instance, in Euripides' *Hecuba*, the captive princess Polyxena, condemned to die, attempts an appeal to Odysseus to spare her life. His non-verbal response is evident from the opening words of her speech:

> Odysseus, I can see you hide your hand
> Under your cloak, and turn away your face
> To stop me touching you. You need not worry.[8]

There are many such references as this. In addition, we have indications of stage behaviour in the scholia, the body of learned commentary which grew up round the texts as they were copied, recopied, and edited from one generation to another. Many of these annotations deal with historical, literary, or grammatical matters (and some of them are remarkably silly). A small proportion, however, offer pertinent comments on performance. For some reason, the most useful come from the scholia on Sophocles.

There are some hazards in using them as evidence. It is rarely possible to assign a date to any given comment. The scholiast who wrote them may be referring to the original production, to a fourth- or third-century revival (by which time the theatre had greatly changed) or to even later. The scholia do, however, help to build up a general picture, and some of the most useful offer a comparison of actors' changing methods over the years.

Secondly, we have visual evidence, mostly in the form of vase painting. Theatrical illustration first made its appearance on vases at the end of the sixth century. The quasi-dramatic processions of Dionysus were so portrayed; and from then on the theatre, its scenes, themes, and characters, provided an inexhaustible source of inspiration for the Greek vase painter. Some paintings indisputably illustrate plays in performance. A larger number are at least theatrically related, offering a composite of scenes from the play or the associated mythology. In this body of illustration one would expect to see the gestures of ancient acting reproduced, in one form or another. The evidence, however, must be approached with caution. We can rarely be sure whether a painter is reproducing exactly what he saw in the theatre, or whether he is interpreting it according to his own painterly conventions. T. B. L. Webster summarizes the problem thus:

> For pre-dramatic performances and for classical drama painted vases are an essential source of information. One must never approach a Greek vase expecting to derive the same sort of information from it as one would derive from a coloured photograph of a first night. The Greek vase painter is an artist and often a very good artist. A Greek artist in the archaic and classical period always wants to tell more than he sees. . . . Sometimes he forgets the appearance of the actor and draws the character as he imagines him, or produces a figure which is partly character and partly actor. Sometimes he adds figures which do not appear in a particular scene, because they make the story clear. He may paint the situation described in a messenger speech and yet put it into a stage setting and give the characters actors' clothing to show that the story was told in drama. These pictures then are seldom completely accurate realistic representations of a stage scene, but it would be foolish to reject them because they are the records of an intelligent artist rather than of a stupid camera.[9]

One might add, ruefully, that the 'coloured photograph of a first night' is not necessarily accurate either. The hazards of theatrical illustration have not been dispersed by photography. Illustrators may frequently recompose a scene to suit their own format. The resulting picture may not be a factual record of the scene, but a translation of the scene into another medium.

Thirdly, we have the evidence of a kindred art, that of oratory. In the ancient world, oratory was a formal art demanding careful composition, long rehearsal, and histrionic presentation. For the Greeks, oratory and acting were different aspects of the same art; or perhaps it would be more accurate to say, the same art before two different kinds of audience. We have ample testimony to this. First, there is a widely believed ancient tradition that the greatest orators received instruction from actors. Demosthenes was said to have learned public speaking from the actor Andronikos, or, in another version, from the great Polos himself. Another story has Demosthenes paying a large fee for lessons in breath control to the actor Neoptolemos.

The two disciplines were closely allied. There are two celebrated instances of actors who turned to a political career – the conduct of politics, of course, being largely a matter of public speaking. The most famous is Aeschines, the fourth-century opponent of Demosthenes. It is clear from what we know of him that he used his stage training to full advantage in addressing the political assembly. Demosthenes sneers at him, but behind the sneers one may sense a real appreciation of his power. He had enjoyed a promising career as an actor, and worked with some of the greatest stage personalities of his time. By 343 BC he had abandoned the stage for politics. His first office was an elective clerkship – it has been suggested that he read documents to the *boule* and *ekklesia*, for which his stage training admirably suited him – but by the age of 42 he had already acquired political influence and was able to use his theatrical connections to advantage when his former colleague Aristodemos began peace negotiations with Philip of Macedon.

The language and style of Aeschines' speeches show close affinities with the stage, and it is clear that his former career made it easier, not harder, for him to rise to eminence. Modern comparisons are instructive. The modern world no longer thinks so highly of actors in politics; and this tells us much about shifting cultural attitudes towards the theatre. Another prominent statesman, Archias of Thurii, the captor of Demosthenes after the debacle of 322, had been a tragic actor before taking up politics, taught, we are told, by the great Polos.

There are numerous examples of actors who, without relinquishing their first calling, were pressed into temporary service on political and diplomatic missions. Actors enjoyed both high visibility and a distinguished reputation; the theatrical career was no bar to political eminence. In the fifth century the actor Kleandros was influential in negotiating for the repatriation of Theokritos of Halimos, who had been captured during the Peloponnesian War. In the fourth century another actor, Ischandros, appeared before the Athenian *boule* and *ekklesia* to present certain political proposals from friends in Arcadia. Neoptolemos, one of the reputed tutors of Demosthenes, took part in the peace negotiations between Athens and Philip of Macedon, and helped persuade the city to accept the king's terms; on another occasion he served as Philip's personal emissary. Aristodemos, Aeschines' erstwhile theatrical colleague, was despatched unofficially on a similar mission, and Thettalos, victor at the Dionysia in 347, went as Alexander's representative to Caria to arrange the marriage of the local satrap's daughter. In the third century, Ariston of Syracuse served as political spokesman to his own people.

The tradition is impressive, and continuous. We may safely assume that a theatrical training was a valuable asset to public speaking; that the actor was equipped to lend his skill to debates and political negotiations at need; and that the roles of actor and orator were, to a large extent, interchangeable. It is therefore possible to examine the practice of oratorical delivery for any hints that may illumine our scanty knowledge of fifth-century acting.

Great stress is laid on the importance of *hypokrisis* in oratory by practising speakers and theorists alike. An example is the well-known story of Demosthenes that became a commonplace of ancient literature. An anonymous Greek writer, after quoting the opinion of the actor Andronikos that the words were nothing but the delivery (*hypokrisis*) was all-important, goes on to relate how Demosthenes, asked what was the most important element of rhetoric, replied three times 'Delivery'. Quintilian, in his version of the story, translates *hypokrisis* by *pronuntatio*, the accepted Latin equivalent. Cicero divided *pronuntatio* into *vox* and *motus*, voice and movement, and Quintilian into *vox* and *gestus*, voice and gesture; both the Greek and Latin terms implied the physical movement accompanying the speeches, as well as voice control. The story of Demosthenes is perhaps best known in the form in which Francis Bacon tells it, in his essay *On Boldness*:

> It is a trivial grammar school text, but yet worthy of a wise man's consideration: Question was asked of Demosthenes 'What was the chief part of an orator?' He answered 'Action'. He said it that knew it best, and had by nature no advantage in that he commended. A strange thing, that that part of an orator which is but superficial, and rather the virtue of a player, should be placed so high above those other noble parts of invention, elocution and the rest; nay, almost alone, as if it were all in all.

Bacon speaks with the anti-theatrical prejudice of a later age. Yet, for all his surprise, *hypokrisis*, including gesture, was a recognized part of the ancient orator's technique. Without it, we are told, everything else is useless. Action is a necessary concomitant to words. It must arise naturally from the matter of the speech, strengthen points and underline meanings. The orator Hyperides, who did not employ *hypokrisis*, is noted as someone extraordinary. In the fully developed theory of both Greek and Roman oratory, *hypokrisis* had an assured place.

Acting and oratory, moreover, seem to have developed along

similar lines. The increase in the use of gesture seems to have occurred simultaneously in each. Aeschines has a long digression on the degradation of oratory in his own time. He praises the old orators and compares them favourably with the new, in a passage which resembles Aristotle's comparison of the different generations of actors:

> The orators of past generations, Pericles and Themstocles and Aristeides, had too much restraint to do what we all do now as a matter of habit, namely, to speak with the hand outside the robe. They thought this unseemly, and took care to avoid it.[10]

To speak with the hand inside the robe implies speaking without gesture. There are, corresponding to this, interesting illustrations on theatrical vases where the actor is keeping his hand concealed under his robe. Aeschines himself goes on to refer to the statue of Solon at Salamis, which portrays the sixth-century statesman with his arm inside his cloak. Demosthenes, in rebuttal, casts doubts on the authenticity of the statue, and mocks his rival's historical allusions: 'You can keep your hand open while speaking, as long as you keep it closed while on state business'. But his sarcasm does not diminish the value of the evidence. Aeschines' point is reinforced by his description of Timarchos' speech as a 'gymnastic exhibition', a criticism similar to that made, in the fifth century, of the demagogue Kleon. These strictures are identical in tone with that of Mynniskos on Callipides.

We can deduce something of the actual gestures used by Greek orators. Once again, Aeschines is valuable. His speeches, crammed with personal invective, describe the behaviour of his opponents. He tells us that it was a typical gesture of Demosthenes to put his hand to his forehead. This was also a common gesture of the stage. Elsewhere, Aeschines describes his rival as 'twirling around'. This suggests an animated delivery, and lively physical accompaniment. From Demosthenes' speech against Theokrines, it appears that it was perfectly in order for the defendant to throw himself at his opponent's feet, a theatrical touch still permissible in the lawcourts.

For most of our information about Greek delivery, however, we have to look to Roman sources. The first complete analysis of oratorical gesture appears in the writings of Quintilian in the first century AD, though it is clear, from his own testimony, that the subject had been treated in some detail before. His own description is exhaustive. Throughout, he regards oratorical gesture as developed from the stage. Some gestures he condemns as too theatrical, but still describes them. Others, he says, are too violent even for the stage. But even this is useful for the theatrical historian.

Quintilian offers a complete analysis of all types of gesture permitted to the orator, and the emotion that each portrays. Broadly speaking, he divides his treatise into three parts. A brief introduction is followed by a section on position and movements of the head; this by a section on the arms; and, finally, we have a highly detailed passage on the use of the hands. For Quintilian the hands are all-important. He describes their value in a long passage which is worth quoting if only to show the importance of gesture to an ancient orator:

> The other parts of the body aid the speaker. The hands, I might almost say, do the speaking by themselves. With the hands we demand, we promise, we summon, we dismiss; we threaten, we entreat, we show abhorrence and fear; we say yes, and we say no. We use them to show joy and sadness, hesitation and confession, limit and abundance, number and time. The hands urge, the hands hold back; the hands applaud; the hands show admiration and respect. They point out places and people. They lend themselves to adverbs and to pronouns.[11]

The difficulties of using a manual of oratory composed in the first century AD to illustrate the acting technique of the fifth century BC are self-evident. But Quintilian's study is by no means irrelevant. He writes as an historian. He is well-acquainted with the background of his subject, and its relevance to Greek as well as Roman practice. He tends to hark back to his predecessors, and can write knowledgeably of gestures attributed to Demosthenes. He refers to the *veteres artifices*, the orators of former times, and, to take one example, attributes a particular gesture to Kleon, the fifth-century politician: 'The gesture of slapping the thigh, which is believed to have been first used in Athens by Kleon, is a familiar one. It is appropriate to indignant speakers, and wakes up the audience.'[12] This statement harmonizes well with what we know of Kleon's style from earlier sources, and thus gives some authority to Quintilian's references to the past.

We may thus, perhaps, assume that the gestures of Roman oratory were grounded in the Greek past, and that Quintilian's treatise represents a continuous tradition. More pertinently, there is a close affinity between the hand gestures described by Quintilian and those portrayed on Greek vases. In many cases the resemblance is too exact to be coincidental. At long remove, then, we have another source for Greek acting.

Our last source for Greek acting is the dance. In the early theatre the poet was his own choreographer, as well as his own actor. The first known writers of Athenian drama – Thespis, Phrynichos, Pratinas, Choerilos, now merely names to us – were all called dancers by their contemporaries. Plutarch records the boast of Phrynichos, that he invented 'as many dance-figures as there are waves on the sea'. Aeschylus was equally productive. Sophocles was himself an accomplished performer, who danced with his lyre round the trophy erected at Salamis.

Greek dancing was – as often today – highly mimetic. It aimed not so much at providing a rhythmical movement of abstract patterns as at a direct, often broad imitation of persons and activities from everyday life. Plutarch outlines the system on which it was based. The dance was an enchainement of steps and attitudes (*schemata*). Dancers were required not merely to hold graceful positions but to represent some definite person or emotion. Plutarch, who gives the fullest account, is, of course a later writer; but he echoes more brief descriptions written centuries earlier by Plato and Aristotle.[13] This particular concept of the dance is common to Greek writers both early and late.

Accordingly we know of dances representing a wide variety of subjects. Dioskorides mentions an Aristagoras who 'danced a Gallos', a eunuch priest of Rhea. There were the *pyrriche*, a war dance in full armour; a cyclops dance; a dance representing the gait of old men; and the *skops* or *skopema*, which seems to have represented men searching or looking out.

Dramatic dances were numerous and known by a variety of names. The *knismos* or *aklasma* seems to have been an exotic dance originating from Persia. The *eklaktisma* was a woman's dance, apparently of bold and abandoned character: a sort of Greek can-can, it involved kicking the legs above the head. Another highly lascivious dance, mentioned by the comic playwright Kratinos and Aristophanes, was the *apokinos*, or shimmy. Other dances, such as *dipodia* and *krinon, igdis* or *igdisma*, remain little more than names.

Out of this bewildering complexity three main types of dramatic dance emerge. These were the *emmeleia* for tragedy, the *cordax* for comedy, and the *sikinis* for satyr play. The latter two were appropriately wild. The *emmeleia* was more restrained. It could be danced by an individual performer. Aristophanes, in *The Wasps*, demonstrates this through the person of the drunken Philokleon, who parodies various styles of dancing. From Herodotus we have the story of Hippokleides, who danced to win his bride; he began with an *emmeleia*, which was acceptable, but then, flushed with success, went on to wilder and wilder gyrations which shocked his prospective father-in-law into forbidding the match: 'Hippokleides, you have danced away your wife'.[14]

To what extent can dance be used to supplement our knowledge of acting? We know that dancing was highly mimetic; is there any evidence that acting was, in the broadest sense, balletic? Fortunately there is. Plato, evidently drawing on his own observations, testifies to a rhythmic connection between speech, delivery, and movement: 'In general, no one who is using his voice, whether in song or in speech, is able to keep his body wholly at rest'. This statement occurs in a long passage on the use and abuse of dancing.[15] As Plato goes on to voice disapproval of the theatre, of actors in general, and of comic actors in particular, we can say that in his mind acting and dancing are already connected: mention of one leads him automatically to talk about the other.

The plays themselves offer more concrete examples. In Euripides' *The Phoenician Women* Jocasta, characterized as old, slow, and weary, comes out to greet her long-absent son Polyneices:

> How shall I speak to you, how show
> In motion and in words the joy
> That wraps me all about? How find
> In dance the pleasure that I used to know?[16]

This conjures up a vivid stage picture, and gives us evidence irrefutable: Jocasta actually expresses her joy to the fullest extent by breaking into an ecstatic dance. The tone of this passage recalls the invitation addressed by the chorus to old Hecuba in *The Trojan Women*:

> Dance, mother; turn your aged feet
> This way and that, with my feet
> In the dance that we so love.[17]

In both these examples, there is nothing incongruous in old age dancing. The conventions are the same as in classical ballet. In *Coppelia*, the doddering Doctor Coppelius dances as nimbly as young Franz. In Greek tragedy, dance is simply one of the actor's modes of expression, and is accepted as such.

Dance in the theatre may thus be seen as a counterpart to song. In passages of heightened emotion, the language shifts from the iambic trimeters normal for speech and dialogue to more agitated lyric metres. This is normally observable even in translation: the lines are shorter, the rhythms more complex. Greek actors, in fact, punctuated their roles with arias: when Antigone goes to her death, she *sings* of her sorrow. We can surmise the same relationship between dramatic movement and dance. At high points in the action, normal movement quickens into dance rhythm. We can therefore apply the *schemata* of Greek dancing, so far as they can be identified, to Greek acting as a whole.

We have two lists of such *schemata*. Both are late: one is given by Pollux,[18] the other by Athenaeus,[19] and to some extent they duplicate each other.

Pollux's list – he specifies that these are the *schemata* of tragic dancing – runs as follows:

Upturned hand
The basket gesture(?) Greek *kalathiskos*
Downturned hand
Passing the log
The tongs
Somersault
Dropping on all fours(?) Greek *parabenai tettara*

Here 'upturned' and 'downturned' hand are self-explanatory. As will appear later, they can probably be identified with gestures of prayer. *Kalathiskos* may imply holding the hands above the hand, basket-wise. 'Passing the log' suggests that the hands were held equidistant from each other and moved across the body, presumably with a turning movement of the body itself. The somersault sounds incongruous by modern standards, in a style of dancing said elsewhere to be grave and dignified; it serves to remind us that Greek tragedy was not necessarily solemn. 'The tongs' presumably means crossing the legs. *Parabenai tettara* remains obscure. If it does mean 'dropping on all fours', it suggests the movement of the Priestess of Delphi, terrified by the Furies at the opening of Aeschylus' *Eumenides*:

> Things terrible to tell, things terrible
> For eyes to look upon, have driven me
> Out from Apollo's house again.

> My strength deserted me; lock-limbed
> I crawled away, could walk no more.
> An old woman afraid is nothing, she is
> A child again.[20]

Similarly, in Euripides' *Hecuba*, the blinded Polymestor scrabbles on the ground, frantically searching for his murdered children's bodies:

> Where shall I go? Where shall I stand?
> Where shall I run for shelter?
> I go upon my hands and knees,
> Crawling like an animal.
> Shall I turn to left or right
> To find them, get my hands on them,
> These women, Trojans, murderers?[21]

Athenaeus extends Pollux's list with several other figures, as well as duplicating most of those already given. He does not specify that these are all tragic schemata. The *kallabides*, especially, seems to have been a wanton comic dance. But the *xiphismos*, 'sword-thrust', is particularly interesting. Several ancient lexicographers agree in making it a recognized posture of *emmeleia*.

Skops, *skopeion*, and *skopos* appear to be identical, or at least very similar. This gesture has already been mentioned above; Athenaeus describes it as 'putting the head to the forehead, in the manner of someone looking out', and assigns it to satyr plays. He quotes a lost play by Aeschylus; we could perhaps assign the gesture also to the chorus in Sophocles' fragmentary *The Searching Satyrs*, as they hunt for Apollo's stolen cattle. The only other figure identifiable from Athenaeus' list is *strobilos*, 'pirouette'. Again, this may not seem suitable for tragic dancing; but again we must remind ourselves that ancient and modern notions may be wide apart here, and that Demosthenes, at least, used such a gesture in the middle of a serious speech.

These, then, are the sources from which we may hope to reconstruct at least some of the characteristics of Greek acting. None of them is sufficient by itself. All present enormous gaps in our understanding. The literary evidence is often late, and need not necessarily be valid for the century in which the plays were written. The visual evidence may be distorted by the individual artist's interpretation. Nevertheless, when we consider all these sources together, one will often help to fill omissions in another, and when the same information is provided by two or more, it is safe to assume that they are a representation of stage practice.

Of one thing, at least, we can be certain: that the art of Greek acting had to respond to certain basic conditions imposed by the Greek theatre. If one were to ask how the Greek actor differed from his modern counterpart, certain obvious answers would immediately suggest themselves. Greek actors wore masks, modern actors, on the whole, do not. Greek actors spoke in verse, modern actors, on the whole, do not. Greek casts were all male, but modern plays use actresses as well as actors. The list would be a long one. There is, however, one fundamental difference which underlies and, in some measure, explains the rest; a difference which is so great that, paradoxically, it is not often noticed. This is the factor of size.

Greek theatres were, by modern standards, enormous. The theatre of Dionysus in Athens – the structure in which we are chiefly interested, for it was here that the surviving works were first performed – held some 15,000 people in antiquity. It is hard to recognize this now. Most of the upper tiers have vanished, eroded by time and disturbance. We have to imagine the auditorium as it was in its prime, with curvilinear tiers of stone benches rising up the steeply sloping hillside, illuminated by the sharp spring sun, until they met the abrupt face of the Acropolis. A substantial proportion of the population of Athens – perhaps as much as half – could watch the play at one sitting. This may be the only explanation needed for the Greek theatre's failure to offer extended runs. In normal circumstances, a playwright could expect only one performance of each work in Athens in his lifetime. Some plays might be revived in local festivals, at smaller centres. A playwright might occasionally be invited to stage his plays in another city, as Aeschylus was doing in Sicily on the occasion of his death. But the only known work to enjoy a repeat performance in Athens during the author's lifetime was a comedy, Aristophanes' *The Frogs*, in 405 BC. Usually, it would appear, everyone who wished to see a play could be accommodated at one performance.

Nor was this size peculiar to Athens. The theatre at Corinth, almost as old, now totally ruinous, held some 16,000 people in antiquity. The theatre in Epidauros, built in the fourth century on fifth-century principles and the best surviving ancient theatre in Greece, held about 20,000 spectators when first constructed, 14,000 today: today's spectators are larger, and demand more room, for audience comfort is a modern innovation. The largest known theatre in mainland Greece was that of Megalopolis, in the central Peloponnese. This was a purpose-built community, erected by Thebes as a buffer against Spartan military encroachment, and given a typically unimaginative bureaucratic name, Big City. Its theatre, intended as a magnet for a larger area, is said to have held 46,000 people. And the largest theatre in the wider Greek-speaking world was at Ephesus, in what is now Turkey, with a staggering 55,000 capacity.

There were of course smaller structures. Some of the deme theatres still to be found dotted about the countryside of Attica held only a few thousand, or a few hundred. The fact remains, however, that the theatres which represented the norm for major centres, and for which the dramatists had to write, were huge. In this respect there is no comparison between an ancient theatre and a modern one. For us, a large theatre is the Metropolitan Opera House in New York, the Guthrie Theatre in Minneapolis, or the Olivier in London's National Theatre: theatres which hold 2–3,000 people. The Greeks would have considered these buildings insignificant; recital halls, merely, for a solo artist. The best comparison in our world to the ancient theatre is the football stadium or bullring.

The statistics are impressive. Their implications are more so, for they affected the way in which the plays were written. Large theatres imposed certain constraints on the author. They dictated the ways in which he could communicate information to his audience. In the same way, the theatres controlled the behaviour of the actors, and Greek actors were unable to do several things that the modern actor takes for granted.

The most important question was visibility. In such a large space, how much could actually be seen? The answer is, comparatively little. Webster calculates the scale of the performance thus:

If for the moment we accept the Periclean theatre as depicted by Pickard-Cambridge, the area between the projecting wings, the 'stage' proper, was 45 feet wide, the same as Drury Lane; the width was increased in the fourth century to more than 60 feet. The distance from the front of the 'stage' across the orchestra to the front row of spectators was 60 feet in the fifth century and over 70 feet in the fourth century; in Drury Lane it is only 48 feet from the front of the stage to the centre of the dress circle. The back rows of the Theatre of Dionysus were about 300 feet from the stage. This means that an actor six feet high would look about three and a half inches high to the spectator in front and three quarters of an inch high to spectators at the back.[22]

In such surroundings an intimate rapport between actor and audience was impossible. Facial expression – indispensable to the modern actor – was useless. Even without the mask, which by bright colouring and exaggeration helped to overcome the disadvantages of distance, any subtle play of features would be lost in such a vast expanse. As modern performance experience shows, the actors' faces are reduced to meaningless blurs.

Small gestures would be equally useless. Open-air theatre, in any culture, demands a certain magnitude of performance. The actor's movements must be conceived on a grander scale. In a theatre holding 15,000, this was even more essential. We can assume, then, a repertoire of gestures that we would now consider operatic rather than legitimately theatrical; exaggerated by the standards of indoor, intimate acting and designed to be clear, meaningful, and immediately comprehensible. Our combined evidence suggests precisely such a range.

The most common emotion in Greek tragedy is grief, and its attitudes are consequently the best documented. There are several ways of expressing it. The most vivid occurs in Euripides' *The Madness of Heracles*. Here, the hero of the title has murdered his wife and children in a fit of insanity. Restored to his senses, he realizes what he has done, and his grief is so intense that he can no longer bear to be part of the living world. He signifies this by throwing his cloak over his head, removing himself from others' eyes and them from his. His old friend and ally Theseus later persuades him to uncover his head, and re-enter the land of the living.

This gesture has a long stage history. It seems to have been one of Aeschylus' favourite devices. The ancient *Life* of the dramatist says that he showed Achilles veiled, to indicate his grief. According to Aristophanes, Aeschylus allowed it to develop into a cliché; in *The Frogs* we are told that his Achilles and Niobe 'never showed their faces' but stood silent in their grief.

Euripides employed it on several occasions. In *Orestes* the hero asks his sister why she weeps, and muffles her head. In *The Suppliant Women* Theseus asks Aethra why she weeps and throws her veil across her eyes. Aristophanes parodied him, no less than Aeschylus, for this. In his *Thesmophoriazusae* Mnesilochus, acting out a parody of Euripides' *Helen*, hides his face from those around him. Niobe and the mourning Clytemnestra are so represented in art; and on at least one occasion the gesture found its way into the lawcourts. Aeschines mentions a speaker confounded by his opponent as 'covering his face and running away'.

The gesture thus fulfils the basic requirements of the Greek theatre. It is unambiguous, it is instantly and vividly evocative, and it can be seen at a distance. It also has important psychological implications. Greeks associated light and life, and could not envisage one without the other. Where the Bible distinguishes between 'the quick' (i.e. the moving) and the dead, Greeks spoke of 'the seeing and the dead'. Zeus, god of the living world, is also lord of the bright sky, and his name is cognate with the word for 'day' in various Indo-European languages. Hades, his brother, god of death and ruler of the Under-world, is king of a land where the sun never shines, and his name means 'the blind one' or 'the unseeing one'. For a tragic character to veil his face and cut off the sunlight is thus a powerful visual ex-pression of the death-wish.

It may also be linked with one of the most famous moments in all Greek tragedy, the self-blinding of Oedipus in Sophocles' *Oedipus the King*. Here the protagonist, by his own admission, strikes out his eyes because he can no longer bear to look upon the world that has betrayed him. He gives himself a living death. Though he remains alive – as he says, his wife-mother's suicide was too easy a way out – he strips himself of everything that made life worth living. The blinding may be indicated by a change of mask. We have no evidence for this. But among its many levels of meaning, it shows the conventional stage gesture for extremes of grief carried to its cruellest extent.

Other indications of grief are less drastic. The most common was to drop the head and look at the ground. As a general principle, in masked acting, the position of the head makes a strong statement; any deviation from vertical and frontal is immediately significant. Thus, in *Antigone*, Creon speaks of the heroine as 'You whose face is bent to the ground.' Agamemnon speaks similarly of Iphigeneia in Euripides' *Iphigeneia in Aulis*; and a particularly clear example occurs in *The Madness of Heracles*, where Heracles admonishes his children not to grieve, but to look up to the light. There are numerous other examples, and Aristophanic parody shows how familiar it was. The gesture is amply recorded on vase paintings where the hands are either supporting the lowered head or raised to the forehead in the conventional attitude of melancholy.

Mourning, though an extension of grief, has certain specific gestures of its own. These derived from everyday practice. Distress at the loss of a loved one was expressed by tearing the hair, cheeks, and garments. Such self-mutilation is already mentioned in Homer. By the sixth century, it was causing so much harm that Solon prohibited this savage and primitive ritual as part of his funerary reform. The custom still survives in African and Asian countries; and in modern Greece, mourning is still a far from passive business.

In the theatre, the ritual of mourning survived as a stylized representation of its former self, in much the same way as the smiting of the breast which accompanies the *mea culpa* of the Catholic liturgy recalls an older, sterner penance. Thus, at the opening of *The Libation Bearers* we have a whole chorus performing the action:

> Forth from the palace gates, as I was bid,
> With urns I come, with drumming hands,
> Torn cheeks, the nails' fresh furrows
> A talisman of red,
> And in my heart old sorrow;
> With rending of my robes, with fingers tearing
> Wild at the linen on my breast
> In grief of glad days gone.

So too the chorus of elders at the close of Aeschylus' *The Persians*, in antiphonal dirge with their leader Xerxes. For individual characters in mourning we have, conspicuously, Hermione in Euripides' *Andromache*, who tears her hair, her cheeks, and finally, despite her nurse's protests, begins to rip off her clothes. Mourning on the tragic stage was a vivid and vigorous performance. Vases show the gestures both in non-dramatic dances, and in scenes inspired by plays; and though we would not expect these movements to be reproduced in oratory, there is something reminiscent in Quintilian's prescribed gesture for penitence: the fist is clenched and brought towards the breast.

One of the most familiar of ancient gestures, as well as one of the best recorded, is that of supplication. The petitioner kneels at his interlocutor's feet, throws one arm around his knees and with the other hand grasps his chin or beard. This is the meaning of 'I beg you by your beard' so often heard in Greek tragedy; readers unaware of the gesture are sometimes puzzled by this. The gesture does not seem to occur in Aeschylus, which supports the assumption that early acting was largely statuesque and declamatory. In later plays, however, there are examples in plenty: in Sophocles' *Philoctetes*, Philoctetes to Neoptolemus; so too, in *Oedipus at Colonus*, Antigone to Polyneices, who tries vainly to escape. The point of the gesture was that, once one had locked one's respondent in such an embrace, it was impossible for him to escape. In the passage quoted earlier from *Hecuba*, Odysseus manages to do so. He sees Polyxena coming, hides his hand beneath his cloak, and turns his head away. As with the familiar gesture for grief, any movement of the masked head makes a strong statement. There are few things so forbidding as a masked face turning away and refusing to listen. Thus, for example, Oedipus refusing to listen to his son in *Oedipus at Colonus*:

> POLYNEICES But there is a power who sits by Zeus' throne,
> Compassion, who is present in all our doings,
> Who stands by you now, father. . . .
> Why are you silent, father?
> Say but a word. Do not avert your face.
> You do not speak. You do not even grant me
> The courtesy of answer. Is it yes or no?
>   (to ANTIGONE and ISMENE)
> Blood of my blood, and flesh of his flesh,
> Try, both of you, to move my father's silence,
> This stubborn and inexorable silence.[23]

For prayer we have different gestures, depending on what deity was being prayed to. A vase illustration of scenes from *Hecuba* shows Polyxena kneeling, her arms above her head. This gives us one of the most familiar forms of worship: the arms stretched forward, the palms turned up (perhaps as in Pollux's 'upturned hand'). In Sophocles' *Electra* the heroine utters a great cry to heaven; and the scholiast notes 'Simultaneously with the cry, the actor must look up to heaven and stretch up his hands.'

There was a different procedure for addressing the chthonic powers, the gods of death and the Underworld. Here, the speaker struck the ground with his foot. Cicero gives us, at long remove, a quotation from Sophocles' lost tragedy *The Successors*, where the shade of Amphiaraus is thus appealed to. We can also reasonably assume it in the chorus of *The Persians* when they invoke the ghost of their former king Darius, and in *Medea* where the protagonist is working herself up to kill her children:

> Do not do this, my heart, do not do this.
> Spare them, unhappy heart, let your sons go.
> They will live with you in exile and make you glad.
> No! By the fiends that dwell in Hell below
> It shall never come to this, that I allow
> My sons to be insulted by my enemies.[24]

Joy is, for obvious reasons in this kind of drama, a less well-chronicled emotion. But there does seem to have been an appropriate gesture for it. We have already seen how, in *The Phoenician Women*, Jocasta expresses her joy at reunion by dancing round her son. Something similar occurs in *The Libation Bearers*. Orestes, just returned to his homeland, has shown his sister Electra proofs of his identity. His own words make it clear that she has made some violent demonstration here: 'Contain yourself; do not be overcome with joy.' And in Sophocles' *Electra*, Chrysothemis, Electra's sister, enters 'with all haste, full of joy, setting decorum aside'. Electra later speaks of her as 'fevered'. We know from other sources what decorum, and the lack of it, meant for Greek womanhood. A respectable girl was expected to walk slowly and discreetly, and not draw attention to herself. Chrysothemis has forgotten her manners. She is making rapid movements here.

We have no direct evidence for the gesture, but the connections with the dance are suggestive. We know the pirouette was a recognized dance figure. Athenaeus includes it in his list of *schemata*, and Aristophanes mentions the sons of the poet Karkinos, tragic dancers, as famous for their pirouettes. From Aeschines, we know that Demosthenes employed it at a moment of high excitement in a public address: 'And again, when you whirled around in the circle on the platform and said . . . .' It is at least possible, therefore, that it may be the gesture we are seeking here.

Vase evidence suggests the gesture for expressing fear and horror. One arm is half outstretched, the hand upraised with palm outwards as though to drive the object of horror away. The other hand is brought in towards the body. The body itself recoils; the face is usually turned away. Thus we have several illustrations of the Pythia, Apollo's priestess at Delphi, recoiling from the sleeping Furies, recalling the opening of Aeschylus' *The Eumenides*.

In its best-known example, the gesture seems to have been copied for the familiar ivory statuette of a tragic actor from Rieti. One arm has been broken off, but must originally have been extended. The right arm is bent, with the hand half clenched and lying against the breast; the shoulders are slightly hunched, and the whole figure is expressive of fear and revulsion. Centuries later, Quintilian describes a remarkably similar gesture of the Roman orator. 'We express detestation', he says, 'with palms turned away, to the left side.' And, elsewhere, 'Hunching the shoulders is rarely appropriate [for the orator]. It contracts the neck, and gives a self-deprecating, servile, and almost deceitful look when speakers use it to show wonder, reverence, or fear.'[25]

To swear an oath, the characters join hands. So in Sophocles' *The Women of Trachis:*

HERACLES Then first of all, place your right hand in mine
HYLLUS You ask an oath of me? You do not need it.
HERACLES Do as I tell you. Quick, give me your hand
HYLLUS Then here it is. I do as I am bid.[26]

In *Iphigeneia in Aulis* Menelaus grasps Agamemnon's hand and goes on to swear; in *The Children of Heracles* Iolaus tells the children to give their hands to Demophon and Acamas and tells them to reciprocate, as a pledge of friendship. Neoptolemus and Philoctetes similarly exchange a handshake in *Philoctetes*. The heroine of *Medea* can invoke two familiar stage gestures when she recalls Jason's unfaithfulness to her:

This my right hand, that you wrung so often,
These knees at which you fell; how I am deceived
By a false lover, cheated of my hopes.[27]

In the same vein there is a common gesture for embrace and greeting. In *Oedipus at Colonus*, Oedipus embraces Antigone and goes through the motions of kissing Theseus' head and hand a few lines later. Directing experience suggests that, when two masked figures embrace, they seem almost literally to grow into one; unmasked actors, in a similar action, retain much more of their individual identity. In Sophocles' *Electra* Orestes and his sister embrace, while in Euripides' play of the same name Electra mistakes her brother's out-stretched arm of greeting for a threat; they truly embrace later. And, among numerous other examples, Iphegeneia embraces her father Agamemnon in *Iphigeneia at Aulis*, and he asks for a kiss and to have her hand.

Threats were often accompanied by weapons. In *Philoctetes*, when Odysseus and Neoptolemus quarrel, they drop their hands to their sword hilts, and we may imagine the opponents confronting each other in a formal menacing attitude. Later in the play Philoctetes threatens Odysseus with his bow. Similarly, in Euripides' *Electra*, as noted above, Orestes carries his sword in a manner which Electra interprets as a threat to her. In the same author's *Ion* the protagonist, warding off the embraces of Xuthus, threatens him with his bow. The sword-thrust (*xiphismos*) was a recognized dance-figure, numbered among the attitudes of the tragic dance, and must have been a conventional gesture of threat and striking. Such highly formalized attitudes – the weapon hand raised, the knee slightly bent – appear on vases. Orestes is shown in such a conventional posture, advancing to attack his mother Clytemnestra.

We have noted the indecorous movements that expressed joy. Similar wild motions show pain, sickness, and madness. Aeschylus, as usual, is comparatively restrained in this. In *Philoctetes*, however, the degrading malady of Sophocles' hero is vividly displayed. Philoctetes stands stock still; he cannot speak; he struggles with Neoptolemus, gazing wildly at the sky; and he finally drops to the ground, overcome by pain, where he sinks into a coma. A second fit comes later in the play. In *The Women of Trachis* Heracles is poisoned. He awakens to dreadful agony; he writhes and struggles, he cannot control his limbs, and the Old Man and Hyllus have a struggle to hold him down.

Euripides frequently employs such horrific touches. Particularly pathetic is the sick-bed scene that opens his *Orestes*. Orestes lies weak and helpless, unable to stand upright without his sister's support. His looks are wild; he cannot stand for long, but has to lie down again almost immediately. When his madness strikes him again he 'rolls his eyes wildly' (presumably signified, in a mask, by tossing the head), shudders violently, and has to be restrained by Electra's arms around his waist.

In *Hippolytus*, Phaedra, sick to death with love and half out of her mind, has to be supported by her nurse.

PHAEDRA Prop up my body, raise my head.
   I have lost all will to move, my dear.
   How thin my hands and arms are. Hold them.
   This crown is too heavy. It hurts my head.
   Take it off, and let my hair fall free.
NURSE There, there, child. Do not toss
   And turn so, you will hurt yourself.
   A queen should not excite herself. Think who
   You are, and it will give you strength to bear it.
   Pain and suffering are our mortal lot.
PHAEDRA The mountains! I want to go to the mountains.
   The pinewoods where the hounds run, hunting
   The scent of racing deer.
   Gods, this is joy, to run with the hounds,
   And weigh the heft of the spear in your hand
   And toss your hair back, and let fly.[28]

The ancient commentator points out that the action must suit the word here. 'At this point the actor must use agitated voice and gestures; on the line "I go to the wood" he must leap up, as though Phaedra were going herself, and so in the following lines.' The passage is, of course, a lyric one. Vigorous motion accompanies the agitated vocal line.

The point of this scene, and of others like it, is that it represents a breach of stage, as well as real-life, decorum. Phaedra is a queen, and should comport herself with dignity. She is a woman, and should efface herself as women are expected to do. And, from the actor's point of view, the character suddenly explodes into motion. This passage punctuates the normally sedate and studied sequence of movements and gestures with a display of violence. The disorder in Phaedra's mind is reflected in the disorder of her movements.

As a great deal of Greek tragedy is occupied by long speeches, exhortatory, narrative, or forensic, we would expect a range of gestures in conjunction with them: in this element of tragedy the speaker's and the actor's art are clearly one. For hand gestures to accompany speech, our principal source is Quintilian, again with the proviso that he was writing centuries after the event. In important points, however, his testimony is supported by earlier Greek sources.

Quintilian comments on the use of the arms in lengthy passages and in narration, as follows:

In continuous and flowing passages a most becoming gesture is slightly to extend the arms with the shoulders well thrown back and the fingers opening as the hand moves forward. But when we have to speak in a specially rich and impressive style ... the arm will be thrown out in a stately sidelong sweep and the words will, as it were, expand.[29]

This movement almost exactly parallels one described in the scholia on Euripides' *Orestes*. The protagonist is addressing a lengthy speech to Menelaus: 'At this point', says the commentator, 'the actors raise one hand'. This point, it should be noticed, is one where Orestes' words must carry special weight.

Use of the hands, *cheironomia*, was of great importance. In one development, it led to mime. Xenophon, talking of a gifted dancer, says that 'his neck, his legs, his hands, his whole body was in movement'.[30] The dance *schemata* listed by Pollux and Athenaeus include two hand-positions, upturned and downturned. Vase paintings show the latter commonly used as a gesture of deprecation. A similar gesture listed but not explained by Quintilian also appears on the vases with the same significance. Here the first two fingers are kept apart without inserting the thumb, while the remaining two point inwards; even the two former must not be fully extended. This gesture occurs several times in a familiar illustration, the Apulian krater known as the 'Persians' vase and clearly related to Aeschylus' play. Here the council of Persian elders warns Darius against his proposed expedition to conquer Greece. Three of the counsellors make the gesture, one with a gloomy expression, standing immediately in front of the seated king.

Conversely, the upturned palm denotes encouragement. On the 'Persians' vase one of the counsellors, who seems to be contradicting the others, makes this gesture to one side. On an amphora from the Naples Museum, probably illustrating *The Libation Bearers*, Orestes addresses Electra with his arm outstretched and the palm uppermost. It is reasonable to see in this a gesture of encouragement. This is exactly the gesture noted by Quintilian:

There is also the unusual gesture where the hand is cupped and raised above shoulder height, with an encouraging motion, as it were; but the shaking of the hand now generally adopted by foreign schools is acceptable for stage use only.[31]

A gesture of modesty or surprise is described by Quintilian: 'The thumb and first three fingers are gently brought to a point; the hand is brought close to the mouth or breast, then relaxed palm downwards and slightly advanced'.[32] If Quintilian is right in attributing this gesture to Demosthenes, and not merely venturing a guess, it would probably have some affinity with the stage. Additional testimony comes from a krater from Polenza showing Sophocles' *Thyestes*. On the left of the picture, which shows a suppliant before the king, stands a woman with her hand to her mouth as if in trepidation.

Identification of the less important hand gestures cannot be certain. In some cases, the resemblance between early pictures and late oratorical treatises may be only accidental. Nevertheless, in the more important cases the similarity is striking. Enough evidence is available to show us that the techniques of Roman oratory represented, at the very least, a continuity of tradition from the fifth-century theatre. In preparing a reconstruction of the historical acting style, Quintilian's descriptions would form an excellent basis.

About comic acting there is less to say. We can assume that, in action as in language, comedy was closer to the everyday. We can also assume that, as a large part of comedy consists of tragic parody, the gestures of tragedy would be parodied also. We can point to various specific acts of comic business: the gesture called the 'goose', for example, which involved making a clacking beak with two hands, indicating that nonsense was being talked; or the recurrent sight-gag of the comic stage, creeping up to another character and singeing his behind with a lighted torch.

For tragedy, however, the evidence suggests a system of standardized gestures, each portraying a specific emotion. These gestures appear to have been reasonably close to those of real life. They had not evolved, as happened centuries later in the Japanese religious drama, into a cryptic gestural language which only initiates could understand. Our visual evidence indicates that the Greek gestures were clear, simple, and intelligible to the average observer. They were, however, generic. There seems to have been little variation between one character, or one type of character, and another. Rather, the same gestures appear to have been used across the board. By analogy with similar styles of acting in other times and places, therefore, we may infer a system of gestures learned as part of the actor's physical discipline, and applied as appropriate; a system, moreover, not evolved from the actor's individual consciousness, but assumed, as mask and costume were assumed, to convey a meaning in broad terms to an immense audience.

This is consonant with our other impressions of Greek tragedy. Even at so distant a remove from the original performances, certain dominant characteristics stand out. The visual effects of Greek tragedy are always broad, simple, and powerful. Subtlety has no place here. We think of the massed chorus of Persians invoking the ghost of Darius; of the impact of the chorus of Furies, in Aeschylus' *Eumenides*; of Agamemnon treading a carpet which is the colour of blood up to the door of his palace (an effect designed to be seen from above, as virtually all the audience would have seen it); and, similarly, the broken body of the boy Astyanax cradled in his father's shield in *The Trojan Women*.

The mask itself is a generalizing device. It eliminates individual distinctions and works in broad terms. Problems that exist for actors playing Greek tragedy in unmasked modern productions did not exist in the original. For example, one of the hardest problems, in modern revival, is the casting of Jocasta in *Oedipus the King*. The actress must look equally convincing as Oedipus' wife and as his mother; it is almost impossible to find one face that will serve for both. Sophocles' own production, however, eliminated the problem. Oedipus and Jocasta both wore masks. One said 'man', the other 'woman'; and the dramatist could work plausibly with the various relationships between the two, mother–son, husband–wife. In comedy, some masks were clearly made to resemble individuals. As evidence we have Socrates in *The Clouds*, and the famous story of the mask-maker who was reluctant to make a likeness of Kleon. But the texts suggest that these too were generalized, in the sense that they were exaggerated to the point of gross caricature.

Costumes, too, appear to have been generic. Aeschylus' costumes were said to have been copied for the use of the priests of Eleusis. This suggests a set of formal robes for acting in, rather than any sort of theatrical costume as we would now understand the term. Vase illustrations, too, suggest costumes that were, at the most, indicative of different types of character. Functions were indicated by simple properties or costume accessories. A king carried a sceptre, a warrior a double spear. Heralds wore an olive wreath, travellers the *petasos*, or broad-brimmed hat. Of more subtle distinctions, or indeed, of costumes designed individually for each new production, there is little sign; we have indications that actors had their personal stock of

costumes which were an important part of their professional equip-
ment and could, presumably, be used for any play as appropriate.
Euripides seems to have been the first to have introduced individual-
ity in costuming: to have dressed beggarly characters in rags (if this,
indeed, is what he was doing) and, perhaps, Medea in an exotic
costume to demonstrate her un-Greek origins. But the resentment
with which his innovations were greeted shows how deeply rooted the
older tradition was.

This generalizing tendency carries over into other aspects of production. We see it clearly, for instance, in matters of age. It is
impossible to look at a Greek character and say 'He is 38'. The plays
do not allow of such precision. Characters fall into well-marked
groups. They are old; they are in the prime of life; or they are very
young. Old in Greek tragedy means very old indeed, another case of
exaggerating for stage effect. Any character described as aged bears
every mark of extreme senility. His strength fails him, his legs cannot
hold him. He limps and stumbles. He often enters supported by
others. The Old Man in Euripides' *Electra* complains of the steep
climb to his home and of how he must drag his old feet and palsied
limbs up the slope. We can hardly doubt that a vivid pantomime
accompanied these words. Similarly Hecuba, in the play to which she
gives her name, has to be helped from her tent by servants:

> Help the old woman out of door, my children,
> Lead me, Trojan women, hold me up; I was
> Your queen once; now I am a slave like you.
> Hold me, carry me, help me along.
> Take my old arms and let me lean on you.
> Your arms shall be my crutches
> To lend motion to my feet,
> One first, and then the other.[33]

In *The Phoenician Women* Teiresias is led by his daughter and supported
by Menoeceus; his knees are failing him, and he is out of breath. In the
same play Jocasta talks of her dragging feet, and in *Ion* the old servant
has to be supported by Creousa. In such matters, as in most things
visual, Greek tragedy painted on a large canvas, with a big brush.

3

THE ACTOR HEARD

Subtlety was left to the human voice, which was, both for actor and playwright, the principal means of expression. Once again, this was a function of the space available. Although not much could be seen in the Greek theatre, everything could be heard. The acoustics of these theatres were excellent as, indeed, they still are. Epidauros, the best surviving example, is particularly famous in this respect. Every word spoken in the orchestra can be heard in the upper tiers. So can the striking of a match, or a coin dropped on the central altar-base; these are tricks the tour guides regularly perform for visitors.

At Epidauros, at least, the reverse is also true. Noise from any section of the auditorium can be distinctly heard in the others. A rowdy audience can ruin the performance. We recall the tradition, dating from the early days of the theatre before the buildings had assumed permanent stone form, that audiences drummed their heels on the wooden benches to show their disapproval of a play. In a theatre with naturally good acoustics, this must have been devastating. It illuminates the necessity, both for tragedy and comedy, of embodying attention-holding devices, and the dangers of allowing a huge crowd to be distracted. The largely irrelevant prologues which open Aristophanic comedy were probably intended to quieten the spectators down. It does not matter if the first few speeches are not heard. The subject matter of the play is introduced only when attention has been secured.

Not every theatre, of course, had acoustics as good as those of Epidauros. But even in structures now largely ruinous, the spoken word still carries to the limits of the seating with extraordinary clarity. This is all the more remarkable since the Greeks seem to have been self-taught in acoustics, working empirically and with no foundation of theoretical understanding. Aristotle remarks that the voices of the chorus were made less distinct when straw was spread in the orchestra. For him this was a discovery; to us it seems obvious. As late as Vitruvius, who wrote in the first century AD, it was still being debated whether wood or stone was acoustically better for theatre construction. Majority opinion was in favour of wood.

But whether by accident or design, words spoken in the theatre could be heard. They were addressed, moreover, to an audience that knew how to listen. A large proportion of the Athenian public was non-literate. Reading and writing were not, as for us, the fundamentals of education. Public speaking, however, was. The average citizen spent a good deal of his working week in the public discussion by which the city-state operated. In the voting assembly, the *ekklesia* held regularly across the valley from the theatre in the Pnyx, in a structure that closely resembles a theatre, the citizen would have been exposed to the finest orators of his time, and called upon to speak himself. In the committees that concerned themselves with particular acts of business, and the juries, huge by modern standards, that sat in judgement in the courts, he would have grown used to hearing arguments and weighing verbal testimony. Public speaking was the key to advancement. When Aristophanes wrote *The Clouds* he was composing not so much a satire upon Socrates as a dramatic treatise on the power of rhetoric, and its dangers. Strepsiades, the comedy's debt-ridden protagonist, can think of no better solution for his problems than the acquisition of a glib tongue. The caricature of Socrates to whom he turns for help earns his living by instructing men in speech. In *The Clouds* both philosophy and education are equated with rhetoric.

Familiarity with the spoken word thus communicated itself to the plays. So, by the same token, did a prejudice against writing. In Homer we find writing presented as an arcane art, tainted with the possibilities of evil. By the time we reach fifth-century tragedy, this picture has hardly changed. Both in tragedy and comedy, the act of writing is presented as esoteric, mystical, and, *ipso facto*, suspect. In Euripides' *Iphigeneia in Tauris* the princess, Agamemnon's daughter, has been supernaturally preserved from her apparent sacrifice at the outset of the Trojan War. Whisked away to the barbaric northland, she presides as a priestess over savage rites, though still longing for her lost home in Argos. Her brother, Orestes, and his friend Pylades, arrive on these inhospitable shores. Brother and sister do not recognize each other; but, learning that the visitors come from Argos, Iphigeneia determines to send back one of them with a message to the land of her birth. She entrusts Pylades with a letter. In the play, it is made clear that she has not written this herself. Writing, apparently, is not something that a well-brought-up princess would be expected to do. One of the other captive women has done it for her. Pylades, entrusted with this missive, is nervous of handling it. A letter fills him with foreboding. Supposing he should lose it? He therefore demands to have it supplemented by a spoken message, from which comes the recognition of brother and sister. The implications could hardly be more plain. Writing is secret, sinister, and fraught with dangers. The spoken word is clear and honest.

In the same author's *Hippolytus*, Queen Phaedra, driven mad by love for the stepson who rejects her, hangs herself and leaves for Theseus, her husband, a suicide note accusing Hippolytus of raping her. The tablet is discovered on her body. Read by Theseus, it is taken as incontrovertible evidence. On this basis, the king condemns his son to banishment, and delivers the curse that will destroy him. Of course, the tablet lies. Soon afterwards, one of Hippolytus' servants comes to narrate his master's death. He reports how a monster rose from the sea to execute the curse, and drove Hippolytus' horses insane, so that their frenzied gallop threw him on the rocks and killed him. The messenger concludes his speech thus:

> I am nothing but a servant here, my lord;
> But I can never bring myself to think
> That there was any malice in your son,
> Not if all the women in the world
> Should hang themselves, or every pine on Ida
> Be turned to tablets to be written on,
> For I know virtue in him when I see it.[1]

Here, once again, evil is seen as vested in the act of writing, and the tablet is accessory before the fact.

In the same light, we may view the lying letter sent by Agamemnon to his daughter in *Iphigeneia in Aulis*; it promises her marriage to Achilles, when in fact she is being lured to her death. In comic vein, we have an example in *The Clouds*. Socrates, attempting to educate his rustic pupil, asks him:[2]

You're taken to court. They fine you a small fortune.
Tell me how you'd get out of that one.

Strepsiades replies:

> Haven't you seen in the druggists' shops
> That beautiful transparent stone
> They use for lighting fires? ...
> ... I'd get my hands on one
> And as the clerk was writing down the charge,
> I'd stand at a distance on the sunny side
> And burn up the letters ...
> ... It's wonderful
> To wipe out an enormous fine like that.

Eliminate the writing, Strepsiades believes, and you eliminate its harm. By the same token the Statute Seller in Aristophanes' *The Birds*, attempting to market his collection of written legislation for the new colony, is driven off with threats and blows.

Non-literate societies cultivate good memories; it is the only way that things can be recorded. The effects of this, too, are obvious in the Greek theatre. Plays feed upon themselves. Virtually every work we have contains allusions to other plays, verbal echoes, and visual and aural reminiscences. When Strepsiades welcomes his son home from Socrates' academy, he parodies a lyric from Euripides' *Hecuba* written a few years before. Euripides' *Electra* reverberates off Aeschylus' *The Libation Bearers*, a work of the previous generation. Perhaps most impressive among a multitude of examples is a famous passage from Aristophanes' *The Frogs*, which once again goes back to Euripides.

In 428 BC, Euripides had written *Hippolytus*, the story of Phaedra's incestuous passion for her stepson. In the play, she confides her secret to her nurse, who in turn swears Hippolytus to silence and then tells him. The following dialogue ensues:[3]

HIPPOLYTUS O mother Earth! O rays of golden sun!
  Such words should not be heard on human lips!
NURSE Peace, peace, my son, or somebody will hear you!
HIPPOLYTUS How can I hear such horrors and be silent?
NURSE Yes, I beg you, by your strong right hand.
HIPPOLYTUS No. Keep away. I will not let you touch me.
NURSE I go down on my knees. Do not destroy me.
HIPPOLYTUS I thought you said your words were innocent?

NURSE But not for all the world to hear, my son.
HIPPOLYTUS Fair words could only gain by the repeating.
NURSE You swore your oath to me. You must not break it!
HIPPOLYTUS It was my tongue that swore, and not my mind.

This last line, as we know from ancient commentaries, immediately became notorious. Euripides was accused of justifying perjury, and the passage was seen as yet another example of his fondness for subverting traditional moral values. The charge is hardly substantiated by the play. Hippolytus dies precisely because he does *not* break his word. All the same, the charge stuck. How vividly the line was remembered is demonstrated by *The Frogs*.

In this comedy Dionysus, God of Tragedy, descends to the Underworld to resurrect Euripides, lately deceased. It is the only way, he says, that he can keep the art of tragedy alive. But, after presiding over a debate in Hades between Aeschylus and Euripides, he changes his mind, and decides to take back Aeschylus. Euripides is furious. He snarls:

> Remember all the gods by whom you swore
> To take me back with you, and choose your friend.

Dionysus replies:

> My tongue has sworn. But I'll choose . . . Aeschylus![4]

The punchline, placed in so prominent a position, assumes that the whole audience will grasp the allusion. But *The Frogs* was written in 405 BC. Aristophanes is confident that his audience will remember quotations from a play written twenty-three years before.

To some extent this retentiveness derived from the limited output of the Greek theatre. Restricted to three festivals a year, plays were noteworthy events, well remembered because of their comparative scarcity. Each production was eagerly anticipated, avidly watched, and treasured in the memory. Points of high interest, like the *Hippolytus* scene quoted above, could be discussed years afterwards. As in other respects, our own theatre offers no true comparison. In many places the theatre is, or can be, an everyday event. It is fed into our homes; we need only to cross the room to switch on the television set. We have grown blasé through surfeit. A recent survey shows that any television programme, no matter how good, fades from the popular memory in a mere eight months. For the Greek theatre, a fairer

78

modern comparison might be the more selective festival experience. An audience which returns yearly to Salzburg for the Mozart operas, or to Bayreuth for Wagner, is able to retain sharp memories of personalities and performers, and compare records over a long span of years. So, in another frame of reference, do aficionados of cricket in England, and baseball in the United States. The Greeks preserved such memories of plays.

This is not, however, the only explanation. Clearly, the Greeks possessed a level of aural attentiveness far superior to ours. We have evidence of this from the earliest period of Greek literature. The complex structures developed by the bards who recited epic presuppose an audience with the intellectual sophistication to follow them: an audience habituated to perceiving parallels, identifying verbal echoes and assonances, and following the intricate liaisons out of which such poems as the *Iliad* and the *Odyssey* were constructed. This, like other qualities, carried over to the fifth century. Quite obviously, Greek audiences were trained to listen to a play in a way that modern audiences are not. The plays, like the Homeric poems, are interwoven with intricate verbal patterns. A line at the end of a speech will pick up a thought at the beginning. A scene late in the play mirrors one from early on. Modern scholars trace these patterns by close application to the written text. An ancient audience was expected to attain the same results by hearing the play, and hearing it only once.

This combination of superb acoustics and an alert, aurally receptive audience produced actors who knew that they could rely on the spoken word. Throughout the history of the Greek theatre, a good actor and a good voice were synonymous. Aristotle defined acting as being 'concerned with the voice, and how it should be adapted to the expression of different emotions'.[5] Similarly, he conceived of the appreciation of acting as being purely a matter for the ear; he coupled it with music, as a kindred art.[6] To Demosthenes is attributed an illuminating dictum: he said that 'actors should be judged by their voices, politicians by their wisdom'.[7] According to Zeno, the actor should have a powerful voice and great strength;[8] while Plato characterized the actors, whom he would have expelled from his ideal state, as 'fine-voiced'.[9]

These general reflections were supplemented by numerous notices of individual actors throughout ancient literature. The voice was always the main object of criticism. Hegelochos, the actor who played the title role in Euripides' *Orestes*, was mocked by Plato the comic poet for his poor voice. It was, apparently, not pleasant to the ear. Nikostratos' excellent delivery of messengers' parts made his name pass into a proverb. Sophocles was restricted to a limited range of parts by his small voice, and according to one source it was by overstraining it that he died.

In the fourth century as in the fifth, *euphonia*, good voice production and delivery, was the hallmark of the accomplished actor. Demosthenes constantly refers to his rival Aeschines, the actor turned politician, as *euphonos*, and this cannot have been wholly sarcastic. Aeschines must have been a young actor of considerable promise: he attracted the attention of two of the greatest actors of his time, Theodoros and Aristodemos, and joined their company to play important roles in revivals of Sophocles and Euripides. At some stage in his career he joined Simylos and Socrates, indifferent provincial actor-managers popularly known as 'the roarers'; from this period may have derived the tendency to rant so often derided by Demosthenes. Theodoros himself was praised for his voice by Aristotle. What distinguished him from other actors was that it seemed quite natural, not assumed. Neoptolemos, 'head and shoulders above the rest in loudness of voice and reputation', is said to have given Demosthenes lessons in breath control, and to have been well paid for them. Dionysios of Syracuse assembled for a festival 'those actors who possessed the finest voices', whose 'excellence of delivery astonished those who heard them'.

In accordance with the importance attributed to *euphonia*, any fault or blemish was severely criticized by a knowledgeable public. It was not necessary to shout to be heard. The secret lay in controlled delivery. Some actors doubtless had their tricks, like the zither-players mentioned in Roman times by Vitruvius who 'when they wish to sing with a louder tune, turn to the wooden scenery and, with this assistance, gain resonance for their voices'.[10] But on the whole, such devices, or systems of amplification described elsewhere by Vitruvius, were unnecessary. An able actor could achieve his effects without assistance and without strain, and shouting, the mark of a bad actor, was deplored. Pollux, the late lexicographer, lists a whole string of terms describing specific faults in an actor's voice.

Individual mistakes in delivery and pronunciation were quickly seized upon by a keen and critical audience. Modern opera singers dread performing in Parma, the legendary 'lions' den', where audiences unmercifully boo the smallest failing. Every Athenian audience seems to have been like that. One of the favourite jokes of the fifth-century theatre concerned the actor Hegelochos already mentioned above, who played Euripides' Orestes. In line 271 of the play, instead of 'After the storm I see a calm [*galen' horo*]', he recited 'after the storm I see a polecat [*galen horo*]'. This seems to us a mild joke at best, but the comic poets would not let it alone. It apparently had the same effect on an Athenian audience as a diva singing a wrong note in a Puccini aria would have for us. The value of the anecdote, however, lies in what it tells us about the acuteness of the Athenian ear. Hegelochos' gaffe involved no more than a misplaced elision which, to us, seems barely perceptible. A similar tale is told about the actor Cleomachos, who sounded an unnecessary 'h' in a tragic passage.

Voices were carefully nurtured and trained. Aristotle preached the necessity to watch one's diet, if the voice were not to be ruined. Other writers gave the same advice. Roast meat, it was believed, was not good for speakers. Thus the epithet *opsophagos*, 'eater of roast meat', when used of an actor was a term of abuse. We might almost translate it 'ham'. The comic poet Plato described Aeschylus' actor Mynniskos in this way.

Once again, we are talking of a tradition that continued through Roman times. Cicero refers to an exercise of running up and down the scale, used by the Greek tragedians. A century later, we have Suetonius' description of the emperor Nero, a keen amateur performer. We are told how the emperor lay on his back, with lead weights on his chest; how he purged himself with laxatives and vomiting; and how he abstained from fruit and other food considered harmful to the voice. Before we dismiss this as the product of a decadent empire, we should remember that one of the most notorious court cases in fifth-century Athens concerned a choir trainer who inadvertently poisoned a boy chorister (in this case, for a non-dramatic performance) by administering potions designed to strengthen his vocal chords. Actors rehearsed their voices right up to, and in the intermissions of, the performance. The comic actor Hermon missed his entrance at a competition because he was trying out his voice outside the theatre.

Inevitably, in some cases, the means became the end, and technical virtuosity degenerated into mere display. It was this vulgarization to which Plato objected in the fourth century:

And other types of men will be all the readier to vary their style the worse they are, and will think nothing too demeaning for them.

They will seriously try to represent in public all the things they were talking about. We shall have the noises of thunder and wind and hail, and of wheels and axles; the notes of trumpets, pipes, whistles, and every possible instrument; the barking of dogs, the bleating of sheep, and the twittering of birds. All these will be represented by voice and gesture, and narrative will play a small part only.[11]

Plato's strictures had their basis in fact. One Theodoros – probably the famous actor of that name – was famous for his squeaking pulley imitations, and Parmenon for impersonating pigs: hence the story that Parmenon's rivals smuggled a real pig into the auditorium; when it squealed the audience shouted 'Good, but nothing like Parmenon.' The pig was then released, and Parmenon's claque confounded.

Another striking characteristic of ancient acting was the amount of energy expended in performance. Greek acting seems to have imposed a far greater physical strain than modern. Actors prepared themselves by constant discipline. Zeno's dictum, that an actor needs a powerful voice and great stamina, has already been quoted. Some actors, like Apollogenes, were successful athletes too. It may be relevant that Euripides was an athlete before he turned to the stage. His sport was boxing, in which he won a victory at Athens. Once again, this insistence on the actor's physical qualifications prevailed until Roman times. Cicero could say that 'philosophy is as necessary for the speaker as the gymnasium for the actor'.

Their training throughout seems to be more like athletes than performing artists. We have seen how they were forced to abstain from certain kinds of food and drink, maintaining a careful diet. Plato saw this as a humiliation, and considered the performers' dignity as lowered thereby. He suggests as a milder alternative for the training of competing choruses in his ideal state total abstinence from wine for adolescents, and moderate drinking only for men under 30.[12] Modern actors would find this severe enough. Other kinds of indulgence were equally forbidden. No sex before the performance; no sex at all, in some cases. Plutarch tells an apt anecdote of Theodoros:

There is a story of the wife of Theodoros, the tragic actor, who was not able to sleep with her husband because of the approaching festival. When he came home from his victory, she threw her arms round him and said [in an appropriate tragic quotation] 'Son of Agamemnon, now you may!'[13]

But although their indulgences were limited, actors in training were carefully looked after and given every luxury that would not be harmful. Plutarch quotes with approval the criticism of an anonymous Spartan, who said the Athenians were wrong to spend on the theatre sums of money that would support whole fleets and armies. The generals, he says, often ordered their troops to bring uncooked rations when they were about to go into action. Sea captains issued their crews with a meagre sustenance of barley, cheese, and onions. But the chorus-trainers in the theatre gave their performers eels, young lettuce, beef, and marrow, pampering them and keeping them in luxury while they trained their voices. The defending chorus-master in the poisoning case was unable to oversee the training personally. He therefore appointed no fewer than four people to look after them, one of whom was deputed to buy anything the poet or the other trainers ordered.

Actors needed their strength. In performance, the costume alone would have imposed a heavy strain. Acting in masks is also hard, hot work. Aristotle bears witness to the great thirst of Parmenon after taking part in a contest: 'So also those under great strain are thirsty. That is why they wash their mouths out and swallow greedily, as Parmenon the actor used to do.' It is recorded as a cause for wonder that the great Polos played eight tragedies in four days at the age of 70.

These requirements certainly do not indicate straight acting as we know it. Rather, they suggest a combination of opera and ballet, with emphasis on the former. In the descriptions of Greek acting given above, comparisons with opera have inevitably suggested themselves. The similarity is inescapable. The Greek actor needed, above all, a powerful and finely trained voice. He needed the physical stamina to support his voice, and carry him through a series of roles in mask and heavy costume. The actors' gestures themselves, as we have been able to reconstruct them, appear like operatic gestures, designed to open the diaphragm rather than constrict it.

One common gesture is, perhaps significantly, conspicuous by its absence. In tragedy, characters hardly ever sit down. Even those like Hecuba, complaining of their feeble bodies and their aching limbs, are not given chairs. They may fall down, and frequently do. But the only case of a character sitting is at the opening of *Oedipus at Colonus*, when the blind protagonist, led by Antigone, finds a place to rest.

Father. Poor father. We are coming to a city.
There, in the distance, I can see the watchtower,
And this is surely sacred ground, where vines and laurels
And olive trees grow wild; a haunt of birds,
Where nightingales make music in the coverts.
And here there is a shelf of rock. Sit down.
It has been a long day's journey for an old man.[14]

But he does not sit for long. By line 30, he is already on his feet again.
It is surely no coincidence that, in the modern theatre, the movement
that opera singers most hate is sitting down. Mimi and Violetta can
sing on their deathbeds; but sitting does harsh things to the voice.

In temperament the famous Greek actors certainly resembled
prima donnas. Stories of their conceit and professional jealousies are
legion. One will suffice here: 'The tragic actor Theodoros summed up
the matter not too badly. He had never once allowed anybody to
appear on stage before he did, not even one of the inferior actors. He
used to say that audiences are most attracted by the first thing they
hear.'[15] There is also the curious tradition recorded by Cicero, that in
the Roman theatre small-part players subordinated their voices so as
not to detract from the principal. Caruso would have approved.

We may, perhaps, venture one more surmise. Opera singers are
usually more concerned with technique than with content. Their
questions about characterization tend to be rudimentary. They do
not interpret a character; they merely present a character already
fully realized in the composer's conception. With the various
demands competing for the Greek actors' attention, it is likely that
they did the same thing.

Exactly how Greek actors used their voices we do not know. Portions of the script, as already noted, were sung. The actor delivered
solo cries at moments of high tension, or sang in concert with the
chorus: notably in the *kommos* passages, the formal dirges and laments
where the voices of principals and chorus were interwoven in extended threnody. Conspicuous examples are the lament over the
murdered body of Agamemnon, in Aeschylus' tragedy of that name,
and the three-part dirge delivered by Orestes, Electra, and the chorus
in its sequel, *The Libation Bearers*. There are many others.

The nature of this musicality is lost to us; the scores have perished.
But we have suggestions throughout antiquity that it was not confined to the lyric portions of the play. On the contrary, what we now
think of as spoken dialogue may well have been chanted with a strong

musical beat, and have been closer to our operatic recitative than to common stage speech as we now know it. Metrical analysis shows how verse patterns change to suit the mood. The usual metre for actors' speeches was the iambic trimeter, a line of six feet based on the iambus ($\cup$ –); a metre that comes close to the iambic pentameter with which we are familiar from Shakespeare, though using a longer line. Modern translators who retain the Greek six-foot line in English, as does Richmond Lattimore in his translation of the *Oresteia*, give actors problems; the line is longer than they have been trained for. This is another indication of the Greek actor's *bel canto* expertise, and his powers of breath control.

At moments of particular intensity, however, the metre may shift, without bursting fully into song. Euripides is particularly fond of the trochaic tetrameter, an eight-foot line based on the trochee (– $\cup$), which he employs regularly in such passages. Thus, in his *The Madness of Heracles*, the usual actor's metre is the iambic trimeter, illustrated by this passage from one of Megara's speeches:

> Fortune did not cheat me in my father.
> His riches were a byword. He possessed
> A kingdom such as makes the long spears fly
> In lust to overthrow its proud possessor.[16]

But in the centre of the play, the goddesses Iris and Lyssa descend upon the house to turn the hero mad. This supernatural apparition is signalled by a shift into trochaics, which can be roughly conveyed in translation:

> We come for one man only, and make war upon his house,
> Him that they call the son of Zeus and of Alcemon
> Destiny preserved him till his weariness and toil were done
> Zeus would not allow that I or Hera should ever do him harm.[17]

Similarly, in the *The Bacchae*, the god Dionysus has appeared in mortal shape, only to be imprisoned in the palace of Thebes. He frees himself by means of earthquakes, and manifests himself to his worshippers in a burst of trochaics:

> Rise, you Asiatic women. Are you overcome with fear?
> Are you all prostrate with terror? Yes, you have the look of those
> Who have witnessed Bacchus' frenzy devastating Pentheus' house.
> Now the anger has departed. Courage, on your feet again.[18]

Beyond such rudimentary observations, however, we can say little about the sound of the sung or spoken word. A tradition of the operatic nature of Greek tragedy, however, remained for centuries. It inspired the western world's first operas, which began as attempts to restore Greek drama to the stage; it passed into the repertoire of French playwrights of the seventeenth century, whose actors chanted their lines, rather than speaking them; it was the foundation of the 'special voice' school of acting which, in tragedy, dominated the theatre for centuries, and insisted that subjects of magnitude demanded a delivery that was formal, elevated, and distinct from the speech patterns of everyday conversation.

Some aspects of the tragic actor's vocal performance, however, we can be more sure about. It is obvious that the level of vocal impersonation was far less than we are now used to – if, indeed, it existed at all. There are few significant differences of vocabulary between one type of character and another. Speech patterns are not changed to show sex, age, or social status. Old men, young men, women, slaves, and warriors, all subscribe to the same standard level of tragic diction. In *The Bacchae* the messenger from Mt Cithairon, who reports the terrifying onslaught of the worshippers of Bacchus, at one point characterizes himself as a simple, tongue-tied peasant.

> Then one among us, who had been in town
> And had a way with words, said 'Fellows
> Of these hills and holy places, what
> If we should capture Agave from these rites
> And take her as a favour to the king?'[19]

The implication is clear: the man who proposed this scheme was an urban dweller, more communicative than his friends from the countryside; the other herdsmen, including the messenger who delivers this speech, are slow by comparison. And yet, of course, this supposedly halting messenger delivers a long speech which could not be more articulate: a torrent of impassioned rhetoric.

Particularly, tragic actors did not use dialects, even where the plot called for them. In Aeschylus' *The Libation Bearers* Orestes and Pylades lay a plot to gain entrance to the palace:

> Accoutred like a traveller I'll come
> Before the outer gates, with this man here
> Whose name is Pylades, my friend, the bounden

86

> Champion of me and mine. We'll both
> Assume the accent of Parnassus, and talk
> The way men do in Phocis.[20]

When he eventually reappears, however, and presents himself at the gates, it is obvious that he has done nothing of the kind. Greek dialects involved more than a change of accent. They were virtually different languages, with different vocabulary, grammar, and syntax. It is apparent from the written text that the 'disguised' Orestes is still using the same standard Attic–Ionic Greek that he (and everyone else) uses for the rest of the play.

Other scraps of evidence, and reasonable surmises, support this absence of vocal realism. It was said of Polos that there was no difference in the grandeur of his delivery between the roles of Oedipus the king and Oedipus the beggar, or in that of Odysseus in rags. For one prominent actor at least, then, vocal characterization seems not to have been a necessary element of performance. And in one major way, casting worked against such realism: female parts were played by men. This prevailing masculinity seems to have affected the writing. We notice that the principal female characters are, at least by Greek standards and probably by ours also, highly masculine. They plan, they organize, they dominate; they are strong themselves, and impart their strength to others. Thus Clytemnestra, Jocasta, Medea; thus even Hecuba, Andromache, and Phaedra. The secondary female roles in tragedy come closer to the conventional Greek idea of womanhood: Ismene, Polyxena, Chrysothemis. It seems reasonable, therefore, to assume a lack of vocal characterization here also. It might be argued that Sophocles, whose weak voice barred him from some roles, seems to have appeared in women's parts, and this implies a difference in delivery; but Pollux, in his list of vocal failings in an actor, gives 'woman-voiced' as one of them.

Once again, a parallel with opera suggests itself. Not, of course, in the distinction between male and female; but certainly in the distinction between ages. In *Rigoletto*, old Monterone sings as lustily as the young and virile Duke. Musical demands are paramount, and an old character does not sing in an old voice.

Greek comedy, in this as in most other ways, pursued a greater realism. Aristophanes makes rich use of dialects. In his *The Acharnians* the Megarian and Boeotian speak with the accents of their own places. Athenians and Spartans are distinguished in *Lysistrata* while in

The Trojan Women Menelaus the Spartan, Hecuba the Trojan, and Agamemnon the Argive all speak the same Attic–Ionic Greek. In Aristophanes' world not to speak Greek as the Athenians do is automatically funny; his outlanders perform the same function as Irishmen, Italians, or Swedes in traditional American popular comedy, or comic Frenchmen in English farce. Not to speak Greek at all – like the Persian ambassador in *The Acharnians*, or the barbaric Triballian in *The Birds* – is funniest of all.

Though we cannot be certain of the sound of theatrical speech, we can point with confidence to its uses. In a context where more could be heard than seen, where the ear was sharper than the eye, and where the voice was the actor's principal instrument, the playwright was accustomed to convey in language things that in more intimate theatres would be left to visual effects.

One elementary example is character identification. How do we know who an entering character is? In the modern theatre we know, perhaps, because our programme tells us; it lists 'Characters in order of appearance'. The Greek theatre had no programmes. Alternatively, we make deductions about what sort of character this is from the way he walks, talks, and dresses. The Greek theatre lacked such distinctions. We find, therefore, that almost invariably a Greek character announces himself by name, or is announced by someone else, either another character or the chorus.

Such announcements may have different levels of formality. At the simplest, we have an example from *Antigone*. The chorus of elders enters, singing the *parodos* which marks the formal opening of the play. They conclude with:

> But here is our country's ruler,
> Creon, Menoecus' son, our new lord
> By the gods' new dispensations.
> What counsel can he be pondering
> That he summons the elders by general decree
> To meet in special conference together?[21]

Creon then enters to begin his speech. It will be noticed that the introduction, in this case, serves a double purpose; the chorus identifies Creon and also, in case it should still be necessary, itself.

Other examples of this type include a later entrance from *Antigone*. Following a *stasimon*, a burst of choral song, the chorus announces:

> But here comes Haemon, your youngest son.
> Does he come to grieve for the doom that has fallen
> Upon Antigone, his promised bride,
> To complain of the marriage that is taken from him?[22]

Similarly, in Aeschylus' *Agamemnon*:

> I see a herald from the shore, a wreath
> Of olive shadowing his face; the dust
> Upon him, mud's confederate
> And thirsty sister, shows he is no mute
> Whose signs are smoke and mountain timber burning
> But come to tell in words more clear 'Rejoice!'
> Or else ... what else I do not love to speak of.
> May the first good signs have double surety![23]

They contrast the human messenger, about to appear, with the beacon fire that has already been seen, proclaiming the fall of Troy.

Such formal choral announcements, which both introduce characters and contain a hint of the coming action, remind us that the Greeks divided tragedy into *stasima*, choral songs, and *epeisodia*, episodes or acted scenes; and that the literal meaning of *epeisodion* is an entrance upon the scene, an interruption. The meaning goes back to an earlier kind of tragedy that was still primarily choral, though punctuated with arias; and the pattern of the formal introduction seems to derive from this.

On a lesser level of formality, we see characters identifying themselves, or being identified by others. Thus Oedipus, at the opening of *Oedipus the King*:

> My children, in whom old Cadmus is reborn,
> Why have you come with wreathed boughs in your hands
> To sit before me as petitioners?
> The town is full of smoke from altar-fires
> And voices crying, and appeals to heaven.
> I thought it, children, less than just to hear
> Your cause at second-hand, but come in person –
> I, Oedipus, a name that all men know.

Shorter and simpler is the introduction of Pentheus in Euripides' *The Bacchae*. Cadmus and Teiresias are already on stage. Cadmus sees his grandson coming, and says:

> Teiresias, since your eyes are bound in darkness,
> Give ear, and I shall speak of things to come.
> Pentheus is hurrying towards the palace,
> Echion's son, my chosen heir in office,
> Angry, excited; what news does he bring?[24]

Simpler still is the introduction of Teiresias in *Antigone*. He enters as the elders of the chorus conclude their song, but unannounced by them. His identity, however, is made amply clear in the dialogue that follows:

> TEIRESIAS Princes of Thebes, we come here side by side,
>   One pair of eyes between us; that is how
>   Blind men must walk, supported by a guide.
> CREON What news have you for us, old Teiresias?[25]

On the lowest level of formality, introductions may be worked almost at random, and with an air of naturalism, into the dialogue. Euripides, who tended towards a greater realism of language than other dramatists, favoured this approach. Thus, in *Medea*, Jason does not make his appearance until the play is one third over. We have heard about him from the beginning, but have not yet seen him. When he finally presents himself, Medea is alone with the chorus. He ignores them and angrily accosts her:

> I have noticed many times, this not the first,
> How wilfulness runs on to self-destruction.
> You could have kept this city as your home
> By obeying the decisions of your betters,
> But futile protests send you into exile,
> They do not worry me. You can go on
> Forever saying Jason is a scoundrel;
> But when it comes to slandering your rulers,
> Count yourself lucky you were only banished.[26]

Here the self-introduction is apparently natural but really artful; Jason has effectively identified himself, within a few lines of his entrance, no less surely than if the chorus had said 'Here comes Jason'.

However the introduction is made, however, it must still be made; and we find that, as a general rule, it happens within eight lines of a character's first appearance, and usually sooner than this. Significantly, characters who change their costume off-stage are introduced again on their re-entrance. In this theatre the eye is fallible; the audience must not be deluded into thinking, even for a brief moment, that a new costume means a new character. This does not happen often in Greek tragedy. Costume changes are restricted. But there is a famous instance in *The Bacchae*. King Pentheus, the sworn enemy of Dionysus, has fallen victim to the god's hypnotic power. Dionysus urges him to dress as a woman, so that he may spy on the Bacchae celebrating their wild rites on the mountainside. Pentheus struggles feebly, but it is clear, on his exit, that the god has convinced him:[27]

> Indoors, then. There I shall make up my mind
> To put on armour ... or to follow your advice.

Dionysus follows him into the palace; the chorus sings; and Dionysus reappears. His first words make it clear that the next character we see will be Pentheus in change of costume:

> Where is the man who lusts for things forbidden
> Who hungers after strange rites? Where is Pentheus?
> Come from the palace, show yourself to me,
> Dressed like a Maenad, in a woman's guise!

Not even the slowest-witted member of the audience could fail to follow that.

A particular problem involves the identification of off-stage voices. The audience instinctively identifies sound with movement, and voices with characters already present on the stage. An off-stage voice could disrupt this pattern and cause confusion. Thus, when such interruptions occur, it must be made crystal clear who is talking. *Medea* gives us some important examples.[28] In the prologue Medea's old nurse, and the tutor of Medea's and Jason's children, are gossiping in front of the palace. The children are with them, but do not speak. Suddenly Medea's voice is heard from inside the house; it is instantly identified by the nurse:

MEDEA (*off*) Oh I am wretched and oppressed with troubles.
　I wish I were dead, I wish I were dead.
NURSE What did I tell you, dear children. Your mother
　Is stirring her heart, and her anger with it.
　Get along indoors as quickly as possible.
　Don't go within sight of her, don't come near her,
　Beware of her temper, the wild beast lurking
　In that desperate mind of hers.

The same thing happens a little later, when another off-stage cry from Medea interrupts the conversation between the nurse and the chorus of Corinthian women:

NURSE Home! There is no home, that's past and gone.
   Jason is wrapped up in his new wife,
   And my mistress sits pining away in her room
   And her friends can say nothing to comfort her.
MEDEA (*off*)
   I wish
   That lightning from heaven would split my head open!
   What have I to live for now?
   Why can I not leave this hateful life
   And find repose in death?
CHORUS Zeus, heaven and earth, do you hear
   How the wretched wife is weeping?

A particularly tricky problem occurs later in the same play, when the children are heard crying inside in the house as their mother prepares to murder them. Here it is essential that the identification be quickly and effectively made, as the children have now been established in the audience's minds as silent characters; though they have been on stage repeatedly, they have not yet given tongue. The voice used for them may be an adult actor's that has already been heard as other characters in the play: perhaps the actor who plays Medea (off-stage too at this point) doubles as the children here. So we have:

CHORUS Do you hear them? Do you hear the children crying?
   Oh wretched woman, woman possessed.
1ST CHILD (*off*) What shall I do? How avoid my mother's hand?
2ND CHILD (*off*) I cannot tell, dear brother; we are dying.[29]

Similarly, in *The Bacchae*, the off-stage voice of Dionysus must be clearly identified by the chorus, as he calls down destruction on the palace of Pentheus:

DIONYSUS (*off*) Listen to me, listen to my voice,
   Bacchanals, O Bacchanals.
CHORUS That voice! I know it! Dionysus' voice!
   The god is near, and he is calling me.
DIONYSUS (*off*) Again, again I call you, I
   The child of Semele, the son of god.

CHORUS My lord! My lord and master!
    Come to us now, make one, and join
    Our company; O god of thunder, come![30]

The necessity for identification of characters, then, is paramount.
This rule is only rarely broken. When it is, some good reason may be
seen. Characters not immediately identified by name tend to be those
whose costume is so distinctive as to leave no doubt. These are
principally divinities, familiar to the audience through their distinctive attributes; Athena with her goatskin aegis, her helmet, and
her spear, Heracles cowled and cloaked in lionskin, and carrying his
club. We may suspect the same technique at the opening of Euripides'
Alcestis, where the prologue is spoken by the god Apollo:

> Palace of Admetus, where I toiled
> To earn my daily bread; a god in bondage.
> Zeus was at fault in this. He slew my son
> Asklepios. With his thunderbolt he struck him.

These oblique references to the familiar story of Apollo's bondage
would by themselves be enough. But as we soon learn, he is also
marked by his usual attribute of bow and arrows. A familiar deity
appears in familiar guise, and hardly needs direct identifications.
Death, on the other hand, who soon comes on the scene to claim his
victim, is named by Apollo the moment he appears.

Characters name themselves, and one another. They also give
verbal indications of their movements. We have seen earlier how this
habit of describing in language what characters are also, presumably,
doing provides a valuable source of evidence for stage business and
actors' behaviour. Evidently, the playwrights felt a necessity to rein-
force movement by description; it was not safe to trust the eye alone.
Characters also talk about their own emotions, and those of others.
Mask and distance deprived the actor of facial expression. Words
provide a meaningful substitute. Thus in *The Libation Bearers* Electra,
seeing her brother's lock of hair, which was cut off in mourning, cries:

> The full tide of my anger now
> Has come, it is a knife to rend my heart.
> The dyke is down, the tears fall from my eyes
> Unslaked, my grief is at the flood
> To see this hair.[31]

We know that she is crying because she tells us so. There was no other way the Greek audience could know.

There are many similar examples. In *Antigone*, as the heroine is led away to her death, the chorus announces:

> It is my turn now. At a sight like this
> The voice of the laws cannot hold me back
> Or stop the tears from falling down my cheeks.[32]

Earlier in the play, we have already had:

> Look, the gates open, and Ismene comes
> Weeping for love and sisterhood. . . .
> Her face flushed red, and tears
> Fall on her lovely cheek.[33]

In *Oedipus at Colonus*, Antigone sees Polyneices approaching:

> This must be he. The man from another land,
> Without an escort. And he makes his way
> In tears. There is no holding them.[34]

Later in the play, Oedipus upbraids his own son:

> It was you that banished me – me, your own father,
> Left me homeless, made me wear these rags
> That now you weep to see, when change of fortune
> Had placed us in the same predicament![35]

And in *Medea*, Creon on his first entrance addresses the protagonist as 'You with the scowling face, who hate your husband'.

Description, then, necessarily replaces depiction. The examples listed above are simply part of the larger condition of the Greek theatre: a place where language did most of the work. In tragedy, language defines and colours the setting in the imagination of the audience. It paints word-pictures on the blank stone of the *skene*, just as it paints emotions on the unchanging mask. Language extends the action in space and time. It works, primarily through the messenger speeches, to convey things otherwise unstageable.

Messengers in Greek tragedy are usually anonymous. Proper names are reserved for the principals, the aristocracy. But the messenger's roles are often the most important in the play. In the fourth century, when the Greek theatre was established on a professional basis and had developed its own star system, some actors chose the messenger parts in preference to all others. They knew what would make the greatest impact on the audience. Thus, we have such vivid descriptions as the battle of Salamis, in *The Persians*; the storm which destroyed the Greek fleet, in *Agamemnon*; the tearing apart of Pentheus, in *The Bacchae*. All of these are verbal *tours de force* of the highest order. They make their effect by enlisting the imagination of the audience.

A further modern parallel suggests itself. In this respect, the Greek playwright may be compared to the radio scriptwriter. The latter works in a medium where language is not merely the preferred, but the only, channel of communication. All necessary information must come through the words. The writers have similar responsibilities in both forms. Setting must be sketched in language. Characters must be easily identified, and kept distinct from one another. Any necessary physical action must be talked about; without the talk, the audience is baffled.

An index of this similarity appears in the ease with which one form can be translated to the other. Greek plays can be adapted for radio with minimal change; usually, with no change. When one is dealing with a more visual playwright – an Ibsen, or a Chekhov – gaps in understanding immediately appear. Without the audience's power of sight, characters blur into one another. Vital dramatic moments disappear, because they depend for the effect upon the eyes alone. But the Greek tragedian was a radio writer *manqué*. He had already, because of the peculiar problems of his theatre, solved the difficulties of a form that the world would take another two millennia to invent.[36]

If Greek plays are primarily talk, however, the talk must still be shaped and organized; and it is the distinctive pattern of this talk that has caused most difficulties for later readers and audiences. The language of Greek plays tends to mould itself into structures of complex and self-conscious formality.

Large portions of Greek tragedy, as we have seen, were sung. These included most of the material assigned to the chorus – though not, probably, those passages where the chorus, in iambics, talks to characters directly – and lyrics for delivery by actors. What remains (though here again we must remember that a strong musical component existed, even in what we now think of as spoken passages) may be divided into three categories: extended speeches, dialogue, and debate.

Of these, the first presents few difficulties. Greek tragedy is manifestly rhetorical; it spoke to an age for which rhetoric was as natural as

writing is to us. The plays bristle with testimony to the power of the
art. In Aeschylus' *Agamemnon* Clytemnestra exalts the power of Persuasion, which has enabled her to lure her husband to his doom; she
looks upon it almost as a deity, constraining men to do its will. In *The
Eumenides*, at the conclusion of the trilogy, Athena pays her tribute to
the same force, though it has now been transformed into a force for
good; Persuasion has enabled her to move the Furies, and change
them from baneful deities to a more benevolent presence.

This sets the tone for subsequent Greek tragedy. As the importance
of rhetoric in Athenian society increased (dating, it is generally
asssumed, from 462 BC, when jurisdiction was handed over to the
large, popular courts) references in the plays increase accordingly. In
the most rhetorically conscious dramatist, Euripides, they abound.
Jason, confronted by a furious Medea, treats her as a rival
rhetorician:

> I must show myself no mean speaker, so it seems,
> But, like the seawise steersman of a ship,
> Close-haul my canvas, lady, and run before the storm
> Of your verbosity.[37]

In *Hippolytus* Theseus, abusing his supposedly incestuous son, laments the power of speech that so often conceals wrongdoing:

> And every man should have two tongues to speak with,
> One for the truth, and one for lighter things.
> Then the lying voice would stand convicted
> And we should recognize the voice of truth.

Similarly later:

> This boy was born with an enchanted tongue!
> First he offers violence to my bed
> And then he tries to charm me from my anger.[38]

In *The Bacchae* Teiresias reproves Pentheus' tirade against the god
Dionysus in a speech which warns of the dangers inherent in oratory:

> An eloquent speaker who knows his ground
> Can easily make an impressive case.
> You make a pretty speech. It sounds convincing.
> And yet there is no sense or logic in it.
> An orator who lets his passions rule
> His head may prove a danger to the state.[39]

Aristophanes composed a whole comedy, *The Clouds*, about contemporary philosophy, which for him was virtually equated with rhetoric. Strepsiades, plagued with debt, can see no hope of escape except in learning how to lie convincingly in court; Socrates, to whom he turns for assistance, is a master of 'making the worse case appear to be the better'; the showpiece of Socrates' academy is a forensic display by True and False Logic; and the play concludes with a debate in which Strepsiades' son demonstrates, through Socratic reasoning, why he should be allowed to beat his father. In *The Acharnians*, Dikaiopolis, pursued by an angry chorus and in danger of his life, can think of only one defence: he will deliver a persuasive speech to them.

The plays are faithful to their society in that they are permeated with rhetoric. It is no surprise, then, that the characters also borrow the forms of public rhetoric: another demonstration of the close affinity between the political assembly and the theatre. The extended speeches found throughout Greek tragedy, and frequently in comedy also, are organized according to the same principles which would govern stock speeches in public life. In an age which viewed rhetoric both as an art and as a formal discipline, the speeches of the theatre work with conscious artifice upon an audience accustomed to the same procedures in the *ekklesia* and in the lawcourts. We find the same types of speech, and the same organization into the conventionally accepted component parts: proem, narrative, proof, conclusion. When the Priest of Zeus appeals to Oedipus, in the prologue of *Oedipus the King*, to save his city from the plague, he is using the same forms of address as an orator would have used to make the same appeal before the body politic. The mechanics of speech-making transfer easily and naturally from one arena to another. It is not surprising that, centuries later in a long tradition, Seneca seems to have composed tragedies as handbooks for oratorical instruction.

Although our view of the importance of rhetoric in society has changed, and although we now prefer naturalness to artifice in a public speaker, the speeches of Greek tragedy are not offensive to modern ears. They still have force and conviction in the theatre. Greek tragic dialogue, however, is less immediately acceptable. It seems – particularly in translation – forced and artificial to the point of absurdity; it invites parody, and provokes questions as to why it was ever used.

In modern plays, we are accustomed to dialogue which reproduces the patterns of everyday conversation. It gives the impression of being random, irregular; characters talk at varying lengths, interrupt each other, leave sentences unfinished. Greek tragic dialogue is clearly nothing of the kind. It adopts a strict form, *stichomythia* (literally, telling a story line by line) in which the characters converse in alternating verses, the speaker changing at the completion of each line. This is the antithesis of realistic dialogue. Each line has the same length, the same weight; only on the rarest of occasions does one character interrupt another; the effect is hieratic and antiphonal. Here is a typical example, the quarrel between the sisters in Sophocles' *Electra*:

ELECTRA Run to your mother. Tell her everything.
CHRYSOTHEMIS I will not join you. But I will not hurt you.
ELECTRA You despise me, and you may as well admit it.
CHRYSOTHEMIS I only warn you what you must expect.
ELECTRA Then I must follow what *you* think is right?
CHRYSOTHEMIS As long as you are sensible you will.
ELECTRA How can you be so right, and yet so wrong?
CHRYSOTHEMIS There, you have named your own predicament.
ELECTRA Do you deny that right is on my side?
CHRYSOTHEMIS There are times when it is dangerous to be
    right.[40]

The single-line pattern is the most common. Sometimes we see a two-line pattern, as in a dialogue between the same two characters earlier in the play:

CHRYSOTHEMIS Orestes has come home! He has, I tell you!
    I saw, as clearly as you see me now.
ELECTRA You fool! have you gone mad? Or are you making
    A mockery of your troubles, and my own?
CHRYSOTHEMIS I do not! By our own father's hearth I swear it!
    I have not come to mock you. He is here.
ELECTRA What is the use? Where did you get this story?
    How can you believe all that people tell you?
CHRYSOTHEMIS No one told me. I saw it for myself.
    The signs were clear. I can believe my eyes!
ELECTRA How can you be so sure? What did you see?
    These are the ravings of delirium![41]

Sometimes, more rarely still, there is a half-line pattern; and sometimes variations are combined, to give the impression of an argument

98

accelerating in tempo and mounting in intensity, as in the quarrel between Oedipus and Creon in *Oedipus the King*:

CREON Then what do you want? My banishment from Thebes?
OEDIPUS No. Not your banishment. I want your death!
CREON There speaks a man who will not listen to reason.
OEDIPUS No. You must show the world what comes of envy.
CREON I think you must be mad.
OEDIPUS And I think sane.
CREON Then hear me sensibly.
OEDIPUS Hear you, a traitor?
CREON Suppose you are wrong?
OEDIPUS Kings must still be obeyed.
CREON Kings but not tyrants.
OEDIPUS City, oh my city!
CREON My city also. I have rights here too.[42]

Whatever specific pattern we are talking about, however, the regularity is constant; this is stage dialogue orchestrated like music.

It must be admitted that translation makes the stichomythic form even more patently artificial. Greek is a highly inflected language. A word in one line can pick up a word in another through agreement of number, case, and gender; English requires repetition of key words to make connections clear. For this reason, some translators abandon the form entirely, reducing the dialogue to the looser patterns of colloquial English.

This, however, does not solve the basic problem. We have here a highly artificial dialogue-structure, even for verse drama, which presents some difficulties in its use. It is a legitimate question why this convention should have arisen, or why it should be so strongly adhered to, when it departs so far from the patterns and rhythms of normal conversation. It may be argued, of course, that Greek tragedy, itself a highly artificial form, was not interested in reproducing naturalistic conversation patterns, any more than it was interested in realistic costumes or stage settings. Yet we have it on ancient authority that the prevailing metre of Greek tragedy was employed because it reflected, even while it modified, the pattern of non-dramatic speech; we are told that the iambic was used because of all metres it approximated most closely to the rhythm of everyday utterance. If the Greeks adhered so closely to the norm in one way, it is hard to see why they departed from it so conspicuously in another.

It might be argued, too, that other types of drama have used non-naturalistic verse forms because of literary fashion – forms which seem to impose no less difficulty than does *stichomythia*. The French rhymed Alexandrine is sometimes quoted as an example of this. Yet, for all its artificiality, the Alexandrine can be shown to have considerable dramatic utility. Here the rhyme form and balanced utterance are no mere external ornaments but the expression, in little, of the delicate symmetry of the play as a whole. (The same case can be made for *stichomythia*: the balance of answering lines, like the strophic–antistrophic responsion of choruses, reflects the balance implicit in the drama.) The Alexandrine compresses passionate sentiment within an arbitrary and limited vocal expression, just as the passions of the French heroes and heroines are constrained within the strict social *milieu* in which they operate. And here there is an obvious point of difference. Where the Alexandrine encourages tautness and compression, *stichomythia*, by its nature, encourages redundancy. Often, the necessity for preserving the regular alternation of lines involves the insertion of a verse that is, for all practical purposes, otiose. What, if any, were its compensations?

A clear example occurs in Euripides, *Medea*, vv. 667–87. This is part of the dialogue between Medea and Aigeus, King of Athens. Medea, troubled by her husband's desertion, asks her visitor what has brought him to Corinth.

AIGEUS I have been visiting Apollo's oracle at Delphi.
MEDEA What took you there, to earth's prophetic centre?
AIGEUS To enquire how children might be born to me.
MEDEA What, are you still without a son, at your age?
AIGEUS Yes, by some whim of providence I have no heir.
MEDEA And what did Phoebus have to say about it?
AIGEUS Words too wise for a man to understand.
MEDEA Then may I know the oracle's reply?
AIGEUS Most certainly, for cleverness is what we need.
MEDEA Then tell me, if you may, what Phoebus said.
AIGEUS Not to loosen the wineskin's hanging foot –
MEDEA Until you had arrived somewhere, or done something?
AIGEUS Until I reached my ancestral hearth again.
MEDEA And what directs your footsteps through this country?
AIGEUS There is a man called Pittheus, King of Troezen –
MEDEA Old Pelops' son, with a great reputation for piety.

AIGEUS I want to tell him what the oracle has said.
MEDEA He is a wise man, skilful in such matters.
AIGEUS And the oldest of my military allies.

In the foregoing quotation, the twelfth and sixteenth lines, both
utterances of Medea, clearly seem to be redundant. Medea's repeated
interruptions are not dictated by any burning interest in Aigeus: as
Euripides is concerned to show us, Medea is preoccupied with her
own troubles. The main function of the twelfth line is to keep the
rhythmic alternation of the dialogue undisturbed. Aigeus quotes
Apollo's prophecy; and even in so compact a language as Greek, it
cannot be compressed into one line. It takes two. Therefore, to
preserve the pattern, Medea must have a line intervening. The same
is true of the sixteenth line, which again seems to be occasioned
simply by the fact that Aigeus has more than one line's worth to say.
By modern standards of dramatic fitness these interjections seem
inappropriate. Even if we do our best to rid our minds of modern
preconceptions, it seems difficult to justify their existence on any
grounds other than the purely mechanical; but the structure is paramount, and takes precedence over plausibility. Such instances are
frequent in Euripides, though not confined to him, and we must ask
why the dramatists allowed themselves to be shackled by a form that
permitted such redundancy and bathos.

Answers have tended to probe into the drama's supposed antece-
dents. George Thomson[43] has suggested that *stichomythia* remains in
the plays because it retains the form of some pre-dramatic liturgy. A
priest would intone the question, and the band of catechumens would
respond with a rhythmically equivalent answer. This catechistic
form, Thomson suggests, has passed over virtually unchanged into
drama, with actor and chorus, or actor and actor, taking the places of
priest and initiate.

Sir John Myres offers another, and perhaps more satisfactory,
explanation.[44] He suggests that the stichomythic form reflects a pre-
dramatic riddle process, wherein the correct answer is elucidated in a
series of questions. There are certainly passages in Greek tragedy
which would support this, including one of the most famous, the
dialogue between Oedipus and the Herdsman in *Oedipus the King*,
from which Oedipus discovers his own identity:

OEDIPUS If you will not speak to oblige me, I must make you.
HERDSMAN No, no, for god's sake; you would not harm an old
    man?

OEDIPUS Quick, someone, tie his hands behind his back.

HERDSMAN Unhappy man, what more do you want to know?

OEDIPUS This child he talks of; did you give it him?

HERDSMAN I did; and I wish that day had been my last.

OEDIPUS This day may be, unless you tell the truth.

HERDSMAN I shall do myself more harm by telling you.

OEDIPUS It seems he is determined to waste our time.

HERDSMAN No, no: I told you once, I gave it to him.

OEDIPUS Who? Which one of my people? Where does he live?

HERDSMAN No, master, in heaven's name, ask no more questions.

OEDIPUS You are a dead man if I have to ask again.

HERDSMAN It was a child of the house of Laius.

OEDIPUS A slave? Or one of his own family?

HERDSMAN I am near to saying what should not be said.

OEDIPUS And I to hearing; but it must be heard.

HERDSMAN They said it was Laius' son. But go inside
And ask your wife: for she could tell you all.[45]

This does, indeed, sound like a riddle-formula; one by one, the questions pare away the enigma, until questioner and questioned arrive at the core of truth.

Either of the above explanations may be true; or both of them may be. There is no way of knowing, for they go back to a time before written records had begun, and when drama was evolving out of magic and religious ritual. But even if they are true, they only answer the question 'How?' They do not tell us why. A play is not a museum. Dramas may very well preserve features dating from the remote past. But they do so not simply because these features are old and interesting, but because they are useful. Therefore, in the case of *stichomythia*, we must ask not where it came from, but why the dramatist thought it worth keeping at all costs.

An answer lies, perhaps, in the requirements of Greek stage speech that have already been discussed in this chapter. If we look again at the dialogue between Medea and Aigeus quoted above, we see a conversation between two characters who, as it first appears, could hardly be more distinct. Medea is a young woman, Aigeus a man almost past the age when he can still sire children. In Greek terms, however, the distinction is far less apparent. To begin with, both parts are played by men. Secondly, as we have seen, the level of vocal impersonation was probably far less than the modern theatre has accustomed us to. Thirdly, both these characters were masked, so that audiences could not see their lips move, or indeed see more than the vague outline of a human face.

In such conditions, given conversation that was random and unpredictable, the audience might have had great difficulty in knowing who was saying which line, or when the speaker changed. With the form of conversation regular and predetermined, however, the audience knows that at the end of every iambic line (or two lines, or half-line, whichever pattern has been established) the speaker will change; and the dialogue bounces back and forth between one and the other rhythmically, regularly, and predictably, like a ball between two racquets.

Whatever the origins of *stichomythia*, therefore, it is in this elementary matter of ensuring understanding that the form displays its utility, and to which it probably owes its survival. To ensure comprehension, the form must be retained; and if a character has to say something which takes more than one iambic line, as in the case of Aigeus' quotation of the prophecy to Medea, it becomes necessary for the information to be divided over two lines and for another line to be inserted between them.

This device is of trifling importance in comedy, where lines are often divided irregularly, between two or even three characters. Tragedy seems to have abhorred a pause. The scanty evidence that we possess suggests that delivery was continuous; where pauses occurred, they would have had the same effect as a five-bar rest in a symphony. In comedy, however, audience reaction was a more important factor. There must have been pauses for laughter, and for the interpolation of comic business. Thus, irregular division of lines would have been more feasible.

In tragedy, the necessity for distinguishing speakers makes itself felt in other ways also. When characters address long speeches to each other, the chorus customarily intervenes with a brief comment; as short, perhaps, as two lines. In *Antigone*, for example, Creon and Haemon, his son, argue over the justice of Antigone's punishment. Creon urges the virtues of discipline and public order, to which even one's immediate family must be subject. When he has finished, the chorus comments:

> Unless the years have robbed me of my wits
> You seem to have sound sense in what you say.

103

Haemon, on his side, makes a plea for humility and tolerance. The chorus caps his speech with another couplet:

> Creon, if he speaks to the point, you ought to listen.
> And Haemon, you to him. There is sense on both sides.[46]

These choral interjections, and the many like them, are scarcely cogent additions to the argument. On the contrary, they introduce a note of anticlimax; and once again, we may legitimately wonder why they are there. Probably, they serve the same purpose that we have now attributed to *stichomythia*. They mark the transition from one speaker to another; they serve as a form of verbal punctuation which is readily apparent. Given the conditions of the Greek theatre, it might not always be obvious that the speaker had changed; but it is always clear when the chorus speaks. What they say is immaterial; they are used simply to underline the fact that one speaker has finished, and another is going to begin.

Even when this does not happen; when one speech leads directly into another; the author is careful to avoid confusion. In *The Eumenides*, Orestes seeks protection from the goddess Athena. She is cautious at first, and seeks assurance that he has a claim on her attention:

> But tell me first your country and your birth
> And something of your history; and then
> Defend yourself against these accusations,
> Given that you come here armed in right
> To keep your vigil at my image, as
> Ixion did before, and are entitled
> To a fair hearing. These are my questions.
> It is your turn now. Give me plain answers.

Orestes replies:

> Lady Athena, let me make
> Your ending my beginning, and remove
> This weighty reservation.[47]

From the last lines of Athena's speech, and the opening of Orestes', it could hardly be more obvious that one speaker has finished, and another has begun. Once again, the example of the radio script suggests itself. Where sight is lacking, or is fallible, the information must be left to sound.

4

DEBATE AND DRAMA

In the examination of the typical patterns of Greek drama, and the way they answer the demands of a theatre concerned primarily with the spoken word, it now remains to consider one of the most striking: the prevalence of debate. In both tragedy and comedy, debate plays a prominent part. It replaces action; it often seems to inhibit action. For modern audiences, it is one of the principal barriers to understanding.

The argumentative instinct is strong both in tragedy and comedy. It springs naturally from the temperament of the people. Argument, and the exchange of abuse, were as much part of the ancient Mediterranean world as they are of the modern. The sustained passages of invective and contention which occur in Aristophanic comedy sometimes embarrass western directors; we are not accustomed to such florid, uninhibited exchanges of opinion in our society. For the average Greek and Roman they were part of the normal cut and thrust of conversation. When Aristophanes is performed by modern Greeks or Italians, the invective falls naturally into place.

More relevant to the present discussion, however, are the times when this argumentative disposition coalesces into the form of a set debate. These occur regularly in comedy, sometimes accompanied by actual physical violence. In tragedy they occur regularly also; whatever the story, a debate (*agon*) may usually be found, and more often than not is the heart of the play.

Sometimes the debate is in the nature of a formal trial, virtually a play within a play, made necessary by the demands of the plot. In tragedy, the most conspicuous example is the trial of Orestes in *The Eumenides*. Here, the debate is a natural outcome of the action. Orestes has come to Athens to seek dispensation from Athena. She creates the Court of the Areopagos to hear his case. Athena herself presides;

Apollo is summoned as counsel for the defence, and the chorus of Furies represents the prosecution; the verdict is decided by the drawing of lots among a jury selected from the citizens of Athens, and Orestes is acquitted on an equal division of votes. The mechanics, language, and manners of the court are designed to remind the audience of their own familiar procedures, and to link the fortunes of the legendary hero with the operation of Athenian justice. Scarcely less formal, though in a different context, is the trial of Helen by her fellow-prisoners in *The Trojan Women*. Here, though the court is an irregular one, an *ad hoc* tribunal set up by Hecuba and the others to condemn the cause of their misery, the procedures of a formal trial are evident. Hecuba prosecutes, Helen defends, and Menelaus ironically presides.

Comedy offers similar examples. In *The Knights* the formal *agon* occupies the greater part of the play. Here it is a political debate, not a forensic one, but Aristophanes still takes pains to equate it with practices familiar to his audience from their everyday lives. The argument between the Paphlagonian and the Sausage-Seller for the stewardship of Demos is modelled on debates between similar political antagonists in the Pnyx, where the actual *demos*, the voting population of Athens, sat in judgement. *The Clouds* is a comedy about the use or misuse of rhetoric, and set debates occur plausibly within the action of the play. The first, between the allegorical figures of True and False Logic, is offered as a demonstration to a new pupil by Socrates in his academy. Each offers a speech in self-defence; each produces evidence to support his case; and True Logic, at the end, admits defeat. The second debate, which ushers in the play's conclusion, is scarcely less formal, though placed in a domestic setting. Pheidippides demonstrates his mastery of Socratic techniques by offering to justify his right to beat his father. Strepsiades accepts the challenge of debate:

PHEIDIPPIDES Choose your weapons! Which argument do you want?
STREPSIADES Which argument?
PHEIDIPPIDES The better or the worse?
STREPSIADES By Zeus, I've really had you educated
   In arguing with justice, if you can prove
   This one – that it's upright and honest
   For fathers to be beaten by their sons.
   All right. Let me begin at the beginning.[1]

Thus Strepsiades launches his speech and Pheidippides his refutation; and the father, who had so delighted at the triumph of False Logic when it was on his side, is mortified to hear it used against him. The two debates run parallel, and give a structure to the play.

The Wasps contains a play-within-a-play, a miniature jury trial. To cure his father's mania for law and condemnation, Bdelycleon has him preside over a trial between two dogs, one accused of stealing cheese from the other; tricked into acquitting the defendant, Philocleon is thus cured by shock therapy, and sees the error of his ways. The second half of *The Frogs* consists of an extended debate between Aeschylus and Euripides to decide which is the better playwright. Although the matter is literary, many of the questions are political, and the debate is staged as a formal trial with Dionysus and Pluto, god of the Underworld, presiding. Evidence is offered in the form of quotations from plays.

Such examples, offered as self-contained episodes within the main action, present no problems to the modern understanding. Courtroom scenes have always been good drama. We may point to such modern instances as *The Trial of Mary Dugan*, *The Caine Mutiny Court-Martial*, *The Andersonville Trial*; to the popularity of television courtroom drama; and to our own, more recent, classics. Perhaps *The Merchant of Venice* offers the best illustration of how a good courtroom scene never fails. The trial of Antonio has been played countless times, and every schoolchild knows its outcome; yet the scene still exercises its fascination in the theatre. A trial scene is a gift to any playwright. The Athenians, temperamentally inclined to litigation, were as aware of this as anyone, and were not slow to take advantage of any such opportunities in the stories they chose to dramatize.[2]

These are, however, not the only cases. There are a number of others where no legal trial is involved, and where the forms of debate seem not merely gratuitous but, to modern audiences, highly inappropriate. Granted that the Athenians were litigious, granted that rhetoric was fashionable, we must still ask why the trial/debate formula is applied to scenes wherein the subject matter does not seem to lend itself to such treatment. William Arrowsmith has neatly assessed the extent to which the tragic form relies on forensics:

> If we require an idea of the Greek tragic theater at all, it seems to me that the clue might best be taken from the very charge of rhetoric so

particularly brought against tragedy, and against Euripides in particular, ever since the time of Schlegel. Over and over again, that is, the late fifth-century tragedy seems to suggest as its informing image a theater shaped more by the law-court than by the altar. In this theater, the *agon* is viewed essentially as a trial, and the characters, with all the tricks of sophistic rhetoric, put their cases in opposed speeches – often of identical length, as though timed by the waterclock of the Athenian dikastery. The audience in this theater sits as jurors, not merely a panel of five hundred jurors, but the full *Heliaea*, the sovereign judicial assembly (*ekklesia*). No appeal, no matter how emotional, is debarred, and each character in his plea speaks with the formal passion of a man whose life and fortunes hang upon his words. But it is a formal and rhetorical passion, below which we can glimpse, as the jury must, the personal passion and the real motives glozed by the rhetoric and often exposed in action. . . .[3]

This rhetorical influence is present from the earliest times; its dominance of late fifth-century tragedy merely reflects the extraordinary rapidity with which the study of rhetoric was gaining ground, and the way in which it was making its mark on every aspect of society. A striking example is the quarrel scene in *Medea*, when Jason and Medea meet in a scene of angry accusation. Here we have one of the most passionate of all encounters, between the wronged wife and the faithless husband, the one demanding her rights, the other anxious to establish his good faith. There is passion enough in the words, yet from the form of the speeches they might be attorneys arguing a case in court. They begin with opposing speeches of equal length. Medea makes her own case, listing point by point the benefits she has brought to Jason:[4]

> Let me begin my tale at the beginning.
> I saved your life, as every single Greek
> Who sailed with you on board the Argo knows,
> When you were sent to tame the bulls that breathed
> Fire, and kill them, and sow death in the field.
> The dragon, that encircled with its coils
> The golden fleece, and watched it without sleeping,
> I killed for you, and lit your path to safety.
> For you I left my country and my home
> And sailed to Iolkos and Mount Pelion

> With you, and showed more eagerness than sense.
> I brought on Pelias the worst of ends,
> Death at his children's hands, and ruined his house.
> All this I accomplished for your worthless sake
> To be abandoned for another woman,
> Though I had borne you children. Were I barren
> You might have some excuse to marry again.

Jason answers her points with his, in a reasoned defence:

> So much for what you say about
> My labours. You began the argument.
> For your reproaches on my royal marriage
> I'll show you first of all how clever it was;
> Second, how prudent; third, that I am your sons'
> And your best friend. Please do not interrupt me.

This is not the way in which an estranged husband and wife usually converse. The argument has an unnatural formality. There is little pure abuse, little wilful wrangling. Instead, we have an orderly arrangement of evidence on either side, a neat pattern of confrontation and refutation.

In *Hippolytus*, which appeared a few years afterwards, the same formula is used in even more unlikely circumstances. Phaedra, young wife of Theseus, has fallen desperately in love with her stepson, Hippolytus. Rejected by him, she commits suicide and leaves a note accusing him of raping her. The 'trial' is then conducted over her dead body. It is in fact a parody of a trial. Theseus doubles the roles of judge and prosecutor. His speech calls on the dead in evidence:[5]

> You think that this will save you? No,
> It is the clinching witness of your perfidy.
> Beside her testimony, all your oaths
> And protestations falter, and you stand condemned.

Hippolytus defends himself in a formal address whose shape and substance seem to spring directly from the lawcourts:

> Father, your anger and your wild suspicions
> Leave me dismayed. You make a good case, surely
> But look more closely, and the flaws appear.
> I am not skilled in public rhetoric,

> But in the circle of my peers I am
> Less diffident. And the reverse is true:
> Those who are tongue-tied in wise company
> Are glib enough when they harangue a mob.
> But in the present misadventure I must give
> My tongue free rein. Let me begin with your
> Insinuations, when you thought I had
> No word to save myself. You see this sky,
> This earth; they look upon no mortal,
> Think what you will, who is more chaste than I.

He goes on to give evidence of character and to argue, logically, that he would have had no interest in seducing Theseus' wife. His father counters with the written proof, the tablet, and pronounces sentence:

> You have stated your conditions. Then accept them.
> Out of this country you must go, and spend
> Your days in banishment and exile.
> You have done wrong. Now you must pay the price.

The scene reads as a formal trial, then, where the situation seems to demand a more passionate and less coherent encounter. Artemis, when she rebukes Theseus at the end of the play, still uses legal language:

> You did not wait for proof, did not
> Consult the auspices; there was no trial, no time
> To sift the truth, but in unseemly haste
> You laid your curse upon your son and killed him.[6]

Hecuba, Euripides' next play, offers an even more striking case of passionate action confined within legal forms. Hecuba's supposed friend, Polymestor, has murdered her son for his gold. Though now a captive in the Greek tents, she contrives a terrible revenge, blinding Polymestor and killing her two sons. Alarmed by Polymestor's outcry, Agamemnon, leader of the Greek army, comes to investigate. At this point the action assumes the pattern of a formal trial. Agamemnon is judge, Polymestor plaintiff, and Hecuba defendant; and we have the curious spectacle of a man who has just suffered ghastly mutilation, who a moment before was grovelling on all fours like a tortured beast, offering a set speech in accusation of his tormentor, adorned, as Arrowsmith says, with all the devices of sophistic rhetoric.

Although examples are prolific in Euripides, Sophocles provides them too. The centre of *Antigone* is a debate between Creon and his son Haemon. Creon has sentenced Antigone to death; Haemon has intended to marry her. Thus the stage is set for a doubly passionate encounter: king against subject, father against son. But there is no wild argument, no physical violence. Instead, we are offered a pair of set speeches. Creon opens with a defence of discipline. Respect for parents is equated with law and order in the state; deprived of these things, society falters:[7]

> Yes, keep this always in your heart, my son,
> To obey your father's word as law in all things.
> For that is why men pray to have
> Dutiful children growing up at home,
> To repay their father's enemies in kind
> And honour those he loves no less than he does.
> But a man is sowing trouble for himself
> And enemies' delight, no less, when he
> Sires sons who bring no profit to their father –
> . . .
> A man who sees his family obey him
> Will have authority in public matters.
> But if anyone offends, or breaks the law,
> No word of honour shall he have from me.
> Whoever the state appoints must be obeyed,
> In little things or great things, right and wrong
> . . .
> So let us all stand up for law and order.

Haemon, in his studied reply, makes an appeal for moderation and resilience:

> You see how trees that bend to winter storms
> Preserve themselves, save every twig unbroken,
> While those that stand rigid perish root and branch,
> And also how the man who keeps his sails
> Spread taut and never slackens them, overturns
> And finishes his voyage upside down.

Only after this does the argument degenerate into angry bickering. For the most part, a passionate confrontation has been compressed into verbal decorum.

And perhaps, of all examples, the most curious is in the satyr play *Cyclops*, where Odysseus and the one-eyed monster Polyphemus debate solemnly and formally the rights and wrongs of eating Odysseus for breakfast.

The answer to this problem – our problem, not the Greeks' – is the same as that suggested above for the phenomenon of *stichomythia*. We are dealing here with a theatre whose main weapons is words, and which must relegate the other aspects of histrionic art very much to second place. Given the nature of Greek dramatic costuming and the distance separating audience from action, the dramatist must *tell* the audience everything they need to know: hence the need for a stylized verse form to make the whole comprehensible without sight. Medea cannot show the audience that she is angry, or hurt, or derisive; she had to tell them in good plain words. A modern actress, playing the quarrel scene with modern acting techniques, would need to say far less than Euripides makes her say. She could express with a shrug or a look what the poet must express in a line. (It is instructive in this respect to compare the *Medea* quarrel scene with the same scene in a modern play on this theme, and see how much more economical the modern dramatist can be in his language.) But in the Greek theatre, if a point is to be made it must be made verbally. The dramatist's art lies in his ability to unfold an argument, to make each step in his plot clear by words alone, and in seeking an 'informing image' he would surely turn to the lawcourts, where a similar premium is placed upon clarity and precision of expression and upon the orderly arrangement of evidence. In this his audience would have found it easy to follow him. The average Greek was trained to listen. Reading was the exception rather than the rule. Writers reached the mass of people not by publication, but by giving public recitals of their work. In modern times the ear has grown lazy. We learn more quickly through the eye, and are gradually losing the art of listening to an involved argument. The Greek was forced to listen, and to commit to memory anything he wished to preserve. Moreover, many in the trained audience would have been trained speakers themselves. In the Athenian democracy, all major decisions were made by the public assembly, the whole body of citizen voters, and not (as in modern systems) by delegated representatives. The man who could sway the assembly by skilful and persuasive oratory was the man in whose hands the ultimate power lay. Rhetorical ability was the key to public advancement, and the history of Athenian government is the history of its most accomplished orators. The average Athenian citizen, even if he had never spoken himself, would, by constant attendance in the assembly, law courts, and committees through which the democracy functioned, have been exposed to the finest speakers of his time. He would have become familiar with the organization of material in debate, and a master of the forms of argument. Thus, in composing scenes in this manner, the dramatist was working within a frame of reference with which his audience was wholly familiar, and talking to them in a way that he could be sure they would understand. By the use of the trial-debate formula, he transmitted his material on a wavelength to which they were immediately responsive, and thus minimized the physical disadvantages of his theatre which were themselves the product of its size. This would have been all the more natural in a civilization where the boundary between the stage and the public assembly was never very clearly drawn. As acting was largely rhetorical, so oratory was largely histrionic, and relied far more than it does today on emotional appeal.

This is not to suggest that technical problems were the only reason for the superimposition of the lawcourt image on the dramatic structure. We may find another cause in the philosophical background of the late fifth century; the dramatists were more concerned with asking questions than with offering solutions, and the conception of the audience as a jury, left to form their own conclusions, naturally suggests itself. Nevertheless, the technical problems were important; and by employing the mechanics and conventions of the law courts, the Greeks found a solution acceptable to their audiences and to their own kind of theatre.

In the modern theatre many of these conditions are no longer applicable. When Greek plays are transplanted to the narrower confines of the twentieth-century stage, there is an inevitable scaling down. The sense of distance is gone, and the audience is brought closer to the action. This is not to say that it is more involved in the action; for despite its size, the Greek theatre was in one respect more 'intimate' than our own. The actor was never set apart from his audience. Playing space and auditorium were spatially continuous; the spectators overlooked the action from almost every side, and the actor, set apart neither by the barrier of the proscenium nor by the selective lighting, was always conscious of his audience. This immediate rapport, this continual sense of actor–audience involvement, was one of the most characteristic features of Greek performance. It was particularly important in comedy, where the actor was able to jump out of the framework of the action, address a remark directly to the audience, and return, without any sense of loss of continuity. In modern revival, the plays are normally performed, *faute de mieux*, on a proscenium stage, with actors and audience separated by the 'fourth wall'. And so the modern theatre loses both ways. It brings the audience closer, but separates them from the action by a far more frigid barrier than the Greeks ever had; and, by bringing them closer, it makes many of the Greek stylistic devices redundant, for the audience can now see a great deal more. They have no trouble in distinguishing one actor from another – when the actors go maskless it is always possible to see who is speaking at a given moment. The modern actor can, and will, express much more by facial expression and bodily movement than was permitted to the Greeks. He can convey by a look what the poet had to express in words.

Thus, Greek drama attracts the charge that is so often levelled against it, namely, that it is too wordy. Drama based on the techniques of rhetoric is forced into a framework where rhetoric has no place. Drama written for long-range effect is crammed into too intimate surroundings; and to modern ears aided by modern eyes the poet seems to be saying much more than he needs to say. The same problem arises in the filming or televising of Shakespeare. Shakespeare wrote for a theatre practically devoid of scenic artifice. Here, too, words were the dramatist's principal medium. The scenic background was created by description rather than by depiction. But the camera works in visual, not verbal images.

As well as hearing Shakespeare's description of the Forest of Arden we see real brooks and trees. In *Henry V*, when the battles are over and the warring kings begin to come to terms, Shakespeare has written a powerful speech for Burgundy, the reconciler. He describes the war-torn countryside of France, the neglected fields and the ragged children. When Laurence Olivier filmed the play, he was forced, because of his medium, to give this speech some visual accompaniment. Thus, while Burgundy orates, the camera leaves the royal court and moves through the scenes he is describing. We see the fields as he speaks of them, overgrown with weeds; we see the children leaning sullenly on a gate. In the film of *Hamlet*, again under Olivier's direction, while Queen Gertrude describes Ophelia's suicide, the camera shows us the death as it happens, with the body floating, Millais-like, downstream. While these effects have their own visual beauty they are at odds with the play. Words or pictures would by themselves have been self-sufficient; we need one or the other, but not both. The visual image makes the description redundant.

It is in films of Greek tragedy that one becomes most conscious of the disparity between what the ancient author provided, and what the modern audience expects. Greek tragedy was essentially a long-range medium, dealing primarily in words; film is a close-up medium, dealing in pictures. Significantly, the most successful film of Greek tragedy yet made, Michael Cacoyannis' production of Euripides' *Electra*, achieved its success by facing the problem, accepting the difference, and dispensing with much of the text. Euripides' words are not illustrated by visual images, but replaced by them. Instead of the long prologue recounting the murder of Electra's father and her forced, humiliating marriage, we observe these things, in screen silence.

The problems of film-making simply magnify the difficulties that occur in transposing Greek plays to modern stages and modern concepts. Criticism has been censorious of the rhetorical elements of Greek tragedy; but the fault is ours, for insisting on seeing Greek theatre in our own terms. Viewed in the light of our own stage, and of Greek play production in terms of that stage, the *agon* appears as an awkward convention that stands in need of explanation. Thus has arisen a tendency to explain it in terms of pre-dramatic practice, and to pass it off as something left over from a previous era that has somehow, by accident or by some vestigial ritual imposed, been embedded in the drama. Like the *parabasis*, and like *stichomythia*, the origins of the *agon* have been traced to fertility ritual. The prevalence of debates in drama has been explained as a relic of an original ritual combat, transmuted from physical violence into words. One must doubt very seriously whether the Greeks would have been conscious of the *agon* as in any way extraordinary or deserving of explanation, so closely was it attuned to their own temperament and their everyday experience.

Each age finds its own informing image in the theatre. For the later middle ages it was the sermon which gave a framework to the morality play. For Brecht it was the *café chantant*, the political cabaret, which provided a shape for his *agitprop* dramas. For the Greeks, it was the lawcourts. Rhetoric is the mode of Greek drama, just as singing is the mode of opera and dance the mode of ballet.

The role of debate in Greek tragedy, however, is not confined to

115

specific episodes, however important these may be. It is all-pervasive; it can mould a single speech, or give a pattern to an entire play.

For an example of the former, we may look at the crucial monologue from *Medea* in which the protagonist makes her decision to murder her children. One crime has already been committed: the princess, Jason's new bride, and her father Creon, lie dead inside the palace, victims of Medea's poison. The tutor, ignorant of this disaster, brings the two boys to their mother. She agonizes over them, foreseeing their inevitable parting:[8]

> My sons, my sons; you have a city now
> And home, where when we've said our last good-byes
> You will live out your lives without your mother.
> I go in exile to a foreign land
> Before I have had the joy of seeing you happy.

Torn between mother-love and her frenzy for revenge she vacillates between killing them and letting them go. Her speech develops as an *agon* in which Medea takes each side in turn, arguing with herself in alternating bursts of passion:

> Women, I cannot do it; my heart
> Is faltering when I look at their bright eyes
> I cannot do it, I renounce the plans
> I made before, my children shall go with me.
> Why should I use their suffering to hurt
> My husband, and so doubly hurt myself?
> Not I, not I. I renounce my plans.
> And yet, what am I saying? Should I let
> My enemies insult me, and escape scot free?
> Why what a coward am I
> That can allow my mind talk of relenting.

A little later the same pattern recurs:

> Do not do this, my heart, do not do this.
> Spare them, unhappy heart, let your sons go.
> They will live with you in exile, and make you glad.
> No, by the fiends that dwell in hell below
> It shall never come to this, that I allow
> My sons to be insulted by my enemies.

116

So the tempo of these self-exchanges quickens like the cut and thrust of *stichomythia* in a quarrel scene, accentuated, we need have no doubt, by Medea's physical actions, now embracing her children, now thrusting them away:

> Oh sweet embrace; the scent
> Of children's breath, the feel of your soft skin. . . .
> Go away! Go away! I have no strength to look on you.

The speech is a remarkable technical *tour de force*, as though the actor had two masks with antithetical images, each covering his face in turn. There is nothing else quite like it in Greek tragedy.

Of the debate motif as informing the whole play, however, there are examples in plenty. They have often been overlooked, or at least not given their full importance. The linear development of a play tends to be the most obvious; and modern audiences are, in any case, less adept than the Greeks in sensing the *shape* of a play. But the original audiences were clearly aware of the existence of such a shape, just as we perceive the shape of a sonnet, or a sonata. In Greek tragedy, and to a large extent in Greek comedy, the favoured structure is antithesis. Case answers case, situation balances situation. Dramatic patterns follow language patterns. Greek had a fondness for alternatives. The two most familiar words in the language are also two of the shortest and most untranslatable: the particles *men* and *de*, which can be only crudely anglicized as 'on the one hand' and 'on the other'. Thus Thucydides' famous definition of the Athenian constitution: *logo men democratia, ergo de hupo tou protou andros arche*: in theory democracy, but in practice rule by the principal citizen. Such balanced utterances are fundamental to Greek speech and thought. Linguistic habits, no less than social observances, condition the form of the plays.

The easiest example is also our most extensive one: Aeschylus' *Oresteia*, our sole surviving trilogy. Over this massive work, which took perhaps some four to five hours in performance, we see two kinds of pattern developing. The linear structure is most readily apparent, the story-line beginning with the conclusion of the Trojan War and Agamemnon's return, and ending with the exoneration of Orestes and the domesticization of the Furies as resident deities of Athens.

Although the background information is presented piecemeal, and some important actions are not clarified until the first play is three-quarters over, a coherent chronological narrative emerges. In the opening work, *Agamemnon*, we are offered the picture of a royal house labouring under the burden of a hereditary curse. Although the origin of this curse is not spelled out until the entrance of Aegisthus shortly after Agamemnon's murder, its presence is manifest from the beginning. The curse, as we eventually learn, derived from the previous generation, Atreus, Agamemnon's father, and Thyestes, Atreus' brother and the father of Aegisthus. Jealous of his brother as potential rival, Atreus lured him to the palace in pretence of hospitality, then killed his two small sons and served them to their father, disguised as a banquet dish. Revolted by this involuntary cannibalism, Thyestes cursed the house for evermore.

This gives the background against which the action unrolls. When *Agamemnon* opens, power has passed to the next generation. The king who gives his name to the work is away at Troy. In his absence his wife Clytemnestra rules. We learn that she has lost a daughter by her husband's action; Agamemnon had sacrificed their child, Iphigeneia, to appease the gods and secure safe passage to Troy at the outset of the war. Clytemnestra has taken a lover, Aegisthus, surviving child of Thyestes, and Agamemnon's cousin. When Agamemnon returns, apparently in triumph from the happy outcome of the war, Clytemnestra lures him within the palace, takes him by surprise, and murders him. She and Aegisthus, who has helped to plan the murder, impose their tyranny upon the state.

The second play, *The Libation Bearers*, demonstrates the continuation of the curse into the next generation. Orestes, Agamemnon's son, has been forced to grow up in exile; Electra, his sister, has been reduced to the status of a slave in her own home. They are reunited when Orestes, now a man, returns to his father's graveside, under divine admonition to avenge the dead. A plan is made: Orestes and his friend Pylades, disguised as common travellers, will have themselves invited into the palace and, once inside, will kill Aegisthus and Clytemnestra. The deception works. Aegisthus dies first; Clytemnestra makes a frantic plea as mother to son, which he ignores. The chorus celebrates the return of tranquillity to the palace, only to see Orestes succumb to the sudden apparition of the Furies. He leaves to find sanctuary in Delphi, and the chorus resignedly await the next chapter in their misfortunes.

In *The Eumenides* the action begins at Delphi; Apollo, now become the protector of Orestes, has temporarily lulled the Furies to sleep.

118

He advises Orestes to seek aid and judgement in Athens. Orestes leaves; the Furies, stung to wakefulness by the vengeful ghost of Clytemnestra, resume their pursuit. In Athens, the issue is decided by Athena and her newly-created court of law. Orestes is acquitted and returns to his own people. The Furies are persuaded to change their natures, become benevolent deities, and take up residence in Athens. The trilogy closes on a note of celebration.

Thus the forward movement of the trilogy. It offers a continuous story, the working of the curse on several generations; and of course it offers far more. Although its action is nominally confined to a limited time-frame, in fact it covers centuries: from the ending of the Trojan War to the establishment of a trial by law, and the substitution of newer, more luminous Olympian deities, who represent the civilizing force of humankind. One of the issues stressed by these new deities at Orestes' trial is that the social bond of marriage is no less important than the tie of blood. The tribal laws of a more primitive society exonerate Clytemnestra for killing her man, while Orestes is condemned for murdering his own blood-relation. In a more civilized world, the relationships stand equal, and Clytemnestra is no less guilty than her son.

This progression is denoted, as the trilogy proceeds, by certain dominant images. *Agamemnon* begins, prophetically, with a gleam of light in darkness: the watchman, keeping his long vigil on the roof, perceives the beacon fire that heralds the awaited end of war. Though Agamemnon's own return is thwarted, the sense of light replacing dark persists. We see it in the natures of the gods who dominate the various plays. In *Agamemnon*, the action is controlled by the Furies. Though unseen, they are omnipresent. They are the embodiments of the curse, the 'daughters of old Night', the spirits of primeval vengeance. Clytemnestra sees herself as their instrument. Cassandra, the captive prophetess brought back by Agamemnon from the war, sees them in her vision clustering around the house and fouling it.

In *The Libation Bearers*, however, the dominance has shifted. The god most frequently invoked is Hermes. He was the messenger god who travelled between Olympians and mortals; it was also he who conveyed dead souls to the shore of embarkation for their final resting place, the Underworld. Hermes has a foot in both worlds. He belongs both to the dark and to the light, and is thus a fitting deity to preside over the centre of the trilogy. When the play opens, Orestes is discovered at his father's graveside, praying:

119

> Hermes, warden of the Underworld
> And father's regent, lend to me
> Your strength, and stand my champion, I pray,
> As I set foot upon my land again.

Electra similarly prays to Hermes as she pours offerings above the tomb; and the chorus address the deity as one who brings things to light, who makes the dark world clear.

If Hermes is the god of half-light, *The Eumenides* is given to the radiant Olympians, Athena and Apollo. Apollo is the god of the sun; he is also, in Greek thought, the personification of civilized society, the embodiment of order and harmony in all their aspects. In this trilogy Apollo himself has grown up, has ascended to a higher order of being. In *Agamemnon* he was an off-stage presence, the deity whose prophetic powers worked in Cassandra; and we were asked to see him there as a spiteful and capricious god, a deity in the Homeric manner, subjecting morals to his callous will. But as the trilogy progresses, so does he; at the end, he is established as the guardian of truth and justice. Athena, too, represents the clarifying power of light; she sheds the radiance of wisdom on the action, enveloping and resolving it, transforming the Furies into another type of deity.

Even the language shares in this progression. The Greek of *Agamemnon* is dense, cryptic, ambiguous; it presents notorious difficulties for textual scholars and translators; it is full of half-hints and allusions; at times it is virtually opaque. *The Libation Bearers*, though still not a simple play, is noticeably clearer. In *The Eumenides*, however, the language is transparent. Characters say clearly and precisely what they mean. The language of the trilogy has evolved, just as its issues have evolved. Forces earlier hidden have become manifest; a world in which motives and meanings were clouded and confused has become a world of clarity and order.

Thus, then, the forward progression of the trilogy: from the imposition of the curse to its resolution, from savagery to civilization, from darkness to light. But as well as this, there is another, no less powerful, structure in which play answers play, case matches case, in the familiar pattern of debate.

If we ask why Agamemnon is killed, the ultimate answer is that he is a man cursed. A curse is like an allergy: a cursed man is allergic to trouble, in whatever form it chooses to present itself. Throughout the play we see Agamemnon confronted with a series of choices. Shall he

go to war to help his brother? Shall he sacrifice his daughter for the
fleet's sake? Shall he gratify his wife and walk upon the purple carpet?
In each case he makes a decision which contributes to his demise; but
it would be easy to write a scenario in which he made the opposite
decisions, and still placed himself in jeopardy. If he had not gone to
war, his brother would have hated him; if he had not sacrificed
Iphigeneia, he would have alienated the army. As a cursed man he is
doomed to die whatever happens.

As the play stands, however, the motives for his dying seem to
divide themselves into three. One, clearly, is personal: Clytemnestra's deeply-felt resentment for the loss of her daughter, so movingly
described early in the play by the chorus. This is the burden of her
speech of self-defence over her husband's body, and of the lyric
threnody sung with the chorus:

> And there will be a mourner at his grave.
> No weeping slaves but his own child,
> Iphigeneia, as she should, shall stand
> Where death's sad river flows through weeping fields
> And set a daughter's kiss on his cold brow.[9]

The second motive is political: the desire to replace the moderate
rule of Agamemnon with a tyranny. The king is set before us as one
who, though his decisions may not have been popular, at least worked
in consort with his advisers, and who, on his return, promises to
eradicate evils from the state. Aegisthus, by contrast, enforces his will
with an armed bodyguard, brutally dismisses the protests of the
chorus, and threatens retribution for the future.

The third motive we may perhaps call the supernatural. Agamemnon is shown as a man who has a tendency to trample on divine
observances; who thinks too highly of himself; who is tainted with the
ominous fault of *hubris*. We learn from the herald that, in seeking
Troy, he has laid waste the temples of the city's gods; divine retribution, therefore, is to be expected. In this frame of reference the chorus,
in one of its more gnomic moments, sees Agamemnon's death as a
moral lesson:

> The more he has, the more a man desires.
> Nor lives there anyone so moderate
> To shut the door on fortune. You have seen a man
> So well beloved of heaven that the gods

> Gave Troy to be his prize. Should this man now
> Requite in blood the deaths that went before
> And by his death in turn, avenge the deaths
> Of those that fell to his word: who then could boast
> He bore a life beyond misfortune's reach?[10]

Agamemnon, then, could be said to make a case for its protagonist, Clytemnestra. She is the instrument of divine, and the instigator of human, vengeance; we see Agamemnon's failings through her eyes, and the play concludes with her triumph.

The Libation Bearers, by contrast, makes a case for Orestes, its protagonist. As he lists his grievances against his mother, we see that the arguments are identical. He tells us, at length, of the impact of the supernatural on his life. He has received direct instructions from Apollo; he has been threatened with fearful, physical torment and a lonely, miserable death if he neglects this charge; he has been chosen as the god's emissary to ensure that right is done. He ends by telling us that, even without the god's injunction, he has other causes

> urgent to drive me on.
> Grief for my father – there is weight in this:
> The press of poverty; and my desire
> That the marvel of the earth, my countrymen,
> Whose glorious spirit subjugated Troy,
> Should not bow down before a brace of women.
> For Aegisthus is woman at heart. If I am one
> He soon shall learn![11]

These answer to the motivations of the first play. Orestes' sense of personal loss – his exile from his homeland, the deprivation of his rank and riches – is given urgent expression by Electra, whose life is similarly constrained. Her great grievance is that she has been denied a husband, and compelled to forfeit the natural fulfilment of womanhood. Orestes' political mission is equally clear: the tyrants must be deposed, and a rule by the legitimate power restored. (It should be remembered that Aeschylus wrote for an audience to whom the deposition of tyrants in Athens was still a vivid memory.) *The Libation Bearers*, therefore, gives us Orestes' case; and it matches Clytemnestra's case exactly.

This responsion is emphasized by verbal reminiscences and by similarity of action. In *Agamemnon* the cry of the watchman on the walls wakes Clytemnestra at the coming of the beacon. In *The Libation Bearers* the watchman's similar cry, within the house, alerts her to another coming, the return of the avenger. Both plays conclude with a tableau of death. In *Agamemnon* Clytemnestra stands triumphant over the bodies of her husband and Cassandra. In *The Libation Bearers* Orestes takes the same position over his mother and Aegisthus. The most compelling visual image in *Agamemnon* is the purple – or, rather, blood-red – carpet over which Agamemnon enters the palace to meet his death. This carpet is laid on Clytemnestra's orders; he is hesitant to tread on such rich stuff, but allows himself to be flattered into consenting; it is both the symbol and the culmination of his *hubris*. But when the palace doors have closed behind him, it remains. Nobody removes it. It is in the forefront of our attention for the duration of the play, all the more evident because the audience is looking down upon it. When the doors reopen and the bodies are revealed, this red pathway assumes a new identity. It is now a river of blood, flowing down from the murdered king into the community.

The Libation Bearers picks up this strong visual image. Orestes brings from the murders the robe in which Clytemnestra had entrapped his father, to butcher him: it is dyed red, he says, with the victim's blood. The chorus is instructed to display it: 'Here, take it, spread it in a circle round.' Once more a vivid patch of red is set against the white stone of the orchestra, and we see that Orestes' position was also Clytemnestra's. They both, under pressure, killed someone near to them; and if there were consequences in the one case, there will be consequences in the other.

The trial in *The Eumenides*, therefore, comes not merely as the conclusion of the play, but as the formal expression of the debate that has already taken place within the play. A case has now been made on each side; the third play brings the issues into focus, weighs them, and adjudicates between them. The structure of the trilogy is also the structure of dialectic: statement, counterstatement, and resolution.

This pattern is also apparent in the casting. One of the few things we are specifically told about Aeschylus is that he always took the main parts in his own plays. In the *Oresteia*, this offers a significant division. The leading role in *Agamemnon* is clearly Clytemnestra. She dominates the play; she dictates the action; she has by far the greatest proportion of the lines. (Agamemnon, for whom the play is named, has only one major speech, a passage of *stichomythia*, and two off-stage cries.) Equally clearly, the major role in *The Libation Bearers* is not

Clytemnestra but Orestes. She has only one short speech and little dialogue; he is on stage virtually from beginning to end. In *The Eumenides* the major role is surely Athena, who presides over the trial, declares the judgement, tames the Furies, and invokes the blessings on her city at the end. Clytemnestra appears only briefly, as a vengeful ghost; Orestes, though he has more to do, is shadowed by the deities, and leaves the play before the end.

In modern production the same actress normally plays Clytemnestra throughout, and the same actor Orestes. Their concern is with the linear progression of the play; with the development of a single character through a period of years and a succession of incidents. If Aeschylus' roles were indeed those we have surmised for him, his concerns were clearly other. His interest was in the inner structure; in the pattern of character answering character, and case matching case; in the trilogy as three acts of an enormous debate.

Although the *Oresteia* is the only complete trilogy that we have, the same pattern has been surmised from the remains of others. *The Suppliant Women* shows the daughters of Danaus pursued and forcibly married by their Egyptian cousins. In the lost sequel, it appears that all the women, except one, took revenge by murdering their husbands on their wedding night. In the third play, also lost, the girl who had shown mercy was put on trial by her sisters. The ending of the trilogy must have been very like the *Oresteia*, with the chorus acting *en masse* as prosecutor.

Prometheus Bound presents a more difficult case, as the order of the plays, and even their Aeschylean authorship, is much disputed. Nevertheless, a plausible reconstruction would assume a lost first play, in which Prometheus' actions are seen through Zeus' eyes as culpable. *Prometheus Bound*, the surviving play, then presents the action from Prometheus' point of view, showing Zeus as tyrant and Prometheus as martyr. The lost *Prometheus Unbound*, known to the Romans but no longer to us, presumably offered a reconciliation.

Although later dramatists abandoned the trilogy form, and preferred to offer their three tragedies for the competition as independent and self-contained works, the imprint of debate on the theatre still remained. It is most obvious in the works of Euripides, who of all the surviving dramatists was most clearly susceptible to the impact of rhetoric.

Euripides' earliest extant tragedy, *Medea* (431 BC), established a pattern common to a number of his plays. It assumes as its background the legend of the Golden Fleece, one of the best-known stories of antiquity and still one of the most familiar today. Its ancient popularity is attested by its ubiquity; it was told widely enough, and often enough, to have been established in a version generally adhered to.

The background story is a simple one. Jason, rightful heir to the throne of Iolkos, is sent by the usurper, Pelias, on an apparently suicidal mission, to recover the fabulous Golden Fleece from the barbaric land of Colchis. He builds a magic ship, the Argo, chooses a crew of heroes, and survives formidable navigational hazards to reach his goal. Once in Colchis, he finds the Fleece guarded by an unsleeping, fire-breathing dragon, and by other trials through which he has to pass. Fortunately, the princess of Colchis, Medea, falls in love with him, and uses her magic powers to win the Fleece. Jason and Medea, taking her small brother with them, take ship for Iolkos. Medea's father gives chase, and is about to catch them when Medea kills her brother, cuts his body into pieces, and scatters them overboard. The king delays to gather up the body of his son, and Jason and Medea make a triumphant return to Iolkos. Finding Pelias still hostile, Medea tricks his daughters into killing him. She takes an old ram, cuts it into pieces, places them in a cauldron and speaks magic spells; out of the cauldron leaps a lamb. The girls, believing they can restore their father's youth, do the same to him, with tragic consequences. Leaving Iolkos behind them, Jason and Medea set sail for Corinth.

So much for the popular version of the story. It is typical of Euripides that he begins his play where the accepted tale leaves off. It is significant, also, that in writing a sequel to the Golden Fleece narrative, he was virtually a free agent. Earlier writers had little concern with the aftermath. Surviving sources were contradictory and obscure; popular interest stopped at the happy ending. When Euripides' audience came to see *Medea*, therefore, in the early spring of 431 BC, they were presented with a version of the story that was new to them. We commonly think of Greek tragedy as deriving from Greek mythology. It would be more accurate to see it as part of the continuing development of mythology. The famous story of Medea that we all know starts, almost certainly, with Euripides; and the structure of the play is therefore of particular significance, since it derives from him, and not from any antecedent version.

There seem to have been two versions of Medea's later history before Euripides fashioned his own. Neither was well known, but each survives, almost by accident, in obscure sources. In one version, Jason deserts Medea to marry the princess of Corinth; she then murders the princess and her father in revenge. In turn the people of Corinth kill the children that Medea had by Jason.

According to the other version, Medea attempts to perform for her children the magical process she had earlier pretended to apply to Pelias: to give them eternal youth, and immortality. Again, something fails in the magic – although this time accidentally – and the children die. This in itself could have made an interesting tragedy, though it was not the one Euripides chose to write. Out of the two versions at his disposal – one in which Medea kills her children accidentally, one in which someone else kills them deliberately – he wove a third, in which the children are deliberately killed by their own mother.

The first, and most obvious, function of the play is as myth-criticism. It is cynical, revisionist, anti-heroic; it retells a legendary story through the actions of characters all too fallibly human. In the play Jason is portrayed as a callous, egotistical adventurer. He abandons his wife as soon as a better match presents itself, and justifies his behaviour with shabby and self-serving rhetoric. We look at the Jason of legend and ask if he, too, was not like this. Medea, similarly, is portrayed as a passionate and unbalanced woman whose chief concern is with her own prestige. Rather than allow herself to be humiliated, she will kill her own sons to spite her husband.

Specific incidents in the play recall elements of the legend. In both, innocent parties are killed. Jason's new wife, the princess of Corinth, is in no way culpable; she does not even have a name in the play, but is simply an anonymous figure hovering on the fringes of the action. Though innocent, she has to die, because her death serves Medea's revenge. The children are similarly innocent; their deaths recall the fate of Medea's little brother, another victim sacrificed for selfish ends. Euripides dissects the legend of the Golden Fleece, and asks his audience to re-examine their moral values.

The play, then, looks back to the legend. There is, however, another responsion, equally important, in which the play looks back upon itself.

Medea is a tragedy which falls naturally and obviously into two parts. In the first half, we see Medea suffering. She is a passive figure; things happen to her, and she can do little more than protest against them. The play begins with the Nurse's sympathetic summary of her mistress' past: Jason's ill-starred visit to Colchis, and the trouble it brought to Medea's family, to Pelias and his daughters, and eventually to Medea herself. We learn of Medea's abandonment; the Nurse voices her fears for Medea's children.

The children themselves appear with their slave tutor, mute, frightened witnesses of this domestic crisis. The chorus assembles as Medea's voice is heard off-stage, bewailing her misfortunes, praying for divine vengeance on those who have hurt her; and Medea herself presently appears, to lament the cruel lot of women forced to live in a man's world. To add to her distress, King Creon appears to sentence her to banishment; she is suspect, dangerous, an alien in a Greek world which has closed ranks against her. All she can wring from the unfeeling king is a reluctant promise of one day's grace to settle her affairs, and find some place to go.

Jason makes his first appearance in the play. Their confrontation, bitter and intense, gives Medea no satisfaction beyond the voicing of her feelings. The first half of the play concludes with Jason looking forward to a new wife, powerful connections, and a lasting home in Corinth, while Medea has only exile and penury.

The mathematical and emotional centre of the play is marked by the entrance of a character who has, so far, not been mentioned in the story, and whose appearance is hailed as coincidental. This is Aigeus, King of Athens, an old friend of Medea, who is passing through Corinth on his way home from consulting the oracle at Delphi. Aigeus provides a familiar point of reference for an Athenian audience. Like his more famous son, Theseus, he was one of the famous figures of local tradition. As so often, Athenian tragedy appeals to patriotic feeling, all the more powerfully in this case because Aigeus offers himself in the role of saviour. When Medea reveals her destitution and the perfidy of her husband Aigeus offers her sanctuary in Athens. This unhoped-for suggestion proves to be the turning point in her fortunes.

With Aigeus' departure the second half, or movement, of the play begins. This time it is Medea who is the active agent, the mover; it is she, now, who makes things happen to other people. Her first action is to lay a scheme to trap her husband. She will pretend compliance, and under the guise of friendship send gifts to his new wife. The presents will be poisoned and the princess will die. Medea also announces her decision to kill her children. It is, as she says, the way she can most hurt her husband.

Her plans are rapidly set in motion. Jason, deceived, leads his children with their fatal presents to her new wife. They are accepted; the princess, off-stage, dies, together with her father Creon. After a frantic soliloquy of indecision, Medea sends the children into the house, and there kills them. Jason, told the news, bitterly castigates his wife, whose nature and career he now sees with new eyes. Medea departs for a peaceful, sheltered life in the sanctuary of Athens, while Jason looks forward to the enmity of the Corinthians, a life bereft of wife and children, and a future as perilous as that to which he had earlier condemned her.

The fortunes of both principals have thus undergone a complete reversal. At the end of the first half, Jason was riding high, and Medea cast down; at the end of the second she is secure and triumphant while he is devastated. The staging reinforces this: Medea's final appearance is in a magic chariot swinging high above the earth where Jason grovels. Not only fortunes, but moral values, have been reversed. When Jason deprived Medea of marriage, home, and security, she complained bitterly against the injustice of his action. Now she has done the same to him, and finds it justified. Audience sympathy, also, changes with the events. In the first half of the play we feel for Medea, in the second half we hate her. Jason, cast as the villain of the piece initially, has our reluctant sympathy at the end.

As was noted earlier, *Medea* contains a key scene which is a formal trial in all but name: the first encounter between Medea and Jason, the estranged wife and the husband who has abandoned her, where grievances are met with justifications and argument caps argument. As in the *Oresteia*, however, this debate is merely the focus of a large debate which encompasses the whole play. The second half of the tragedy answers the first, point by point, motif by motif, with almost mathematical exactitude.

Analysis reveals a play-structure no less formal than the structure of the debate itself. *Medea* opens with a sympathetic summary of Medea's past life and present predicament. Then comes the motif of the children, introduced through the agency of kindly servants. Next comes Creon; finally, the Jason–Medea encounter. This brings us to the pivotal point of the play, the entrance of Aigeus. Following this, the motifs of the first half are repeated in reverse order: the second Jason–Medea scene; the death of Creon and his daughter, reported by a messenger; the deaths of the children, encompassed by their unkindly mother; and a closing summary of Medea's life, this time through unsympathetic eyes, those of Jason himself. This sympathy is reinforced by verbal echoes in the play: the repetition of a word, a line, a phrase, reminds us that we have seen this action before, but with the roles reversed.

One half of the play answers the other, just as speech answers speech in a debate. The actions are the same in each; it is the position of the protagonists with regard to these actions that changes. Medea does to Jason no more than he has done to her. He deprived her of security by severing their marriage. She deprives him of security by making Corinth uninhabitable for him, and by killing the children on whom his hopes for the future depend. We are talking of an age where the continuity of the family was important, not out of sentiment, but for self-preservation. A childless man could hope for little comfort in old age. Just as, in the *Odyssey*, Odysseus cherishes his old father and expects that Telemachus will do the same for him, Jason's hopes lie in his sons. When the chorus asks Medea: 'But will you have the strength to kill your children?' she replies with painful accuracy: 'Yes. It is the way I can most hurt my husband.'[12] When, at the play's end, Jason weeps for his dead sons she taunts him with exquisite cruelty: 'You will not miss them yet. Wait till you are older.'[13]

Medea, then, presents a case for either side. It is as though the *Oresteia* had been compressed within the format of a single play, though with one crucial exception. There is no equivalent of *The Eumenides*. No judgement is made, no final assessment offered. Euripides presents us with a bitter conflict for survival, engaged in a world where moral values have abdicated. There is no justice but self-advantage, no right but expediency. Morality fluctuates according to the viewpoint of the agent. Actions which Medea condemns as vicious and unjust when they are done to her, become legitimate reprisals when she performs them on others. In this moral vacuum there is no solution. No god applies an ending, there are no pat answers. Euripides constructs an open-ended debate in which the audience, transformed into a jury, is left to argue the merits of the case long after the play is over. The audience must find its own solution; though perhaps there is no solution.

This same structure, the split play, play-as-debate, becomes a characteristic feature of Euripides' work, and justifies tragedies which critics have traditionally dismissed as broken-backed. *Hecuba* (426 BC) is a case in point. It seems to consist of two separate stories; to such an extent, in fact, that some critics have virtually accused Euripides of

129

running out of material, and patching up with irrelevant matter a story that proved too short for a tragedy.

Hecuba springs from the same events as the more famous *The Trojan Women*: the immediate aftermath of the fall of Troy and the fate of its womenfolk, awaiting shipment to the country of their captors. In the first half of the play Hecuba loses a daughter. The young princess Polyxena is demanded as a sacrifice by the Greeks, to appease the angry ghost of Achilles. Their emissary is Odysseus, portrayed here as a hard and unscrupulous man whose only goals are military expediency and political survival. The innocent Polyxena must be sacrificed to the urgency of the occasion, and Hecuba protests in vain.

In the second half of the play Hecuba loses her only surviving son. Polydorus has been entrusted, during the war, to an old friend of the family, Polymestor, King of Thrace; when the Greek victory was certain, Polymestor murdered Polydorus for his store of gold. Devastated by this treachery, Hecuba contrives revenge. Pretending ignorance of the murder, she lures Polymestor to her tent with the promise of more gold smuggled out of Troy that the Greeks have not discovered. He is asked to bring his two small sons with him. Once in the tent, the women fall upon them, Polymestor is blinded, and his two boys killed.

The stories are linked in several ways: by the continuing presence of Hecuba, which dominates the play; by the ghost of Polydorus, who speaks a prologue to the play as a whole; and by a central scene in which the women, going to fetch water to bathe Polyxena's body, come across the corpse of Polydorus on the shore. Nevertheless, seen as a linear narrative, the play clearly lacks continuity: it appears loosely jointed and episodic, and moves uneasily from one story to the other.

Considered in the same light as *Medea*, however, the disposition of the elements makes sense. The structure is not linear, but diptychal: one half of the play is intended to be balanced against the other, and the play's meaning lies in the contrast. In the first half of the play, Hecuba speaks forcefully against those who would take her daughter from her. Her encounter with Odysseus is itself a self-contained debate, with major speeches offered on both sides. Hecuba seeks protection for Polyxena on the grounds of innocence. The child had no connection with the war; for the victors to use her to secure their ends is monstrous and inhuman. Hecuba offers substitutes. If you must sacrifice a victim from the captive women, she tells Odysseus, kill Helen; it was her misdoings that provoked the war in the first place. Or, she argues, kill me; I am an old woman and my life is over, while Polyxena has hers still to live. Odysseus is deaf to all this. Expediency takes precedence over individual considerations. Polyxena is the appropriate sacrifice, therefore she must die; guilt or innocence are irrelevant to the case.

In the second half of the play the moral positions of Hecuba and Odysseus are reversed. Hecuba, now, is in the position of seeking revenge, and the most appropriate objects to secure her plan are the children of Polymestor. They are as innocent as Polyxena was innocent; too young to have partaken of their father's wickedness, they can in no way be held culpable. This is now irrelevant to Hecuba, as it was to Odysseus before. Expediency decrees that they shall die, so die they do. We hear no more from Hecuba of right and justice. As in *Medea*, morality is variable and right and wrong are apportioned by the stronger.

As in *Medea*, too, this purposeful symmetry is emphasized by verbal echoes and recurrent visual images. The play begins with a dead child, Polydorus, whose ghost forecasts the coming action. It ends with two dead children, the sons of Polymestor, whose bodies are left lying when the other characters have left the stage. As in *Medea* there is no verdict, no summary: the argument continues when the play is over.

In Aristophanes' *The Frogs*, the comedy about tragedy that he wrote in 405 BC, Aeschylus and Euripides are represented as agreeing on the purpose of drama – to educate the public – but disagreeing on method. Aeschylus believes that tragedy should instruct by offering noble and inspiring examples for the community to emulate. Euripides believes that instruction occurs when the audience is forced to exercise its mind. Socrates, Euripides' contemporary, formulated philosophy out of discussion. Euripides educates by debate. A characteristic feature of the plays, and of the society that produced the plays, gives shape and logic to the plays themselves and generates a form of tragedy very much of its time and place.

5

PLACE AND TIME

Of all the factors that have warped our understanding of Greek
drama, the most pernicious has been the so-called 'Unity of Place'.
This doctrine, erroneously attributed to Aristotle by the scholars and
critics of the Renaissance, and embraced as gospel by neo-classical
playwrights, came to be applied, by fallacious hindsight, to the Greek
plays that were in Aristotle's own past. Its existence has propagated a
host of needless problems.

Unity of Place, as commonly understood, asserts that the action of
a Greek play transpires in a fixed location which, once established,
cannot be departed from. In fact, the plays themselves seem not to
grasp this principle; or, if they do, it is purely as a matter of convenience. Nevertheless, the influence of Aristotle has been so strong,
and the reverence paid to him so persuasive, that scholars have been
forced into agonized head-shakings over what actually happened in
the Greek theatre. Much ink has been expended on the number of
guestrooms in Clytemnestra's palace, to justify the comings and
goings in *Agamemnon* and *The Libation Bearers*. Long articles have been
written to explain why when Heracles, in *Alcestis*, leaves Admetus'
palace for the heroine's tomb, he does not immediately bump into
Admetus, who is returning from the same place. The Dutch scholar
Van Leeuwen finds himself confronted with an apparent impasse in
Aristophanes' *The Acharnians*. Dikaiopolis, the inventive and peace-
loving protagonist, is seen celebrating the rural Dionysia with his
family in the country. Threatened by an angry chorus, he seeks aid
and succour from Euripides. How can we justify this apparent propinquity? Euripides' house is apparently only a few feet from Dikaiopolis' farm, and the latter's retreat is immediate. After much
cogitation, Van Leeuwen moves to a solution. We must imagine, he

132

ponderously conjectures, that Euripides has moved from Athens and taken up temporary residence in the country.

If we look at the plays, instead of what people have said about them, a very different pattern appears. The facilities offered by the Greek theatre were of the simplest: an open space (the circle of the orchestra) and a closed space (the *skene*). This combination seems to satisfy the basic needs of play production, and reappears in other times and cultures: we see the same relationship between *platea* and *domus* in the medieval theatre, or between open stage and tiring house in the Elizabethan. The open space offers scope for the performance, and the closed space, the stage house, serves a multiple purpose as dressing room, a place from which actors may make their appearance, and a focal point for action.

In the Greek variant of this combination, certain local societal associations appear. Greek society was, primarily, an open-air society. Meetings, assemblies, courts, tribunals, business dealings, and religious ceremonies commonly took place outdoors, in the full light of the sun. Greeks slept on their roofs (as they still tend to do) and carried on a good deal of their private life in the streets. Conversely, indoors is often tainted with furtiveness and suspicion. What cannot be openly seen is potentially dangerous.

This feeling washes over the plays. What is good, honest, and open tends to happen outside; what is sly, furtive, and malicious, inside. In *Agamemnon* the palace is a place of festering evil, that the king enters to meet his doom. In *Antigone* the heroine, seeking conversation with her sister, leads Ismene 'outside the courtyard', rather than, as we would, to some private and protected place indoors. In *Medea*, the house is a demonic place from which Medea's voice is first heard threatening and which ultimately sucks her children inside to their destruction. There is more here than dramatic convenience or the fact that, in the usual glib phrase, 'the Greek theatre cannot show interiors'. It represents an attitude of mind.

The plays show us that these bare elements can be given specific identification at will, to suit the needs of any particular drama; and that setting is identified, just as characters are identified, verbally. Once again we are reminded that this is primarily a theatre of language. A character, as we have seen, needs to be identified, for the convenience of the audience, on first entrance. In just the same way, the setting is identified, if and when necessary, as the play begins. As with characters also, the identification may be either explicit or oblique. The opening lines of *Prometheus Bound* clearly define the space for the action:

> Now we have reached our journey's end. World's end.
> The Scythian wasteland, the untrodden desert.

Similarly Dionysus, in the prologue to *The Bacchae*, clearly labels the *skene* as the habitation of the royal family of Thebes, with Semele's tomb adjacent:

> Here is the palace; here, the splintered walls,
> Now made her monument by fire from heaven.

Apollo is equally explicit in the prologue to *Alcestis*:

> Palace of Admetus, where I toiled
> To earn my daily bread, a god in bondage

As examples of oblique identification we may consider the opening of *Oedipus the King*. Oedipus' opening address hints at location without specifically stating it:

> My children, in whom old Cadmus is reborn
> Why have you come, with wreathed boughs in your hands,
> To sit before me as petitioners?
> The town is full of smoke from altar fires
> And voices crying, and appeals to heaven.
> I thought it, children, less than just to learn
> Your cause at second-hand, but come in person:
> I, Oedipus, a name that all men know.

It is obvious from this that we are in Thebes; and the presumption is that we are in front of the palace of Oedipus. Subsequent references to characters coming 'from the palace' reaffirm the location. Similarly, in *Antigone*, a number of hints allow the presumption that we are somewhere around the palace of Creon; precisely where is never made clear, because it does not need to be.

'Need to be', in fact, controls the definition of the setting. In a number of cases in our extant plays, the nature of the story-line suggests a fixed location. Prometheus is, by definition, bound, and the action cannot logically move from where he is; in *Agamemnon* the house, wrapped in its miasma of ancestral evil, is the centre of

134

attention, and the action properly swirls around it; in Euripides' *Ion* we are placed firmly in the shrine of Delphi at the beginning, and we remain there until the end.

It cannot be emphasized too strongly, however, that this is a matter of convenience, and not of rule. There are other significant examples in which the story-line calls for a shifting setting. The assumed location may change as the play proceeds; and, once again, given the basic simplicity of the Greek theatre plan, the change is easily indicated by appropriate verbal reference. Such changes may be major or minor, striking or subtle; but they are all effected in the same way.

Sometimes a setting is left deliberately vague, and brought to a sharp focus later on. This is true of our earliest extant tragedy, *The Persians*. All we can say at the opening of the play is that we are in Persia. There is talk of Sousa and of Ecbatana, but no explicit indication that we are in either of these capitals. Local colour is provided rather by costume and language. The chorus of Persian elders seem to be wearing the official robes of their country, exotic in Greek eyes – at least, they talk as if they are; and Aeschylus puts into their mouths a Greek tinted by an ornate vocabulary, a Greek which, from its artful choice of words and phrases, pretends to be a foreign language: the equivalent, almost, of the German officer in an American- or British-made war film speaking accented English with a few German phrases thrown in. Aeschylus seems deliberately to be generalizing his setting: to be invoking, not merely one particular place in Persia, but the whole idea of Persia; and this for an audience to most of whom Persia would have been as strange and foreign as Samarkand is to us, and to whom King Xerxes would have been the same kind of legendary ogre that Napoleon was to nineteenth-century Europe.

In accordance with this, the words used to define the setting are deliberately vague. We hear only that we are before 'an ancient building' or 'monument'. Only late in the play, when the chorus and Atossa invoke the ghost of their former king Darius, does the identification become specific. We learn, then, that we are in front of Darius' tomb. But with the return of the spectre to his Underworld home, the location seems to become vague again; and this, too, may be part of Aeschylus' grand design. Although *The Persians* is, on the purely superficial level, a play describing a contemporary event, a glorification of a particular Athenian victory, it is also in more general terms a study of the folly of human ambition and the self-defeating nature of hubristic designs.

At the end of the play, Aeschylus brings its lessons home to the Athenians, no less than to the Persians. The ritual mourning patterns of the closure, as scholars have clearly shown, derive from the practices of Greek society. They speak to the Athenian audience in their own language. Aeschylus shows that he is dramatizing not merely a Persian but a universal human failing. Significantly, too, at the end of the tragedy the distinctively Persian colouration is stripped off. Xerxes enters in rags. The chorus tear their own robes. We are watching mere man, paying the penalty for mortal arrogance; not simply Persian men, but all men. And the essential anonymity of the setting contributes to this. When we needed a general indication of Persia, it gave us Persia. When we needed a specific location in Persia, it gave us that. And now, at the end, when the message expands to embrace the whole world, it gives us what it basically is: an open space, scenically undefined, which is both any space and every space. And all these shifts have been indicated as a function of language.

The Eumenides gives us a similar series of transitions. Its prologue establishes us, firmly and by concrete reference, at Delphi. It is essential for the story that the action should begin here. Thus, we have a history of the shrines, monuments, and familiar places to make the identification certain. Orestes receives instructions from Apollo to seek help in Athens, and his departure ends the Delphic section of the play. This is an important change of location, and is made triply clear: by Apollo's admonition that Orestes should go to Athens; by Orestes' exit and subsequent re-entrance, announcing that he is now 'before the image of Athena' and thus, by implication, in Athens; and by the rare device of removing the chorus temporarily from the orchestra. The Furies *exeunt* in pursuit of Orestes, and re-enter, complaining of the hardships of their journey, hot on his scent. The change of location could hardly be more clear; but it is a change effected by the simplest technical means, and still primarily by language. As long as the setting consists only of a few basic architectural elements, it can not only be identified by the language of the poet, but successively reidentified as circumstances demand. It can easily change, provided only that the audience is kept informed of the change. The stage setting, like the actor's mask, serves as a blank slate on which the author writes, with his evocative language, whatever he wants you to see there.

Once the action has shifted from Delphi to Athens, however, there are other, more subtle changes. In the context of Athenian topography, the statue that Orestes is instructed to embrace presumably alludes to the archaic image of Athens presiding over the Acropolis in the legendary past: the same image whose successor looked down upon the audience in the fifth-century Theatre of Dionysus. If we seek a specific location for this section of the play, then, we must find it on the Acropolis itself. But once the goddess has arrived in person, she decrees the establishment of a court – the court of the Areopagos, named for the rocky prominence on which it stood. It is in this place that the destiny of Orestes is argued out. Clearly, the imaginary location has shifted again; it has moved from the sacred hill and citadel of Athens to the ground beneath, from one hallowed territory of the city to another.

Perhaps the closure of the play introduces yet another supposed change of location. The invitation to the women of Athens to drape the reformed Eumenides with robes recalls the quadrennial procession to adorn the statue of Athena in the Panathenaia; are we then to imagine that we are climbing the Acropolis again? Or are we, alternatively, to imagine the location as shifting to Colonus, where the Eumenides established their benevolent home – that same Colonus, the suburb of Athens, which was the birthplace of Sophocles and which that playwright memorialized in his last work? Two things are, if not certain, at least highly probable. One is that *all* these associations would have been aroused in the minds of the Athenian audience: associations made all the stronger by propinquity of place. The other is that no attempt was made to depict these changes scenically. The anonymous, undifferentiated performance space provided a blank area which could be successively reidentified and which could, perhaps, suggest more than one location at the same time. As commonly in presentational theatre, the characters carried their own space with them: the imagined environment adjusts itself to the flow of the action.

There are other examples of this convenient scenic ambiguity. In *The Libation Bearers*, two specific locations are required. One is the tomb of Agamemnon, where the play opens. We are told that Clytemnestra had him buried furtively and without pomp; in real terms, then, we are to consider his tomb as at some remove from the palace. It is here that Orestes has his reunion with Electra; it is here that the plot is hatched to kill the tyrants. Orestes and Pylades leave the stage to prepare for the coming encounter, and when they reappear, the action is assumed to have shifted to the palace. Orestes hammers on the gates, a porter answers, and Clytemnestra eventually appears.

The brief absence of Orestes and Pylades clearly emphasizes this imagined place-shift, just as that of the chorus does in *The Eumenides*. Some commentators have suggested the departure of the chorus also; an intermission, in fact, to mark a change of scene. But this is an unnecessary expedient born out of realistic preconceptions. The choral *stasimon* becomes a bridging song, looking back on what has happened, and forward to what is now to come. Significantly, too, when Orestes and Pylades have returned, and the palace gates (the door of the *skene*) have become the focal point of the action, the tomb is still imaginatively present. The chorus may still address an appeal to their dead king no less immediate than that delivered by Orestes and Electra earlier in the play. In this open and undefined playing space, which can be, at any given moment, what the author wants it to be, we may be first at the tomb, then at the palace, and then both at the tomb *and* at the palace, though in real terms these places could not coexist.

Even Euripides, whose more realistic preconceptions lead him to be more specific about matters of space and time, can profit on occasion from this scenic ambiguity. The opening of *Hecuba* is a case in point. Where, in this tragedy, are we supposed to be? The action takes place in a prison stockade: the shanties housing the captive Trojan women, as they await shipment to Greece. But where exactly is it? Some sequences suggest that we are on the Trojan side of the Hellespont, in the shadow of the fallen city. Here, on the water's edge, stands Achilles' tomb. Messengers come and go between the tomb and prison camp. Polyxena, Hecuba's daughter, the chosen victim, is led off to be sacrificed at the tomb. There is no talk of ships; she seems to go by land. Ships, in fact, cannot sail. Achilles' angry ghost has stilled the winds, and Polyxena must be sacrificed to appease him. The Trojan war is bracketed between the sacrifices of two innocent girls, Iphigeneia at one end and Polyxena at the other.

The camp, then, is on the Trojan side. In this case, how do we explain the arrival of Polymestor? He is King of Thrace, which is on the other side of the water; he has just arrived, as he tells us, from 'the interior of the country'; he has murdered the son of Hecuba, Polydorus, whose body is found by the women bobbing in the surf – presumably along the Thracian coast. Polydorus' ghost serves as prologue to the action, and seems to locate it firmly in Thrace.

Troy, then, or Thrace? In the context of the Greek theatre, there is no need to specify. It can be either or both, as the action dictates. In *Hecuba* Euripides weaves a tragedy from two separate and distinct sources; he uses two plots, each of which illuminates and comments upon the other. In the same spirit his theatre allows him to fuse two separate spheres of action into a no man's land which is Troy or Thrace according to the demands of the immediate moment.

A subtly modulated example is provided by Sophocles' *Philoctetes*, a play whose Greek protagonist has been abandoned, by his unfeeling compatriots, on a deserted island. Here, the setting is established in great detail because the nature of the place is important to the plot. Its description is placed first in the mouth of Odysseus, who has been sent to lure Philoctetes back to the army; early in the prologue, he speaks to his young companion Neoptolemus, describing the terrain in which the object of their search is to be found:

> So be it. Now, the rest is up to you
> Look for a cave there with a double mouth
> The sort of cave that gives a man two places
> To sit and sun himself. But when the heat comes,
> There's still a breeze drawn through, to let him sleep.
> And not too far below, you'll find a spring
> That he can drink from. Well, there used to be

In Odysseus' words the cave, if not idyllic, at least sounds comfortable. Philoctetes sees it with different eyes. The spring turns to ice in winter. The cave is freezing cold; the wounded protagonist has to drag himself across the rocks to find wood, and rub stone on stone to make a spark of fire; he laps at rain puddles when he needs to drink.

But when Philoctetes is delivered from exile, and it is determined that he shall go to rejoin the Greek army at Troy, his farewell to this blighted terrain becomes positively lyrical:

> Farewell, cave, the partner of my years
> Of watching, waiting; farewell, nymphs
> Of stream and meadow.[1]

A singularly unpromising landscape has suddenly sprouted nymphs; we had not heard of them before.

It is clear what is happening here. The environment adjusts itself to the mood of the speaker. It is benign for Odysseus, baneful for Philoctetes in his misery; but when his fortunes are restored, it smiles. These modulations are possible because the environment is created by words in the first place, and what words can make, words can change.

What words can make, words can also destroy. If we agree that settings are spun by the language of the poet out of the imaginations of the audience, we have an easy solution for the scenes of devastation that occur in the plays. In *Prometheus Bound*, the rock on which the protagonist is pinioned is hurled down to the abyss by an earthquake. In *The Madness of Heracles* a similar earthquake destroys the palace.

> See, see:
> A wind has struck the house, the roof is falling.[2]

In *The Bacchae*, Dionysus conjures up an earthquake to free him from imprisonment in the palace.

DIONYSUS Spirit of earthquake come, unseat the earth!
CHORUS See, in a second Pentheus' palace
  Will be shaken to its fall.
  Dionysus is within the house
  On your knees and worship him
  Look, the columns gape, the great stone doors
  Shiver and tremble; the thundergod
  Is bellowing within the walls.
DIONYSUS Brandish the lightning! Sear the sky with flame
  Burn the house of Pentheus to the ground!
CHORUS Look, look, the flame that burns around
  The tomb of Semele; the fire
  Lit in her honour, that destroyed her.
  Tremble, you Maenads. Hug the ground with fear!
  Down on your knees! For our lord is coming
  To assail the house, the son of god,
  And the mighty shall bow down before him![3]

The vividness of this description created problems for several generations of critics. Clearly, for the chorus, an earthquake has taken place. Equally clearly, argued the critics, the earthquake could not *really* have taken place; there was no way in which the Greek theatre, working outdoors without the aid of modern theatre lighting and mechanics, could have created such an event. The critics pointed out – rightly – that there are some strange things about this earthquake. After it has happened, no one ever refers to it again. Its consequences do not seem to be on view. Characters who enter subsequently do not comment on the rubble and destruction. And, by the end of the play, the palace seems miraculously to have grown again; characters are spoken of as entering to and from the palace.

How to account for these anomalies? One desperate attempt at rationalization argued that there had never been an earthquake in the first place; that the character who identifies himself as the god Dionysus was in fact a mortal guru, working mass hypnotism on the chorus, so that they see an earthquake where there is none. The interpretation may now safely be discarded; it was conditioned by the realistic context of the theatre to which the critics were exposed in their own time; they assumed that, if an event could not be realistically shown, it could not be shown at all. Modern familiarity with more open, and more imaginative, types of staging suggests other alternatives. A generation that can take in its stride Peter Shaffer's stage direction in *The Royal Hunt of the Sun*, 'Pizarro and his men cross the Andes', has no trouble in seeing how the Greeks, by use of language and imagination, could conjure an earthquake out of thin air. The storm is said to happen; therefore it happens. All we need do is to allow the Greeks the same imaginative flexibility that we have long taken for granted in Shakespeare. We need no more insist on a visible and mechanically contrived stage storm in *The Bacchae* than we need assume some prodigy of Jacobean hydraulic engineering inundating the stage with water for the first scene of *The Tempest*. Nor does the objection that the palace seemingly grows again have any validity. The doctrine of the immediate moment is in force. An effect conceived in the imagination need have no consequences, if those consequences are unnecessary to the advancement of the action.

In comedy, because of the greater scope and range of the action, the scenic requirements appear to be more complex. Comedy demands a multiplicity of locations. Although *The Knights* is virtually static – we are implicitly or explicitly in the Pnyx for almost all the action – *Peace* whirls us from earth to heaven, and back to earth again; *The Acharnians* begins in the Pnyx before a full meeting of the Assembly, moves to Dikaiopolis' farm, thence to Euripides' house, and finally to the 'open market' established by the protagonist; and *The Frogs* takes place successively before the house of Heracles, in a street, on the banks of the River Styx, on the Styx itself, in front of Pluto's palace in the Underworld, and inside the same.

Because of this, it is often assumed that the scenic background for comedy must have been more elaborate than for tragedy. Most scholars would now agree that the physical requirements for tragedy were very simple: no more than the orchestra, the *skene* with one central door, and the facility for making other open entrances to the right or left. No extant tragedy requires more than a single door, plus the language and imagination that colour it with a specific identity.

Though comedy may seem to require more, we can easily see how the same basic simplicity might apply. In *The Frogs*, the door is first identified as the house of Heracles: Dionysus beats upon it, and the demigod appears protesting. Following Heracles' exit, the action moves into open areas. The procession carrying the corpse to burial defines – if definition is needed – the location as a street. We next know that we are supposed to be on the banks of the Styx, because the language of Dionysus and Xanthias identifies the place for us. This is made certain by the arrival of Charon in his boat. There is no need to imagine elaborate mechanics here. The actors could easily carry the boat along with them, in the manner of the ferrymen in Japanese Noh drama.

For the frog chorus, the most appropriate location would be the orchestra itself, to give scope for the choreography that the script suggests. Following this, the boat returns to land, and Dionysus soon finds himself knocking on the gates of Pluto's palace. Surely we need only accept the simplest explanation: that this is represented by the same door that earlier stood for the house of Heracles, now reidentified after a brief absence. We might also note that the exit and subsequent reappearance of Xanthias (instructed to take the long way round the lake) serves to indicate a major change of scene, in the same way as the disappearance of the Fury chorus in *The Eumenides*.

In some plays the use of a single door makes a comic point that would evaporate with two. In *Ekklesiazusae* (*The Congresswomen*, or *Women in Parliament*) the young man goes to the door to serenade his girl. She calls to him from aloft; he impatiently awaits her coming. At last the door opens; but instead of the young girl, there appears an old hag, who seizes the young man and tries to make off with him. This switch of persons is illogical but hilarious. One door makes a splendid comic point. Two doors would make none at all.

Perhaps we may apply the same reasoning to *The Clouds*. Here two doors seem to be demanded. As the comedy opens, we see Pheidip-pides and Strepsiades in bed. Strepsiades pulls the blankets round his ears and tries to sleep but cannot; he is oppressed by debts and worries and does not know where to turn. Then he has his bright idea.

He wakes Pheidippides and urges him to join Socrates' academy, where he will be taught to lie, cheat, and steal:

STREPSIADES You see that house there, with the gate in front?
PHEIDIPPIDES I see it, yes. But what the devil is it?
STREPSIADES That's Highbrow Hall, the hallowed seat of learning.[4]

When Pheidippides rejects his proposal, Strepsiades decides to enrol as a student himself.

I may be down, but I'm not out yet
I'll say a prayer, stroll down to Highbrow Hall
And register myself. But wait. I'm way over-age
Slow, muddle-minded. What hope have I of learning
How to split hairs, and chop logic? Well, here goes.
What are you waiting for?
Here's the Academy. Let's give them a call.
STUDENT Hell! Who hammered on the door like that?
Don't you have any manners?[5]

As written, the action seems clearly to posit two locations, two doors. We begin before the house of Strepsiades; making his resolution, the protagonist crosses to the other door, Socrates' door, and bangs on it.

But are two doors really necessary? Further consideration suggests that one door could stand, in the manner of *The Frogs*, for two different places in succession. Is it not possible to construct a scenario in which one door stands for both? The action might then proceed as follows. Strepsiades and Pheidippides conduct their initial dialogue before the door. Pheidippides, refusing to accept his father's suggestions, leaves (either through the door or off to one side, it makes no difference). Strepsiades makes up his mind to become a pupil himself. He takes a walk – which need be no more than a small circuit, perhaps in the orchestra. This brings him back to the same door which his knocking, his language, and the Student's angry appearance immediately identify as belonging to somewhere else.

This concept of multiple use is one of the simplest dramatic conventions to assimilate. We find it used plentifully, for instance in the Elizabethan and Restoration theatres, where a single door may assume a succession of identities in the course of the play. The convention that a short walk may stand for a longer journey is a recognized feature of, for instance, the Noh play. It is strange that scholars have been so reluctant to see the possibilities for the Greek theatre also. In the case of *The Clouds*, the use of one door to stand for two distinct places has the added advantage of creating a thematically important visual image. At the beginning of the play we see Strepsiades, in his own house, wrapped in blankets. He is beset by cares and worries; he does not know which way to turn. When he enters Socrates' academy, the philosopher first subjects him, as an initiatory rite, to a parody of Orphic ceremony; then he endeavours to instruct him in music and grammar; and finally, when the old man is totally confused, compels him to undergo an 'autotherapeutic session'.

> Now put on your thinking-cap,
> Look at things from every angle,
> Scrutinize and contemplate.
> If you're caught in a dilemma
> Drop it, change your point of view.
> Honeyed sleep must stand at bay.[6]

Strepsiades, wrapped in a verminous blanket, prodded by nagging questions, cannot cope with what is being demanded of him. When asked how he intends to put his life in order, he can only come up with farcical answers to financial questions.

The visual allusion here, surely, is significant. One tableau recalls the other. Strepsiades wrapped in a blanket in front of Socrates' house, and chattering about his money troubles, recalls the Strepsiades we saw at the beginning of the play similarly occupied at his own door. If both doors are the same door, the association of images is meaningful and powerful. By joining the Academy Strepsiades has, quite literally, got nowhere. He is in exactly the same position as he was when he started.

We began with the pseudo-Aristotelian Unity of Place. We have now transformed this into something else, which we might perhaps call the doctrine of the immediate moment. The scene adapts itself to what it needs to be, for any given portion of the play. If the story-line requires a continuity of place, setting once established can be assumed as continuing in force, as long as nothing is stated to the contrary. If it is desirable that the location should change, this too can be established, in the simplest possible way, by a new set of verbal references. Characters carry their location with them, and remake their space according to their need.

The contrast between Greek and Roman comedy best shows how

the Greek theatre, at its most flexible, could work. In Aristophanes, the plot dictates the setting. The swirl of the action propels the characters through a succession of imagined locations. The scene is constantly re-creating itself. Aristophanes has achieved a quasi-cinematic flexibility without benefit of camera; and he does it by the use of language and imagination.

In Roman comedy, however, the reverse applies. The setting is carefully established at the play's beginning, usually in a narrative prologue. The action is normally located in a street, before a row of houses. These houses are represented by doors – now grown to three from the Greek theatre's one, and now specifically identified as the houses of particular characters. Once this location has been established, the action never moves away from it. Here, the Unity of Place clearly does apply. The setting dominates the action, and imposes its own restrictions upon it.

If this view of the Greek theatre is accepted, one important corollary follows. Once we admit that the location is established largely by language, and changed by language, then it becomes axiomatic that language cannot lie. We have to believe what we are told, or there is no meaningful way in which the play can proceed. If we are informed that we are in front of Creon's palace, this must be true. The 'mass hypnosis' theory of *The Bacchae* cannot work; there is no way in which the chorus can 'see' something which the audience cannot 'see'.

This seems to be supported by other aspects of the Greek drama. Characters for the most part do not lie: about themselves, about their behaviour, about their motives. What they say about themselves is true – unless they make it crystal clear, beforehand, that they are going to lie. Falsehoods are prepared for in advance. Thus, in *Medea*, the protagonist pretends to be reconciled to her faithless husband:

> I should have shared your counsels, been your go-between,
> And had the joy of tending your new bride.
> But we are what we are; I will not say bad,
> But ... women. Yet you should not take bad example
> And answer my stupidity with yours.
> I admit that I was wrong before
> But come to saner judgement now.[7]

Jason is deceived, but we are not. This entrapment has been prepared for in advance. Earlier in the play, we have heard Medea say:

> One of my servants shall I send to Jason;
> And when he has come here before my face
> I shall say soft words to him, that all is well,
> That the royal match he abandons me to make
> Is for my advantage, and a good idea.[8]

Similarly, in *The Libation Bearers*, Orestes and Pylades appear in disguise to inform Clytemnestra that her son is dead, and so gain admittance to the palace. Here again, the plot is set up carefully in advance. Orestes has earlier informed Electra and the chorus what he means to do, and forewarns the audience at the same time. We see the same technique in a later play with a similar plot, Sophocles' *Electra*. We have already seen Orestes alive, and learned of the Tutor's plans to feign his death. When the urn is brought in filled, supposedly, with Orestes' ashes, Electra is temporarily deceived, but we are not. There are other examples, but the point is clear. In a theatre where words are the principal means of conveying information, words have to mean what they appear to mean.

We have questioned the Unity of Place as a valid dramatic principle, at least for the Greeks themselves; it was certainly valuable for their imitators centuries later, but that is another matter. May we go on to apply the same criticism to the Unity of Time? This is another principle attributed to Aristotle, this time with more accuracy. He did suggest, in the *Poetics*, that the action of a tragedy should properly be embraced within one circuit of the sun – a single day, in pre-Copernican terms. Later scholars were to debate, hotly, whether this meant twelve hours or twenty-four, but the general implication is clear: the action of a tragedy should be brief and continuous: like Racine, and not at all like Shakespeare. Stage time should be more or less equivalent to real time.

Like the Unity of Place, the Unity of Time is superficially and misleadingly true. Certainly, the principal action of most tragedies (not all) may be compressed into a compact time span. The playing time of *Oedipus the King* is approximately one and a half hours. Its on-stage action – the information brought to Oedipus and the discoveries he makes about himself – may plausibly be encompassed within that period. As spectators, we are observing ninety minutes – though crowded minutes, perhaps – in a man's life. The events of *Medea* are similarly compatible with clock and calendar.

Similarly, in Greek tragedy characters do not grow old. In the

Oresteia, Orestes grows from infancy to manhood in the interval between *Agamemnon* and *The Libation Bearers*; but no character ages within the limits of a single play. If the Greek playwrights had written descriptive stage directions to their plays – which they did not – they could never have written 'The same scene, ten years later'. Even in the *Oresteia*, although Orestes ages between plays, there is no obvious way in which the other characters do. Clytemnestra and Aegisthus are still, in the second play, what they were in the first. The process of ageing seems to be arbitrary in Sophocles also. We see Oedipus at two points in his life: in the prime of life, as ruler, in *Oedipus the King*, and as an old man in *Oedipus at Colonus*. In the comparison, he seems to have aged centuries. Antigone, however, seems to have grown more gradually. In the earlier play she is still, presumably, a child too young to comprehend what has happened to her family, and to her. Oedipus, bidding farewell to her and Ismene at the play's end, says:

> Children: if you were old enough to understand
> There is much I could say to help you. As it is
> Pray after me: to live with moderation
> And better fortune than your father did.[9]

In *Oedipus at Colonus*, Creon jeers at Antigone for still accompanying her father through the Greek countryside, when she is of an age to have been married. This would place her at about 14; Greek girls married early. Still, the age gap between the two Antigones seems much smaller than the chasm which separates the younger from the older Oedipus.

This sort of comparison, however, is not really relevant. It merely serves to remind us that each play creates its own context, its own time-scheme; that characters live within the world of each play, and that the data may change from one play to another. Within the limits of a single play, be it noted, specific age has no importance. As we have already seen, Greek tragic characters divide themselves into broad age-groups: young, prime-of-life, and old. Shakespeare gives us the seven ages of man, but the Greeks identified three. In *Agamemnon* the aged chorus compare their feebleness to that of a young child:

> Youth and age are alike. When the sap runs green in the body
> Weak limbs are deaf to the call of war. With winter coming
> We use three legs to walk, weak as a newborn babe,
> Wandering through the streets like a dream abroad by daylight.[10]

These two states of weakness are contrasted, implicitly, with the healthy manhood of the Argives sent to fight in Troy.

Similarly, the riddle of the Sphinx which lies behind *Oedipus the King* divides human life into three ages, in language reminiscent of *Agamemnon*: 'What is it that goes on four legs in the morning, two legs in the afternoon, and three in the evening?' The answer is Man; and though the riddle is never quoted in the play, suggestions have been made that the stage picture reproduces this tripartite division at significant moments, particularly in the crowd of suppliants described by the Priest at the opening:

> Why, Oedipus, our country's lord and master,
> You see us, of all ages, gathered here
> Before your altars: some, too young to fly
> Far from the nest; and others bent with age,
> Priests – I of Zeus – and these who represent
> Our youth.

More specific than this, however, we cannot be. In *Antigone*, for example, which sister is the elder? Sophocles gives no information; though modern actresses, more concerned with character, would like to know. In the non-dramatic sources, interestingly enough, the evidence comes out approximately even: half the ancient authors make Antigone older, half Ismene. Sophocles leaves the matter open: such precision is apparently unimportant to him.

To return to the so-called Unity of Time: this principle, only superficially true, begins to break down when we examine the plays in detail. We see this in both subtle and more obvious ways. A number of plays contain actions which could not be temporally continuous, though at first they may appear so. Consider, for example, the old Herdsman in *Oedipus the King*. He plays a double role in Oedipus' life: first as his rescuer when he was abandoned as a baby; second, as the only surviving witness of the murder at the crossroads. It is in the latter function that we first hear of him. Jocasta tells Oedipus that this man

> wrung me by the hand, and begged me send him
> As far as possible from the sight of Thebes
> I gave him his request. Slave though he was,
> He could have asked for more and had it granted.[11]

He is located, then, far from the city; but when Oedipus sends for him, he appears almost instantaneously. He seems to have been waiting just round the corner. Time is obviously compressed here, to suit the needs of the dramatic action. This is no great matter. In the context of performance, it is barely noticeable. We note it here simply as one small rift in the apparent unity of time.

The same compression is seen in antecedent, off-stage action. Describing the same Herdsman, Jocasta identifies him as the sole witness of Laius' murder, and tells what happened to him after this event:

> OEDIPUS Is he with us? Is he in our household now?
> JOCASTA No, he is not. When he came back, and found
> You ruling here in Thebes and Laius dead

Something strange has happened here. In the background story, Oedipus has murdered Laius on the road. He makes his way to Thebes; he finds a widowed Jocasta, and the city ravaged by the Sphinx; he solves the riddle, marries the queen, and ascends the throne. And then, apparently, the survivor returns. Where has he been all this time? Once again, in performance the discrepancy is easily swallowed and barely noticeable. It is simply another indication that time in Greek tragedy is manipulable; that it can adjust itself to the dramatic moment.

An example more often commented upon is drawn from *Agamemnon*. We learn, at the beginning of the play, that Clytemnestra has arranged a chain of beacon fires to leap across the Aegean and give almost instant warning of the victory at Troy. The chorus is at first incredulous:

> What messenger could travel here so fast?
> CLYTEMNESTRA Hephaestus, his beams piercing the night
> From Ida's lonely summit.
> And beacon fired off beacon, as
> the herald flame sped on
> To Hermes' crag in Lemnos. Then Zeus' home,
> mountain of Athos,
> Snatched up the stand torch as third in the race.

So the beacon-fire flashes from station to station, from island to mountaintop

to alight on the crag of Arachnae
Where Argos' neighbour watches; so came here,
True offspring of the fire of Ida.[12]

Convinced by Clytemnestra's ingenuity, the chorus celebrates the victory. At once, however, the beacon is substantiated by a human messenger. He has arrived by sea, a long and dangerous journey; yet his appearance and the beacon's are almost simultaneous. Once again, time bends to dramatic necessity. An extended voyage is compressed into a few minutes. Commentators sometimes suggest that, in such cases, an intervening chorus suggests the passage of time; but it is doubtful whether the Greeks would have thought it necessary to justify the time compression. Such concerns belong to a theatre more realistically conceived. In a theatre where the setting is controlled by the imagination, time, like place, can be what you want it to be.

If time can be compressed, it can also be extended. A famous example occurs in *Antigone*. In the prologue, Antigone announces her decision to bury her brother. Ismene tries to stop her, but Antigone will not be dissuaded. As the prologue ends, it is clear that she is going straight out to perform her act of defiance:

ANTIGONE Go on like this and you will make me hate you.
　　Leave me alone with my stupidity
　　To face this dread unknown. Whatever it may be,
　　Anything is better than to die a coward.
ISMENE Then if your mind is made up, go. You are
　　A fool. And yet your own will love you for it.[13]

There follows the *parodos*, in which the chorus celebrates the end of war, and Creon's inaugural address to his subjects, in which he announces his intentions for the body. The Guard enters, nervous and trembling, to announce that, in defiance of orders, the body has already been covered with dust, as token burial. Creon, furious, orders the Guard to catch the unknown malefactors. They both leave; the chorus sings of human ingenuity, its powers and limitations, in one of the best-known *stasima* of Greek tragedy:

　　The world is full of wonderful things,
　　But none more so than man;
　　This prodigy who sails before the storm-winds,
　　Cutting a path across the sea's grey face
　　Beneath the towering menace of the waves.

And earth, the oldest, the primeval god,
Immortal, inexhaustible earth,
She too has felt the weight of his hand
As year after year the mules are harnessed
And ploughs go back and forwards in the field.[14]

No sooner has the choral song concluded than the Guard returns with the captive Antigone; he describes in detail how he has caught her scattering dust and pouring libations over the body.

This episode has become notorious as the question of the 'double burial'. For it seems that the body is indeed buried twice. The first occasion is reported by the Guard to Creon; on the second, Antigone is caught. Clearly, Antigone performed the second burial. Who was responsible for the first one?

This question has produced a wide spectrum of responses. It has been suggested that the first burial was a divine admonition, a strong suggestion by the gods to Creon that this is what should properly be done; and there is certainly some support in the text for this. Alternatively, it has been suggested that both burials were carried out by Antigone herself; that she performed the first one undetected; and that, wishing to be caught so that her defiance would be known, she went back and did it a second time, when the guards were certain to be watching. This vision of Antigone as haunted by a death wish, however, seems to belong to Anouilh's play rather than to Sophocles'.

Perhaps we can find an easier explanation in terms of the manipulation of stage time. In real terms, we have a single action, temporally continuous: Antigone goes out to bury her brother, and is caught. Sophocles has fragmented this into two actions, temporally discontinuous. The body is buried; Antigone is caught. This permits us to observe in greater detail the impact of the action on Creon; on the Guard; and on Antigone herself. Sophocles extends the action for dramatic effect. By the manipulation of time he achieves, let us say, what a cubist painter achieves by the analytic depiction of space: he allows us to study something from several points of view at the same time.

We should note, however, that even this striking departure from strict logic is hardly perceptible in performance. It becomes apparent from close reading only, and the solutions suggested for it tend to come from scholars, not from actors. In some plays, however, we have massive manipulations of time, which involve not hours but eons;

plays in which the action, far from taking 'one circuit of the sun', sprawls across millennia.

The prime examples here are Aeschylean. In the *Oresteia* we have a trilogy which deals, ostensibly, with the story of two generations. Thyestes and Atreus, whose quarrel was the immediate begetter of the family strife, and the curse upon the house, are both dead. *Agamemnon*, the first play of the trilogy, shows us their issue: Agamemnon, son of Atreus, and Aegisthus, the last surviving child of Thyestes. In the second play, *The Libation Bearers*, the story is continued through the next generation, Orestes and Electra, the children of Agamemnon. The third play, *The Eumenides*, continues with the subsequent history of Orestes, and ends with his exoneration.

In historical terms, however, the action of the *Oresteia* spans a much longer period. It begins with the ending of the Trojan War, to which the Greeks themselves assigned a date early in the twelfth century BC. The war is the product of a feudal era, waged by an agglomeration of individual monarchs with their private armies; it speaks of a time when the old-established Mycenaean communities could still impose their will on the rest of Greece.

The *Oresteia* ends, however, with the foundation of the Court of the Areopagos, the council convened by Athena to decide the fate of Orestes. This jumps the years to bring us into a new era. While we cannot date the formation of this body with historical precision, it seems to stem from the seventh century BC; it is a product of the period when aristocratic government, with advice from assemblies, was replacing the rule of kings; and it belongs to an Athens no longer under the control of other powers, but already an independent centre of government. This apparent tale of two generations, therefore, carries us across some 500 years.

In fact, though, the time span of the *Oresteia* is even longer than that. Spiritually, it begins in the dark recesses of the primitive mind: that forbidding substratum of the Greek world, of which we have occasional glimpses in myth and sculpture, that was peopled by monsters and controlled by fear. The supernatural powers presiding over the first stages of the *Oresteia* are the Furies, the 'Children of Old Night', the Curses. Their code is justice at its crudest; they are embodiments of blood-guilt, the primitive vendetta; they personify the all-destructive family feud, where blood seeks blood until nothing is left.

From these powers of darkness we move to the god of the half-light,

Hermes, and from him to the luminous deities, Apollo and Athena. These are the gods of a new order, the gods of the enlightenment. Instead of retribution they bring the rule of law; instead of superstition, reason. Vendetta is replaced by social order. What we have in the *Oresteia*, then, is no mere tale of two generations, or even of 500 years. It is nothing less than an allegory of the progress of civilization.

The time-scale of Aeschylus' trilogy suits the cosmic nature of his investigations. If we still possessed the complete trilogy of which *Prometheus Bound* is a part, we should no doubt be able to say the same of this too. As it is, we see in the extant drama an action which goes back to the beginning of time, to the struggle between gods and Titans for the possession of the world. We see, by reminiscence, man in his primitive beginnings, as no more than a burrowing animal:

> In the beginning they had eyes but did not see,
> Ears but did not hear: like creatures in a dream
> They lived in chaos all their days, possessing
> No houses brick-built in the sunshine, knowing
> No art of carpentry. They could not tell for sure
> When it was winter, when the spring brought flowers
> Or summer harvest.[15]

It was Prometheus who taught them astronomy, writing and mathematics, metallurgy and divination. Thus *Prometheus Bound* too becomes an allegory of civilization, the focal figure here being Prometheus himself. The action promises a sequel set in the far future, when, after generations have been born and died, a hero will arise to set Prometheus free, and bring about a *rapprochement* between the Olympians and their erstwhile victim, a new age of tolerance and understanding.

We have seen earlier how, in *Prometheus Bound*, the chorus takes a simple central action and expands it geographically until it covers the entire world. When Prometheus cries in agony upon his rock,

> upon the earth's face
> Comes a cry of mourning,
> Lament for the greatness
> And glory past, the grace
> Of you and your kin.

> All mortals that inhabit
> The homes of holy Asia
> Grieving and sorrowing
> Partake of labours.
>
> And the maiden dwellers in the land
> Of Colchis, terrible in battle
> And the Scythians mustered
> At earth's end, the fringe
> Of Lake Maiotis.
>
> And the flower of Araby, who hold
> Their mountain fortress in the country
> Close by Caucasus, savage
> In battle, who whoop
> As spears fly round them.[16]

Literal-minded scholars have asked, from time to time, where exactly the setting of *Prometheus* is meant to be. The answer is that it is everywhere. The lonely figure on his rock embraces the whole world.

Prometheus has a similar temporal universality. It looks back to the creation, and forward to the remote future; and this expansion of time is made possible by the figure of Prometheus, who is coeval with time, who is himself a prophet, and whose very name means Foresight. Just as the earthbound Titan establishes a link between earth and heaven, so his memory and insight assemble past and future, and make them contemporary with the present.

The past is brought before us both by Prometheus himself and his visitor Io, another victim of Zeus, who recounts her own history. Prometheus alone has power to know the future. Prompted by the chorus, he forecasts for himself and Io. She is destined to embark on a journey that will take her across the known world:

> You will come across the host
> Of Amazons, manhaters, who round Thermodon
> Shall live in future time, at Themiscyra,
> Where the sailors' curse, the ships' unnatural mother,
> Salmydessus, sinks her teeth into the sea.
> Then you will reach the narrow portals of the water,
> The isthmus of Cimmeria. Pass by this
> With courage in your heart, and you must then
> Traverse the channel of Maiotis. And

> For all eternity mankind shall tell
> The saga of your passing, for its name
> Shall be yours, Bosphorus. So leaving Europe
> You will make the crossing into Asia.[17]

This speech not merely looks forward in time, but achieves the same geographical expansion we have already seen in the chorus. Io's wanderings will continue, taking her to Egypt:

> On the fringe of the world
> You will come to a tribe of black men, and their home
> Is by the sources of the sun, the River Aithiops.
> Follow along its banks until you reach
> The cataract where from the Bybline Mountains
> There flow the sweet and holy waters of the Nile[18]

Prometheus' fortunes and those of Io will be linked; Heracles, her remote descendant, will come back to liberate him from his bondage. Time in *Prometheus Bound* is closer to geological time than to 'one revolution of the sun'. Just as the setting of the play is the whole world – indeed the cosmos – its time-scheme is eternity.

Prometheus in his own play is the nodal figure drawing together past, present, and future. This device as used in drama reminds us of the concept that anthropologists have defined as 'ceremonial time': the use of ritual or magic, in a place of sanctity, both to summon up the spirits of the dead and to predict the future. Channelled by a shaman of appropriate power, all time flows into the present moment.

In *Agamemnon*, this power is vested in Cassandra. Fatally gifted by Apollo, she can see the palace's dark past, the ghosts of the slaughtered dead, Thyestes' children:

> See where the children sit
> Beside the house, pale creatures of the twilight,
> Slain by the ones they loved, each in his hands
> Holding a portion of that same tender flesh
> That served as food, and show for all to see
> Their bodies gashed and torn, to make a meal
> Whereof their father feasted.[19]

More, she sees the supernatural force behind these murders, the Furies who assume tangible shape for her:

> Here to the house I say there clings a choir
> Chanting a strange discordant symphony;
> Slaking their thirst, and bolder grown thereby,
> On human blood. Here to the house it clings,
> No power can move it, this foul gathering
> Of Furies bred and nurtured in the race.[20]

Looking to the future, she can see her own death, as well as Agamemnon's.

The parallel between 'ceremonial time' and dramatic time is forceful here. It reminds us that, whatever Greek tragedy may have become, it had its roots deep in religious ritual. The orchestra of the Theatre of Dionysus is still, in Aeschylus' time, a place of particular sanctity; the actor is still close to being a priest; the community surrounds the celebration, just as the tribe surrounds the sacred ground in non-dramatic ritual.

Purely as a dramatic device, however, the use of the prophet figure liberates the dramatist from the laws of real time. Through Prometheus' and Cassandra's eyes, we see whole generations pass before us. They are made real in language, just as the stage setting is. For Sophocles, the prophet Teiresias performs a similar function. Through him, assisted by the reminiscences of Oedipus himself, and by the chorus, we view the life of the protagonist from birth onwards. One of the most powerful aspects of *Oedipus the King* is the way in which past action is created for us, simultaneously with present action: past and present continually intertwine, illuminate each other and entangle, until they meet in the dreadful moment of Oedipus' self-realization. It is only the play's immediate action that encompasses 'one revolution of the sun'. Its total action covers Oedipus' whole life from babyhood, and reaches back into the lives of his parents before him.

Although not all plays possess specific prophet-figures, the same techniques are regularly used. Dreams and visions open windows onto a wider world. The chorus, particularly, can divorce itself from present time to enlarge the boundaries of the action. Examples are common, and one particularly impressive one will perhaps suffice. This occurs in *The Bacchae* when Pentheus, dressed as a woman, has gone to spy on the Dionysiac worshippers on the mountain. The chorus looks forward to the immediate future:

> To the mountain, you hounds of madness, run
> Where the daughters of Cadmus dance and sing
> And inflame their hearts against him who comes
> Driven mad in the dress of a woman to spy.
> As he peers from the crannies and clefts of the rock
> He'll be seen by the mother's sharp eye. She will shout
> To the women 'Who comes to the mountain, the mountain,
> To spy on our revels? What mother's son?
> Some lioness bore him, not one of us women,
> Some monster, some Gorgon, some beast of the desert.'[21]

The choral song both transmutes the future into the present and brings remote action before our eyes. When the Messenger subsequently arrives to report the death of Pentheus, he merely tells us what we already know, and have in a sense already seen.

One more recurrent phenomenon deserves to be considered here. This is the blending of time schemes, the way in which the fictional time of the play may merge with the actual time of the audience. An interesting example occurs in Euripides' *Cyclops*, our only complete surviving satyr play.

In this short work, Euripides is heavily indebted to Homer. The familiar story of the *Odyssey* Book IX is preserved almost complete. Odysseus and his men, thirsty and famished, land on the island of Sicily; they begin to carry off the Cyclops' sheep; the one-eyed monster catches them, and imprisons them in his cave; and Odysseus and his men blind the Cyclops and escape by a trick. As this is a satyr play, a satyr chorus is added. So is another traditional character, their bald and paunchy father Silenus. Certain alterations must be made to suit stage practice. But, on the whole, *Cyclops* is faithful to Homer in narrative, mood, and language.

One change – which seems at first to bear out Aristotle – is the compression of the narrative. In Homer, the action extends over three days, as follows:

First day: Odysseus arrives with his men on the Cyclops' island. They discover the cave and sit down to wait.

First night: Polyphemus returns with his flocks, questions Odysseus, and eats two men.

Second day: Polyphemus eats two more men and takes his flocks to pasture. Odysseus prepares the stake with which to blind his enemy.

157

Second night: Polyphemus returns, eats two more men, is made drunk and blinded.

Third day: Odysseus and his men escape.

For dramatic purposes Euripides collapses the three cannibal feasts into one, with the blinding following immediately afterwards. But something strange has happened to the time scheme.

The first indication of dramatic time that we are given comes with the *parodos*. Silenus, as he finishes the prologue, sees the satyrs, his sons, bringing their flocks home from the mountains. It is therefore implied – though admittedly not stated – that this is evening, just as in Homer Polyphemus returns with his flocks at the end of the day.

The next time reference bears out this assumption. Polyphemus, returning from the hunt, accuses the satyrs of idleness. They hang their heads in shame; and when he tells them to hold their heads up, they reply:

> We're looking at Zeus, up aloft in the sky.
> We can see all the stars, and Orion himself.[22]

So far so good; it is now night-time, and the time scheme is consistent. We might note that to set a play in the darkness hours is unusual. *Antigone* opens before dawn, but the *parodos* celebrates the rising sun. Specific scenes in comedy – usually later comedy – imply darkness by the production of lamps and torches. *Rhesus*, with a whole torch-bearing chorus, is the only play whose action takes place wholly at night, and where 'darkness' is important to the plot.

In *Cyclops*, however, the time scheme is almost immediately shattered. Polyphemus proceeds to bellow for his *ariston*; and though *ariston* can mean either breakfast or midday meal (*petit déjeuner* or *déjeuner*) it can never mean a meal eaten in the evening. The problem is compounded by another reference later in the play. When the Cyclops has finished his cannibal feast, Odysseus produces the wine to make him drunk; exuberantly, the monster cries:

> It's pleasant to sit in the sweet long grass

and Silenus, who has his own eyes on the wineskin, answers

> And sip wine in the sunshine, and let the world pass.[23]

In other words, the clock has gone berserk. We are now at siesta time, and seem to be leaping from one part of the day to another with a freedom unparalleled in Greek drama.

What has happened here? Is it merely the dramatist being careless, and forgetting that he has made three feasts into one? Probably not. Rather, we have moved from the fictional time of the play into the real time of the audience – where it is, no doubt, siesta time and where the audience, this being after all a satyr play and the latter part of a long day's festival, is probably sipping a little wine on its own account. This sudden outreach to the audience is made easier by the fact that, as usual, there is no barrier between the play and the spectators; that orchestra and audience are lit by the same sun; and that, consequently, time indicated by one verbal reference can be changed by another.

A more important example comes from *The Bacchae*. This play is set in Thebes, in the third generation after its founding. Its founder and first king, Cadmus, who colonized the site under divine admonition, is now an old man, but still alive, and one of the most important characters in the play. His coeval is Teiresias, the prophet. These two old men belong to the beginnings of legendary history; their presence takes us back to the dawn of Greek time. Other characters are Cadmus' descendants. We hear of one daughter, Semele, who was impregnated by Zeus and gave birth to the god Dionysus. We see another daughter, Agave, and her son, Pentheus, who has inherited the power from his grandfather. Though one is immortal and the other mortal, therefore, Dionysus and Pentheus are cousins, and of the same age. Much is made of the physical resemblance between them. Dionysus is, by definition, younger than Cadmus. The religion that he introduces into Thebes is strange, new, and exotic.

The first episode introduces us to Cadmus and Teiresias, both old, yet willing to espouse the new. Dressed in beast-skins, with wreaths in their hair, they are ready to celebrate the Bacchic rites: they are the only men in Thebes to do so. They reassure each other that they are correct in this.

> CADMUS I am but mortal. When god speaks, I listen.
> TEIRESIAS Ours not to reason with the powers above.
> These beliefs were dear to our fathers, handed down
> From the dawn of time; and they will stand for ever
> Against all arguments of clever men.[24]

In terms of the play, of course, these beliefs have not been handed down from the dawn of time. They could not be. We are still at the dawn of time. And in Theban terms, at any rate, the generation represented by Teiresias and Cadmus had no father. Thebes began with Cadmus. The whole point of the play is that this is a new religion, one which has still to win acceptance.

If these lines make no sense in the context of the play, however, they make very good sense indeed from the viewpoint of the audience. To an Athenian crowd in the late fifth century, these beliefs were certainly as old as time. The worship of Dionysus had been practised from the immemorial past, and continued to be practised still. Euripides' apparent lapse of logic is instead an appeal to contemporary sensibilities. We have slipped from fictional time into real time.

This practice justifies many things in Greek tragedy that might otherwise appear as anachronisms. They justify, for instance, the fact that, in *Prometheus Bound*, Aeschylus, while discussing the cataclysms of the world in creation, can insert an allusion to an event still fresh in the audience's mind:

> [on the monster Typhon's body]
> Etna's roots lie heavy. Far above,
> High on the summit, squats Hephaestus, forging
> The molten ore. And from this place one day
> Rivers of fire shall flow, there shall be waste
> And devastation of the lowlands, all the fertile
> Soil of Sicily: for so will Typhon's anger boil
> And where men once walked the burning streams shall flow,
> For all that Zeus' lightning had cremated him.[25]

The reference seems to be to a recent historical occurrence, the eruption of Etna, in Sicily, in 479 BC.

This practice justifies, too, the apparent anomaly in *Hecuba*. Here a chorus of Trojan women, anticipating their slavery, start to sing of festivals contemporary with the play's audience:

> Or will the driving oarstroke
> Transport me to the islands
> To house my heavy head
> Where first the palm tree grew
> And holiness of laurel
> Keeping green the name of Leto

160

Who was hard delivered there?
And when the girls of Delos hymn
The crown and bow of Artemis,
Shall I be at their side?

Or shall I take up my abode
Where Pallas dwells, in chariot and glory.
To ply and pattern at the loom.
Linking a skein of horses
And garlands, gay devices
As ornament for her saffron robe?[26]

The latter stanza, of course, refers to Athens' greatest festival, the Panathenaia; the former reminds the audience of the festivals of Apollo at Delphi. In recent times these had been allowed to lapse, but were reinaugurated in 426 BC. We seem to have here a contemporary allusion to this reinauguration which allows us to fix the date of the play.

Thus, references to battles of the Peloponnesian War find their way into plays set in legendary times; thus the tyrant Lycus, in *The Madness of Heracles*, can discuss the relative merits of spear and longbow, an urgent debate for fifth-century tactics; thus tragedy, in its own way, is no less topical than comedy, and stories from the long ago can address contemporary issues.

6

CHARACTER AND CONTINUITY

We have suggested that, far from providing the rigid format that the neo-classicists attributed to it, the Greek theatre furnished an ambience that was infinitely flexible. In this imaginative world, the normal laws of time and space were suspended. Both were controlled by the wit of the dramatist.

To a large extent, this free-floating environment conditions plots that are themselves flexible, and can reshape themselves at will, no less than the setting does. We see this most conspicuously in comedy, which does not even have the parameters of a known story to act as a controlling factor. In Aristophanes, the plot may change direction without warning. The first half of *The Frogs* is built on Dionysus' passionate desire to resurrect Euripides. This motivates his journey to the Underworld, and carries him through many hazards to the gates of Hades. Only Euripides will do. He has no time for any other dramatist.

This takes us through to the *parabasis*. But when the principal characters reappear, the plot has radically changed direction. We are informed that Aeschylus and Euripides intend to hold a trial in the Underworld, to determine which is the better playwright. Dionysus has agreed to resurrect the victor. No reason is given for this sudden change of mind. It simply happens. The god who was so passionately devoted to Euripides gives the honour to his rival, and dismisses the younger playwright with a flippant quotation from his own works.

A similarly arbitrary change appears in *The Birds*. This comedy begins with two old Athenians on their way to Birdland; they persuade the birds to build a wall, and starve the gods into submission by cutting off the scent of sacrifices. The scheme works; Prometheus, himself a notorious opponent of the gods, announces that a divine embassy is on its way to treat for peace. Out of the blue, a new element is introduced. Not only must Pisthetairus, the proponent of the plot, take over Zeus' sceptre; he must also marry Sovereignty, Zeus' daughter. The introduction of this figure is unprepared for; it brings a new theme to the comedy when the play is almost over, prompting some scholars to suggest that the marriage element belongs not to drama but to ritual.

Other plays of Aristophanes behave in a similarly disjointed fashion. Scenes follow scenes at random, without logic, almost by free association. It was this apparently unclassical regard for form and structure that condemned Aristophanes to obscurity for centuries. While the influence of Greek tragedy was enormous, the comic writer had few imitators. His work could only be appreciated when a context of humour was provided which made his writing viable again.

This did not occur until the middle of the twentieth century, and coincided, significantly, with the rise of the electronic media. Radio comedy broke away from the literary script to provide a surreal world in which humour defies space, time, and logic. All things are subordinated to the immediate joke, the immediate moment. A context created by suggestion and allusion may change at will. The world of the classic radio scripts – of Fred Allen, of Tommy Handley, of the Goon Show – is very close to that of Aristophanes. Its emergence caused a reappraisal of humour, broke away from the circumstantial, literary anecdote of the nineteenth century, and enabled an ancient dramatist to be rediscovered. The Marx Brothers performed the same function in film: their anarchic *mélange* of parody, satire, and sight-gags, interwoven with direct addresses to the audience, recaptures the spirit of Aristophanes at his most potent, and reveals the same basic characteristic: the sacrifice of consistency of plot to the humour of the immediate moment.

In Greek tragedy the inconsistencies are less apparent, because the story acts as a controlling factor. Drawn from the *publica materies* of myth and legend, it is not the dramatist's invention; it brings its own logic with it. Even here, however, the liberating ambience of the Greek theatre makes departures from strict logic possible. As in comedy, the plot may change direction without warning. We have already seen this in the tragedies that critics label diptychal: plays which do not proceed as a linear narrative but instead embody two actions, two points of view, intended to be matched against each other with a point made by the contrast. *Medea* proceeds to its mid-point, stops, and goes backwards; *Hecuba* offers two distinct stories built around the same protagonist. Even in plays which do proceed by linear narrative, we find loose ends, unanswered questions, gaps of logic, sudden jumps from one scene to another. In *Oedipus the King*, why has Oedipus, apparently, never heard how Laius met his death until the play opens? And why, later in the action, do Jocasta and Oedipus not realize that each is telling substantially the same story? In *Antigone*, how has the heroine heard the edict about Polyneices' death before the play opens, when everything in the play assures us that the decision has been kept secret?

These things are not problems; or, rather, they are only problems if we let them be. They are problems only if we let ourselves believe that *Antigone* was written not by Sophocles but by Ibsen: that is, placed in a simulacrum of the actual world, and governed by the logic of that world. Greek tragedy does not work that way. Freed from such constraints by an anonymous environment, it tends to work from moment to moment, from scene to scene. The immediate dramatic point is all-important, and one scene need not necessarily cohere, in every detail, with the next. The details may adjust themselves for greater cogency. A fact important in one section of the play may vanish from consideration in the next. The facts, like the imagined setting, are fluid and flexible.

By the conditions of their art and training, Greek actors contributed to this conception of a play as a series of individual moments. Some of the other features of the Greek performance that we have studied can easily be paralleled from other cultures. The free-flowing use of time and space characterizes the Elizabethan public playhouse also. *Antony and Cleopatra* carries its action across the ancient world of the Mediterranean, and *Doctor Faustus* tells a tale of twenty-four years. But on the Elizabethan stage, the characters provided continuity. The personality of Lear bestrode his play; although, in the mind's eye, the setting changed from England to Scotland, from blasted heath to Dunsinane, the consistent and coherently developing characters of Macbeth and his lady gave continuity and progression to the drama. It seems unlikely that this was true for the Greeks, or that Oedipus, for example, was regarded as a three-dimensional and fully integrated character in the way that we think of Hamlet.

Several considerations suggest that the Greek approach to characterization was quite different. First, there were the mechanics of casting. Our theatre recognizes doubling and tripling of roles, but for specific reasons. Sometimes this is done to display an actor's virtuosity: Louis Jouvet, Alec Guinness, Peter Sellers, have shown themselves masters at this. More often, it arises from necessity: too many roles for too few actors. It has been wisely said that the minor lords in Shakespeare's historical plays address one another with such scrupulous exactitude of title because the audience had already seen the same actors in three or four other roles already, and might be confused. In either case, however, the normal rule is one actor, one role.

For the Greeks, however, doubling was a way of life. With only three actors, at most, to portray a much larger cast of characters, it was normal for them to appear in several parts throughout the play. Nor need these parts be sequential. *Antigone* provides a good example. The prologue is played by Antigone (actor A) and Ismene (actor B). Both *exeunt*. After the *parodos* Creon enters, probably played by actor C. He makes his inaugural address. Then the Guard enters, to report the burial of the body. Who plays the Guard? Creon (C) is still on stage; it must be therefore A or B. Assuming that it was desirable to keep the same actor as Antigone throughout (though this is by no means certain), the Guard must be played by B, who previously played Ismene. Creon and Guard *exeunt*; there is another chorus; and Guard, B, enters with the captured Antigone, A. Enter Creon to interrogate her; the Guard is dismissed, and Ismene is summoned – B again, presumably, as A and C are still on stage. On this analysis, actor B turns out to be very busy indeed, alternating two quite different roles with minimal time for costume changes. Other permutations are possible, but each requires a similar versatility.

It seems likely that this doubling may at times have had a thematic relevance. In the first half of *The Madness of Heracles*, the hero saves his family from the tyrant Lycus. In the second half, he murders them himself. By a callous and arbitrary switch of fortune, the saviour has become the oppressor. It can hardly be accidental that, in the easiest and most probable role division, the parts of Heracles and Lycus must have been played by the same actor. (They never meet on stage: Heracles goes in to confront the tyrant, and we never see them face to face.) Similarly, in *The Bacchae*, it seems likely that the same actor played both Pentheus and Agave, his mother, who kills him; and that Agave made her entrance with, as it were, her own head in her hands.

Unfortunately, to be certain of this, we need to know whether the audience could identify the same actor in both roles; perhaps by some trick of voice, perhaps a particular mannerism, perhaps by an announcement of casting made at the *proagon*, the ceremony which opened the dramatic festival. And these, unfortunately, are things that we shall probably never know. Nevertheless the suggestion remains tantalizing. There also appear to be some thematic values in two-actor plays. In *Medea*, which is a play about one woman against the world, one actor presumably played Medea, and the other everybody else with whom she comes in contact. In *Alcestis* one actor presumably played Admetus throughout, and the versatility demanded of the other was enormous. He played at least Alcestis and Heracles, two roles which could hardly be more different; probably the old Servant as well; and either Death or Apollo in the prologue.

By the same token, a major role could be apportioned among several actors. Sophocles' *Oedipus at Colonus* presents this problem at its most crucial. If a fourth actor was to be avoided, the role of Theseus must have been shared between the existing three. We have already suggested that, in the *Oresteia*, Aeschylus did not play any of the major roles throughout. Although he played Clytemnestra in *Agamemnon* his role in *The Libation Bearers* is more likely to have been Orestes, leaving Clytemnestra to one of his assistants. This division emphasizes the dialectical structure of the trilogy at the expense of continuity of characterization. A modern actress in the role of Clytemnestra sees the three plays as a whole; she traces the psychology of her character from the blood-lust of the first play, through the wariness and satiety of the second, to the rancour and frustration of the third. Aeschylus probably saw his participation in the play as involving three different parts of a component whole. He was more interested in structure, his modern counterpart in characterization.

This fragmentation of the actor's personality demanded some kind of continuity, if the story were to make sense. Such continuity was provided by mask and costume: in a real sense, they were the character. In our manuscripts, the cast list is entitled *ta tou dramatos prosopa*, 'the masks of the drama'. We know virtually nothing about what fifth-century masks looked like, but we can assume that they were simple and easily identifiable. Behind the mask, the actor would have changed without detriment to the role. To this extent, as in the classical theatre of Japan, the external manifestations *are* the character and the actor is merely the temporary means that gives these manifestations speech and movement. Though the actor may change, the *persona* remains constant. Aristophanes utilizes this fundamental characteristic of his theatre in the beating scene of *The Frogs*. Dionysus has assumed the club and lionskin of Heracles. To anyone who meets him in the Underworld he is, therefore, Heracles. When threatened, he passes the costume to his slave Xanthias, master and man assuming the character in turn. Whoever wears the club and lionskin is for that moment Heracles and taken to be so by the other characters. The costume dictates the comic logic of the scene. Just as, in performance, the tragic costume imposes its own personality on the wearer, so, in the comedy, the Heracles costume dominates its wearers to the extent that their individual personalities seem to blur and mingle. Dionysus is infected by his slave's mortality. He, no less than Xanthias, cries out when beaten.

If we accept this equivalence between mask and costume and *persona*, certain interesting consequences follow. It seems likely, for instance, that a dead character could have been represented by an actorless mask. Thus, in Euripides' *The Bacchae*, a probable candidate for the severed head of Pentheus is the mask which the actor has just worn – in the simplest role-division, as we have seen, the actor who has just finished playing Pentheus and now plays Agave.

This device may have been anticipated by Aeschylus in *The Libation Bearers*. Near the end of this play, Orestes displays the slaughtered Clytemnestra and Aegisthus to the chorus, crying:

> See here the double lordship of this land
> Who killed my father and laid waste his house.[1]

It is usually assumed that the stage picture here parallels the similar tableau near the end of *Agamemnon*. There, Clytemnestra stood in triumph over the bodies of Agamemnon and Cassandra. Here, Orestes stands over his mother and her lover. There are strong arguments in favour of such an exact visual parallel, with the robe in which Agamemnon was slaughtered providing a link between the two. It may well have been displayed in the first play, and certainly is in the second. When Orestes commands the chorus 'Take it, spread it in a circle round' the equation is made between the bloodstained robe and the red-purple carpet on which Agamemnon walked to his death. Given the intricate pattern of repeated images around which Aeschylus constructed his tragedy, it seems desirable that this one should be repeated too. Yet there is some suggestion that the tableau is not exactly duplicated. Earlier in the play, the chorus encourage Orestes by telling him:

> And with Orestes' mind combine
> The heart of Perseus; for your friends
> On earth and under it, perform
> This favour, though it sting you sore.[2]

Perseus decapitated his victim, the Gorgon; and from the language of the chorus after the event, it seems that Orestes may have done the same:

> For you brought liberty to all who live
> In Argos, when you came upon
> This pair of snakes and cut their heads off clean.[3]

Is this to be construed literally? Did Orestes make his entrance holding up the severed heads of his victims? And are these heads then the empty, eyeless masks?

In Greek practice the equation between mask/costume and *persona* indicates a convention whereby any impairment of the former presages some damage – usually death – to the latter. In a theatre which creates its characters from the outside in, the destruction of the costume implies the destruction of the character. Pentheus' fate in *The Bacchae* offers an obvious example. In this play the ritual pattern of *sparagmos*, of tearing apart the sacrificial victim, both underlies and dictates the action. It is foreshadowed by the reference of Cadmus to the fate of Pentheus' cousin:

> Remember Actaeon. Take his tragic fate to heart.
> The mighty hunter. Greater, so he boasted,
> Then Artemis herself. Deep in her forest sanctum
> The goddess heard and punished. He was torn to pieces
> By hounds that had eaten from his hand. Avoid
> His ending. Come here, let me crown your head
> With ivy. We shall praise the god together.[4]

Pentheus does not avoid Actaeon's ending, despite further warnings which grow more insistent as the play proceeds. The *sparagmos* motif next appears in the 'palace miracle', the earthquake which delivers Dionysus from bondage:

> But the god had not yet finished. Bacchus showed his power anew,
> Shook the house to its foundations. Desolate the palace lies.[5]

Soon after this comes the Messenger's report of the action of the women on the mountain:

> They fell upon a heifer lowing,
> With her udders swollen with milk; while others of the women
> Fell on our cows and tore them apart.
> You could see the pieces flying: scraps of carcase
> And cloven hooves were scattered far and wide,
> Torn, bleeding flesh caught dangling in the branches;
> Proud bulls, that but a while before had tossed
> Their angry horns now lay spreadeagled on the ground,
> Felled by a myriad blows of young girls' hands.[6]

So to Pentheus' change of heart, his rapid transformation from Dionysus' antagonist to his dupe, with the change externalized as change of costume:

> PENTHEUS What kind of costume will you put on me?
> DIONYSUS Hair for your head first, long and flowing.
> PENTHEUS What will the rest of my apparel be?
> DIONYSUS A hobble skirt, a fillet for your hair.
> PENTHEUS No! I could never wear a woman's dress.
> DIONYSUS There will be bloodshed if you fight the Bacchae.
> PENTHEUS True. First of all I must survey the ground.[7]

Pentheus thus becomes the simulacrum of Dionysus, and of his mother Agave; but what more nearly concerns our present argument is that by divesting himself of his kingly robes, and perhaps of his mask too, Pentheus disassembles his own *persona* and prefigures his *sparagmos* at the hands of the women on Cithaeron. Dionysus makes explicit the equation between costume change and death:

> Now I go in, to dress him in the robes
> That will serve him as his shroud when he is dead
> Slain by his mother's hands.[8]

We see briefly the new Pentheus, leaping, dancing, the image, so Dionysus urges, of his mother; and so we pass to the Messenger's description of the king's dismemberment, in which costume and body elements are curiously intertwined:

169

His mother flung herself on him.
Thinking she would spare him if she once but saw his face
He bared his head to her, and caressed her cheek,
Crying 'Mother! It is I, your son!
Pentheus! In my father's bed you bore me.
Have pity on me. Pardon my offence
And do not kill me. Do not kill your son!'
But she was foaming at the mouth, her eyes
Were wild and rolling, and her wits were gone.
The god was in her. Deaf to all his pleas
She seized his left arm by the elbow, thrust
Her foot against his ribs, and with one blow
Pulled the arm clean from its socket. She never would
Have had the strength alone, but god was in her hands
And made light work. On the other side knelt Ino.
Picking his flesh. Then Autonoe was upon him
And the whole pack at her heels. As one they cried,
Pentheus screaming, while he still had breath,
And the women bayed their fury. One tore off
An arm, another a slipper, with the foot inside it still;
They tore the very flesh from off his bones,
    and with their hands dyed red
Tossed the bleeding baubles to and fro.[9]

The sense of this speech supports the possibility that when Cadmus
brings the fragments of Pentheus on stage, what we see are the
elements of the dismembered costume. And the play ends with the
culminating *sparagmos*, the riving of the city when, after Dionysus'
judgement, Cadmus, Agave, and the chorus go their separate ways.

A partial parallel to the action of *The Bacchae* is offered by *Rhesus*.
Although this play's date and authorship remain problematical, the
motif of the costume change resembles that in the more famous work.
Rhesus, set in Troy, draws its plot from the intrigues surrounding the
arrival of the eponymous hero, a prominent Trojan ally. As the play
opens, Hector is seen sending out Dolon on a spying mission among
the Greek ships. Dolon announces that he intends to disguise himself.
Under Hector's questioning, he reveals that he will wear a wolfskin,
and go on all fours. In *Rhesus* we do not see the change. We are simply
told that Dolon will assume the wolfskin over his own armour. As in
The Bacchae, however, the nature of the disguise is related to the

character of the wearer, and is attended with the same ill fortune. When Odysseus and Diomedes enter Troy on their own spying mission, we learn from their conversation that they have killed Dolon. We learn also that they bring his armour as the spoils of war. *Rhesus* therefore offers interesting similarities to *The Bacchae*. In both cases, a change of costume is followed by disaster. In *Rhesus* certainly, and in *The Bacchae* possibly, the presence of an empty costume on stage suggests a dead body.

Symbolic dismemberment thus prefigures actual dismemberment, and a change of costume marks a change of state. A similar device appears, with more explicit irony, in the earlier Euripidean *The Madness of Heracles*. As the play opens, Amphitryon, Megara, and her children by Heracles huddle by the altar vainly seeking sanctuary from the tyrant Lycus. Accepting the inevitable, Megara submits, asking only that she may have permission to array her children and herself for death:

> MEGARA And I beg you, to this favour add another;
>   Be double benefactor to us both.
>   Open these doors, for they are barred to us,
>   And let me dress my children for their death,
>   The only legacy their father's house can leave them.
> LYCUS I agree to that. Open the doors, men.
>   Go in and dress. I do not grudge you clothes.
>   When you have robed yourselves, I shall return
>   To make a present of you to the Underworld.[10]

Whether or not Amphitryon joins them in the costume change is unclear. He does not accompany them immediately, but has another speech first; and when the family reappears, the language is ambiguous. In the light of what follows, it is tempting to assume that Amphitryon does not change. Megara and the children, however, certainly do:

> CHORUS See, they are coming now, and they have shrouds
>   Upon them. These are the sons
>   Of Heracles, who once was mighty,
>   And the wife he loved: she leads them
>   Like horses yoked in harness. And the old one
>   Heracles' father.[11]

So Heracles, on his entrance:

> But what is this? My sons before the house
> In winding sheets, heads chapleted with flowers –
> These men assembled, and my wife among them,
> My father weeping?

> These are death's wrappings. Take them off your heads.
> Look up to the sun, and let your eyes
> . Enjoy its welcome. Forget the dark below.[12]

Thus Heracles, at the last moment, brings apparent salvation. He leads them in and, off-stage, slaughters the oppressor. But it is too late. Megara and the children have already been marked for death. They have changed their costumes, their characters have been metaphorically destroyed, and the reprieve can be only temporary. The visual metaphor gains urgency from the fact that they change into real shrouds, not, like Pentheus, into a symbolic one. Once Heracles is touched by madness, they must die. Amphitryon alone survives. The vagueness of the text about his costume may therefore be purposeful. We may be entitled to assume that he does not change when the others do, and that this visual differentiation shows that he will live.

It does not follow that Greek characters invariably change clothes before they die. But if they do, the chances are high that they will. Nor need the change be total. In Euripides' *Hippolytus*, Phaedra, making her first entrance on her sickbed, cries for her crown to be removed:

> Prop up my body, raise my head
> I have lost all will to move, my dear.
> How thin my hands and arms are. Hold them.
> This crown is too heavy. It hurts my head.
> Take it off, and let the hair fall free.[13]

This removal of the crown suggests, on the simplest level, Phaedra's renunciation of the *noblesse oblige* of queenship; the Nurse is quick to remind her of it. In addition, however, the physical disarray becomes the outward expression of the spiritual disorder, and divestment looks forward to coming death. We see, quite literally, a character gradually falling apart.

In *Agamemnon*, Aeschylus offers an example with more complex ramifications. The conqueror, returning to his palace, is tempted by Clytemnestra to walk on the red-purple carpet. After initial refusal, he submits with trepidation:

Then if you wish it so, let someone loose
These shoes from off my feet, these servile ministers
That we do tread on; and I pray
Let no far glance of envy fall upon me
As I set foot upon these tapestries.[14]

There seems no reason to doubt that the act of removing his shoes is actually performed: the eight lines between Agamemnon's command and his entry into the palace seem designed to allow for this, in the usual Greek manner of covering business with dialogue. Shoeless, then, and diminished, he goes to his doom. How literally he is diminished is an interesting question involving the long debate about what Greek actors wore on their feet. The traditional conception of *kothurnoi* boots with high platform soles, designed to add stature to their wearers in the vastness of the Greek theatre, is now generally discredited, partly because of the ambiguity of the evidence and partly because of the impracticality of the device. It is often argued that high-soled *kothurnoi* would impede the movement of the actor. This is demonstrably untrue. If Japanese *onnogata* actors can cope with *geta*, there is no reason to suppose the Greeks less proficient.

The *Agamemnon* scene does raise a specific problem in that, if *kothurnoi* indeed gave the actor extra inches, Agamemnon would have shrunk when his shoes were removed; by realistic standards this would clearly be objectionable. But realistic standards are not necessarily the ones that apply. Considered as a simple stage convention, the effect is surely an appropriate and desirable one. At the very moment in the play when Clytemnestra decisively establishes her dominance over him, Agamemnon shrinks till he is shorter than his wife. We might compare similar effects from other periods of theatre. In the Cambridge (UK) Festival Theatre which flourished before World War II, a production of Shakespeare's *Henry VIII* had Wolsey, in his eminence, mounted on buskins underneath his cardinal's robes. At his fall from grace the buskins were removed, so that he appeared visibly to shrink. A reverse effect is reported for Edwin Booth when appearing as Richelieu in Bulwer-Lytton's drama of that name. When delivering the 'curse of Rome' he rose *sur les pointes* under his robe; simultaneously, the rest of the cast sank to their knees; and it was as if the cardinal had suddenly assumed gigantic stature. More recently we have Patrice Chereau's staging of the death of Fafner in his controversial Bayreuth *Siegfried*. First, the dragon takes Siegfried's sword through his heart; second, the dragon is replaced by the giant who has been masquerading in this shape; third, the enormous *kothurnoi* worn under the giant's robe are removed so that as he dies, he dwindles. There is of course no way in which we can assert that this device was used in Agamemnon, but the parallels suggest interesting possibilities. Whatever arguments may be raised against high-soled *kothurnoi* on philological or archaeological grounds, the arguments from practicality do not deserve to be taken seriously.

Whatever happens here, however, the scene adheres to the convention with which we are principally concerned. Agamemnon removes part of his clothing and subsequently dies. The same thing happens later in the play to Cassandra who, as she bewails her bitter destiny before the chorus, strips herself of the barren symbols of her prophetic art:

> Why do I keep this mockery
> Of trappings still, my wreaths of prophecy,
> My staff? If I must go to death, then you
> At least shall go before me. Go and rot.
> Find someone else to enrich with your curse,
> My part is done. See where Apollo himself
> Is stripping me of my prophetic robes,
> Who watched me when I wore them laughed to scorn
> By friends who turned away from me in blindness.[15]

The allusion may be picked up in *The Trojan Women*, where Hecuba tells Cassandra to cast her temple keys and garlands from her, though Cassandra is not on stage at this point. In *Agamemnon* the robes and garlands, once thrown off, still lie there on the ground; there is no hint that they are removed, any more than is the purple carpet, whose presence now suggests a river of blood pouring from the palace doors. It is possible that when Clytemnestra justifies her double murder, the scattered garments illustrate her references to Cassandra, the symbolic standing for the actual death. Is there, indeed, any necessity to postulate dummy bodies at all here, or is this simply a device with which we have lumbered ourselves from our own more recent and more realistic theatrical traditions?

To Cassandra's action we may compare that of Hermione in Euripides' *Andromache*. In desperation the princess casts aside her veil, tears her robes, and tries to commit suicide. Foiled in the attempt, she leaves the palace with Orestes. Although Hermione does not die, she is as good as dead; her absence leaves a desolation in the house of Peleus, made worse by the death of Peleus' grandson Neoptolemus. We might also note that at the end of the play Peleus undergoes a partial deprivation of costume in the depths of his grief, casting upon the ground the sceptre that seems to have been the invariable token of stage royalty.

One more example deserves to be considered here. This is drawn not from stage action but from a messenger's speech, where all things are possible. Euripides, however, offers several examples of stage conventions colouring reported action, and in *Medea* a lengthy narration is clearly based on the convention we have described. Medea has sent her poisoned offerings to the princess: 'a fine-spun robe, a golden diadem'. They are probably displayed to the audience as the children make ready to carry them, so that the princess assumes tangible form before our eyes and an important, though unseen, character is given a momentary on-stage presence. (In the same way, perhaps, Medea's sons, though present for much of the action, are never heard until the moment before their deaths.) The death of the princess is reported by the Messenger:

> When she saw the gifts, she couldn't hold out longer
> But did everything her husband said. Before the children
> And their father had gone far outside the house
> She took the pretty gifts and put them on,
> And set the golden crown around her curls,
> Arranging them before a shining mirror
> And smiling at her ghostly image there.
>   . . .
> From two directions the pain attacked her.
> The golden circlet twining round her hair
> Poured forth a strange stream of devouring fire
> And the fine-spun robe, the gift your children gave her,
> Had teeth to tear the poor girl's pretty skin.
> She left the throne, and fled burning through the room
> Shaking her head this way and that,
> Trying to dislodge the crown, but it was fixed
> Immoveably, and when she shook her hair
> The flames burnt twice as fiercely . . .
> The flesh dropped from her bones like pine-tears, torn
> By the strange power of the devouring poison.[16]

By a logical extension of the stage convention the costume has become the character so completely that when the princess tries to remove the crown and robe, she tears apart her body too.

If a changed or impaired costume signifies approaching death, a torn or dishevelled costume may signal acute physical or mental distress. The *locus classicus* for this usage is the closure of Aeschylus' *The Persians*. We know the battle of Salamis has been lost; we have heard the consequences for the shattered landforce as it makes its way home through the barren winter; we are assured that the mighty army so triumphantly heralded at the play's beginning has been reduced to a broken handful of survivors. Of this disaster, Xerxes' ragged entrance is the visible symbol. The image of his tattered costume dominates the play's ending. It tells not of the sufferings of a single man, but of a whole host that died; it offers a contrast to the richness of armour and apparel described in the *parodos*; and it suggests the self-flagellation and costume-rending of extravagant mourning in the context of a choral antiphon structured on the known patterns of Athenian keening. Thus in his demonstration of the ragged monarch Aeschylus anticipates by some thirty years a device normally associated with Euripides. There is one curious feature of this scene. If earlier declarations have any meaning, Xerxes should not be wearing rags at all. The ghost of Darius instructs Atossa:

> You, aged mother dear to Xerxes heart,
> Go to your palace, fetch a costume he
> May wear with dignity, and meet your son.[17]

The Queen clearly announces her intention of so doing:

> O heaven, how my troubles come upon me.
> And yet of all my woes this stings me most,
> To hear how shamefully my son is clad
> With nothing fit to bind his body in.
> But I shall fetch adornment from the house
> And take it where I hope to meet my son.[18]

From Xerxes' entrance, however, it seems that she has done nothing of the kind.

> XERXES You see these remnants of my fine array?
> CHORUS I see them. I see them.[19]

Why does Aeschylus prepare for an event that never happens? Perhaps, after all, the two sections of the play are not irreconcilable. Possibly Xerxes makes his entrance in full majesty, carrying the rags with him for display. Alternatively, Xerxes may enter in rags and be redressed by his mother as the *kommos* proceeds. Aeschylus might have intended to remind his audience that in 472 BC the power of Persia was not yet to be considered dead, and that, as the new costume replaced the old, a new army might easily replace the one that had fallen.

Though Aeschylus may have come first, Euripides, by virtue of the familiar Aristophanic parodies, remains the most famous portrayer of ragged heroes. What the comic playwright says is not necessarily evidence, and he seems elsewhere to have identified as particularly Euripidean devices which other dramatists are known to have used: the *mechane* is a case in point. Nevertheless the many instances of the costume joke suggest that, in the minds of the audience, the device was particularly associated with Euripides, and the extant tragedies offer supporting evidence. The surviving works give us Menelaus in *Helen*, and Electra and Orestes in the plays that bear their names; Aristophanes adds Oineus, Phoenix, Philoctetes, Bellerophon, Telephus, and Ino. The references to Bellerophon in tatters upon Pegasus are supported by the scholiast, and to the notorious Telephus by fragments from the work itself.

The tattered hero makes a complex joke. Aristophanes satirizes Euripides as 'beggar-poet' (*ptochopoios*) and 'patcher of rags' (*rakiosurraptades*) with ambiguous allusion to his threadbare heroes and his cobbled verse. In *The Frogs* Aeschylus charges him with using ragged costumes 'so his characters might appear pitiable', and this certainly seems to be the burden of the long scene in *The Acharnians* twenty years earlier. Is Euripides, then, merely seeking greater realism in the theatre, and substituting pathos for the higher *eleos* of earlier drama? If we take Aristophanes seriously, he is. But the comic playwright is always prone to take conventional effects at face value. It is a sure way of getting a laugh. Thus, for him, a deity flying on the *mechane* is simply an actor dangling on the end of a rope; Andromeda bound to an ocean rock is an old man in drag lashed to a post; and it is possible that, in his costume jokes, Aristophanes is simply taking another convention literally. In the light of the other examples we have considered, Euripides' supposed melodramatic innovations may be no more than extensions of, and elaborations upon, an existing convention.

Spiritual disintegration of the character is signified by physical disintegration of the costume. Electra, driven to desperation; Orestes, hovering on the edge of insanity; Telephus, driven to defend himself by threat of child-murder: all are appropriately dressed. By the end of the century the joke seems to have run its natural course. Aristophanes devotes a whole scene to it in *The Acharnians*, but *The Frogs* has only a few passing references. The years between had probably seen the device exploited by others, certainly by Sophocles in *Philoctetes*. By 405 it was no longer unusual enough to warrant special attention.

So far we have confined ourselves to melancholy examples. Although scenes of joy and redemption do not abound in Greek tragedy, there are some instances to show that the reverse effect was possible: that, as in the Japanese theatre, the addition of garments, or the substitution of bright robes for sombre ones, could signify regeneration. One such example occurs in *Helen*, which we have already noted as containing the ragged Euripidean hero. Menelaus staggers ashore from the shipwreck dressed in rags, scraps of sailcloth. Both he and Helen comment amply on this. But when Helen ingeniously contrives his rescue, one of the favours that she seeks from Theoclymenus is a new suit of clothes for him to wear. As she tells us later, she has taken the rags off Menelaus' body, bathed him, and dressed him in new and splendid robes. Thus a new Menelaus has risen from the wreckage of the old. When he leaves the stage he is marked once more for kingship and for glory. Helen, conversely, has changed her white robes for black, and disfigured herself with the conventional signs of mourning for her supposedly dead husband. Her departure may perhaps be equated, in its funereal associations, with that of Hermione in *Andromache*; it marks the death of Theoclymenus' aspirations.

For the most powerful effect of all we may return to Aeschylus and *The Eumenides*. At the end of the play, Athena persuades the Furies to a change of heart. They will remain in Athens as benevolent spirits, and are escorted to their new home by a subsidiary chorus of Athenian women:

ATHENA To all your prayers amen. I shall conduct you
  By radiance of torchlight to your dwelling place
  Beneath the earth, to the dark underground,
  And with us go these women, whose charge it is

To minister to my image. Flower of all the land
Of Theseus, let them come forth now, a noble company
Of maids and matrons, and the older women
Banded together.
Vested in purple, let them come resplendent
To do us honour.
(*or*: Vest them in purple splendour.
Come to do them honour.)[20]

The passage invokes the quadrennial Panathenaia, in which the women of Athens conveyed a newly-woven robe to the Parthenon and draped the statue of the city's goddess. Does this imply an actual rerobing of the Furies on stage, to signify their change of nature? Unfortunately, text and punctuation are dubious here. It is unclear whether the women or the Furies are robed in purple. But in either case the spectacular impact of the scene is the same. If it is the Furies, they are given bright robes to cover the black they have worn since the play's beginning. Change of costume signals change of heart. If it is the supplementary chorus, the effect is collective. Robed in purple, the women surround and enfold the sombre Furies. The resulting tableau is a visual metaphor of the place envisaged by Athena for the Furies in her new dispensation. Fear must still have its place in the scheme of things, but only when vested in civic order. Athena's robes are draped upon the daughters of darkness.

The mask and costume, then, bestow continuity on a role. But behind the mask there is an actor who must continually divide himself and leap from one characterization to another. In comedy, the frenetic role changes beget a moral climate in which duplicity is a way of life; the variety of impersonations required by the performance spill over into the world of the play. In *The Acharnians* Dikaiopolis, trying to engineer a private peace, is pursued by the hostile, warmongering chorus. To give his arguments more pathos, he runs to Euripides for an appropriate costume of tragic rags and tatters. Returning to the chorus, he begins a sequence in which three levels of impersonation intertwine. First, he speaks as an actor – indeed, as Aristophanes himself – in a purely theatrical context, addressing the audience in the theatre:

Ladies and gentlemen, don't blame me if I come,
Dressed as a tragic beggar, in a comedy
To harangue the Athenians on what they ought to do.

179

> Even comedy can tell the truth sometimes
> And what I say may be surprising, but it's true,
> Kleon at least can't prosecute me this time
> For slandering our state when there are strangers present.[21]

These are in-jokes, addressed to the contemporary world of Athens, not the world of the play; the reference is to attempts made by the demagogue Kleon to silence Aristophanes because he had painted an unflattering picture of Athens when there were foreigners in the audience. But this, says Dikaiopolis–Aristophanes, is the Lenaean festival; it takes place before the waters are safe for sailing; we are all Athenians here, and I can say what I like.

Having gone to so much trouble to secure the beggar's costume, therefore, Dikaiopolis proceeds to ignore it throughout his lengthy address to the chorus and through them to the audience. Suddenly Lamachus, the general, the spokesman of the war party, intervenes. Immediately Dikaiopolis retreats behind the protection of his costume:

> LAMACHUS What! You, a beggar, dare to talk like this?
> DIKAIOPOLIS Great Lamachus, have mercy on a beggar
> Who let his poor tongue run away with him.[22]

A few lines later, he is just as eager to deny what he was so eager to assume:

> LAMACHUS A beggar, talking this way to a general.
> DIKAIOPOLIS What, me, a beggar?
> LAMACHUS   Well, who are you then?
> DIKAIOPOLIS I'll tell you. I'm an honest citizen.[23]

Disguises, like masks, can be lightly assumed, and just as lightly discarded. Even within the limits of the single mask, we see a similar ambiguity. In *The Clouds* the charlatan Socrates simultaneously humbugs Strepsiades and admits his own villainy.

Comedy clearly does not cultivate consistency of characterization. Just as characters may adopt disguises or discard them without warning, to suit the needs of the situation, the basic character itself may change. Our own theatre tends to identify one actor with one role. He sees his character as an entity, and pursues its development from beginning to end. The Greek actor, by necessity, saw his roles as a series of interlinked impersonations. He must have been more

concerned with technique than with psychological identification; and
the facility of change between roles induces a flexibility within roles.
In comedy, quite clearly, the character can be whatever the immediate situation requires him to be.

This may extend even to physical characterization. In *The Wasps*
the old man, Philocleon, is described at one point as toothless, and at
another, as having teeth to bite through the net that binds him. Or it
may involve the arbitrary reshaping of mental attributes and attitudes. Early in *The Frogs* we have a confrontation between the god
Dionysus and the demi-god Heracles. Dionysus is presented as the
parodied aesthete, the literary poseur; Heracles appears in his popular comic incarnation as the gluttonous, musclebound, mindless
superman, all brawn and no brain. Dionysus attempts to explain to
Heracles why he wishes to embark on the perilous journey to the
Underworld: he talks of his passion for the tragedies of Euripides, now
dead.

All this is incomprehensible to Heracles. He cannot understand
this talk of plays. The only thing he understands is food. In desperation, Dionysus tries to appeal to him in his own terms:

> Tell, me: have you ever had a mad desire for soup?[24]

The light dawns; here at last is something the demigod can relate to.
'Soup, yes!' he retorts. 'A thousand times!' Thus Dionysus explains
his mission. But, at the end of the scene, the same Heracles who had
apparently barely heard of Euripides can reel off a list of minor figures
in the Athenian theatre:

HERACLES What about Agathon?
DIONYSUS   Gone off and left me.
   A splendid poet, and his friends will miss him
HERACLES Gone where, poor fellow?
DIONYSUS   The Happy Hunting Ground.
HERACLES And Xenocles?
DIONYSUS   Oh, Xenocles be damned!
HERACLES Pythangelus?
XANTHIAS   Nobody mentions me
   Although my shoulder's nearly worn away.
HERACLES But aren't there other artsy-craftsy kids,
   Ten thousand of 'em, writing tragedies
   More chatty than Euripides by miles?[25]

The Frogs is rich in such examples. As Dionysus and Xanthias reach the end of their journey, they are accosted by the ferocious figure of Aeacus, the gatekeeper of the Underworld. An ogre out of Greek nightmares, he heaps abuse on them, threatens them, and finally beats them. There follows the *parabasis*; when it is over, Xanthias and Aeacus are seen chatting on terms of perfect amity. A justifiable transition perhaps; but one that happens with such rapidity that some scholars have suggested that the second figure is not Aeacus at all, but another servant of more amiable disposition.

Dionysus himself undergoes a similar transformation. At the beginning of the play he is represented as devoted to Euripides. He quotes from him; he reveres him; he has even taken the tragedy *Andromeda* to read on military service. Then, in the second half of the comedy, comes the trial. Confronted with Euripides in person, Dionysus professes himself baffled; 'I don't understand', he says, 'what he's talking about'; and he eventually awards the victory to Euripides' arch-rival and diametric opposite, Aeschylus.

The Clouds gives us an equally inconsistent Socrates. Leaving aside the much argued – perhaps too much argued – question of the relevance of the stage caricature to the living philosopher, if we ask what kind of man is the Socrates represented in the comedy we get no clear answer. Or rather, we get three different answers. Depending on which references we select, we can build up three different pictures of the man, each at odds with the others.

First, there is Socrates the businessman, the professor who teaches for a fee. This is how Strepsiades first describes Socrates and his school:

> They'll give you lessons – if you pay their fees –
> In how to make men believe anything you say,
> Whether it's true or not.[26]

He seems to make a handsome living out of this; the demagogue Hyperbolus is mentioned as having spent a talent to acquire his knowledge, and gone on to make a handsome profit on his investment. Admittedly Socrates does not demand money from Strepsiades, or Pheidippides. From the former he receives payment in kind. But there are enough monetary references to make it clear that, for part of the play at least, Aristophanes is concerned with picturing Socrates as a paid teacher like so many of his contemporaries. We may also note that Socrates' spokesman, Unjust Logic, advocates a life of self-indulgence. (We know of course that this is historically false; both Plato and Xenophon emphasize that Socrates taught for nothing. But that is irrelevant to the comedy.)

Secondly, we can string together another set of references to produce a contrary picture, that of a pinchbeck Socrates who is at his wit's end to make ends meet, and lives by petty theft. This is how we hear of him through his student: Socrates, lacking dinner, went down to the gymnasium and, while distracting his audience with some pseudo-scientific hocus-pocus, stole somebody's cloak. This seems to have been a favourite comic picture of Socrates. A contemporary of Aristophanes describes him as not knowing where to find a meal, and as stealing a wine flask. In the present play the chorus describes him frankly as a cheat and a thief, urging him to get all he can out of his dupe; and we see him for himself stealing Strepsiades' cloak and shoes.

Thirdly, we discern a picture which is more sympathetic, and closer to the historical truth. In certain passages Socrates appears as an amiable and absent-minded ascetic. The student tells of the embarrassing incident that Socrates suffered while ruminating on the orbit of the moon, because he forgot to look where he was walking. He is represented in this play (and elsewhere) as despising physical cleanliness. He and his disciples never shave, or rub themselves with oil, or take baths. In this Socrates, indifferent to personal comfort or sensual indulgences, we see a figure closer to the one we know from more sober sources.

How are we to combine these inconsistences within one figure? The answer is that we are not. Logic, consistency, and psychological unity are things the modern actor looks for; they have no place in Greek comedy. Aristophanes' characters are chameleons. They adapt themselves to suit the humour of each passing scene. They are not required to be consistent, merely to be funny. If there is any rule in Aristophanes it is this; that the character changes to suit the joke, not the joke to suit the character.

Let us broaden this generalization, and suggest that the nature of the Greek theatre, and the accumulated conventions of its use, produced, almost inevitably, this attitude towards characterization. The Greek theatre, as we have now seen in a number of respects, was fundamentally anonymous, a blank surface on which the author could construct whatever settings, periods, and actions were appropriate to him. As this was done primarily through language, there were no constraints upon the author other than those he chose to adopt for himself; the story could proceed in whatever direction his imagination took him. For the comic author, there was not even the constraint of a known story. He invented his plots, and could proceed by free association of comic ideas.

We have already made some analogies with film; we may make another here. Perhaps the closest equivalent to the comic world of Aristophanes is the animated cartoon. The animator starts from a blank screen, as Aristophanes started with a blank stage; and he can create on the screen whatever his imagination suggests. Even more importantly, when the point has been made he can wipe the screen clean and start afresh. There is no necessity to retain any image after its immediate comic utility has passed. The cartoon cat chases the mouse. The mouse turns and hands the cat a firecracker. The firecracker explodes; the cat's fur is blown off in the explosion. Once the comic point has been made, however, it would be redundant for the cat to remain naked. As the next sequence begins, the cat's fur has magically grown again. Events are dictated by the laws of humour, not the laws of space and time.

So things stand with Aristophanes. Does Greek tragedy offer any similarities? Both were, after all, performed in the same theatre, and under the same conditions. An obvious difference is the known story, which imposes its own logic and sequence of action. Even this constraint, however, can hardly have been binding. Tragic authors insert variants at will; Sophocles' cast for *Electra* is not the same as for Aeschylus in *The Libation Bearers*, and Euripides combines unfamiliar versions to produce what were for all practical purposes original plots.

The apparent unity conferred by the story disguises the fact that in tragedy changes may occur just as violent and arbitrary as in comedy; characters and incidents may be introduced without motivation, and disappear as rapidly when their immediate purpose is completed. In *The Libation Bearers* Electra is built up as a major character in the first half of the play. She dominates the stage; we see the lurid history of the House of Atreus through her eyes. But once Orestes has identified himself and announced his plans for revenge, we never hear of her again. She is not a 'real' person with a 'real' identity that demands continuous attention. She is there to serve a function in the argument; to demonstrate the personal element in the claims pressing heavily upon Orestes; and once that function is complete, she may go.

Aeschylus feels able to dispose of her as readily as Aristophanes, for example, discards Euelpides in *The Birds*: once they have made their statement, there is no more need for them.

Entrances may be contrived as arbitrarily as exits. That of Aigeus in *Medea* is such a case. It seems to have offended Aristotle for this reason; but Aristotle was conditioned by the more realistic standards of a later century. Aigeus' entrance is indeed unmotivated: he comes as a pat answer to Medea's need; he simply happens to be passing through her city. But his principal function, as we have suggested elsewhere, is to mark the centre of the play, and an important division in the plot. He is important not so much as a character in his own right, but as a punctuation in the argument. Where he comes from, and where he goes, are of little concern. Similarly Creon's entrance in the prologue of *Oedipus the King* has been condemned as arbitrary; his mission is discussed, and he appears prompt on cue. But even to use such words as 'arbitrary' is to introduce realistic standards which do not apply here. The argument controls the characters, not vice versa. It is no more arbitrary for Creon to appear when he is called for than for the flute to appear in a given bar of a Mozart sonata.

As with characters, so with props: comedy and tragedy demonstrate the same liberality of usage. In *The Peace* Trygaius needs an altar to conduct a sacrifice and then cries, with happy serendipity, 'Why! Here *is* an altar, just as we need one'. In *Medea*, the protagonist announces her murderous plan to the chorus: she will send to Jason's new bride the poisoned gifts, 'a fine-spun robe, a golden diadem'. In the chorus that follows, the women urge her not to do this. Athens, the noblest of cities, will never offer sanctuary to a murderess; no mother could so violate the ties of nature as to kill her own children. After the chorus, Jason reappears as summoned. Medea lies to him, protesting her willingness to aid his new union, and her children's cause; she sends the children into the palace, to bring out the gifts.

The question is, when has she found time to prepare them? She has apparently been on stage throughout. It is barely possible that the chorus' appeal is a rhetorical address only, and does not require her actual presence. But the language of the chorus is against such an interpretation.

> How will this city of sacred waters
> This guide and protector of friends, take you
> Your children's slayer, whose touch will pollute

> All others you meet? Think again of the deaths
> Of your children, the blood you intend to shed.
> By your knees, by every entreaty we beg you
> Not to become your children's murderess.[27]

The last two lines suggest a physical presence. Where then did she find time to prepare the poisoned gifts? We cannot assume that Medea has a store of such things, ready for such emergencies. Once again, a realistic causation is not provided, nor is it needed. Dramatic necessity calls the props into being.

In tragedy a certain consistency is imposed on characters by the nature of the script. They are participants in a connected story, and there must be some logic in the sequence of their actions. Even here, however, the piecemeal character of the Greek theatre continues to assert itself. A modern actor, concerned with the psychological unity of his role, looks for smooth and plausibly realistic transitions from one emotion to another. He condemns as contrived any shift of mood that seems too arbitrary or abrupt. In Greek tragedy, as in Greek comedy, such rapid shifts are commonplace. For a striking example, we may consider Euripides' *The Bacchae*. In the first half of the play, Pentheus is established as the dedicated enemy of Dionysus. He denies the latter's divinity; he condemns him as a dissident who has disrupted the social structure of Thebes; he sees in him the source of anarchy and corruption. Even when Dionysus has demonstrated his powers by breaking loose from prison, Pentheus continues to bellow defiance:

PENTHEUS Death and destruction! The stranger I held
  In my stables a moment ago has flown!
  But here he is, in full view of the palace!
  How is this possible? How did you escape?
DIONYSUS Stay where you are. Walk easy with your anger.
PENTHEUS How did you manage to get yourself loose?
DIONYSUS Did you not hear? I said someone would free me.
PENTHEUS Who was it? All the time you talk in riddles.
DIONYSUS He who gave the bounty of the grape to men.
PENTHEUS To steal their minds, and turn them into beasts.
DIONYSUS What you account dishonour is his glory.
PENTHEUS Seal every door and gate! Let no one pass!
DIONYSUS Do you imagine walls can stop a god?
PENTHEUS You know everything but what you ought to know.
DIONYSUS I know the most important thing of all.
  But here is a messenger coming from the mountain.[28]

186

The Messenger brings word of the women waking from their Bacchic slumber, and their ravages upon the crops and cattle. Even this does not deter Pentheus. He threatens war:

DIONYSUS A happy settlement may yet be found.
PENTHEUS How? By letting serfs dictate to me?
DIONYSUS I can bring the women here to you, unarmed.
PENTHEUS What trick is this? What are you plotting now?
DIONYSUS Plotting? Nothing – but your own salvation.
PENTHEUS You have made a compact to preserve these rights.
DIONYSUS I have made a compact, yes. But with the god.
PENTHEUS So. You have had your say. Men, bring my armour.
DIONYSUS Wait![29]

Then occurs an extraordinary change. The word translated 'Wait!' above is itself unusual. It is an extrametrical syllable, a word standing alone, without a full verse line; it is a rare thing in tragedy, and breaks the normally uninterrupted musical flow of the dialogue. Its use here prepares us for the rapid volte-face that follows:

DIONYSUS Would you like to see them, sleeping, on the mountain?
PENTHEUS Yes, That I would give untold wealth to see.
DIONYSUS How has this sudden longing come upon you?
PENTHEUS And yet not drunk. I would not see them drunk.
DIONYSUS But you would gladly see them, all the same!
PENTHEUS Yes. But spying on them, under cover.
DIONYSUS You cannot hide from them. They'll scent you out.
PENTHEUS True. Then I must go there openly.
DIONYSUS You'll risk it then? Shall I conduct you there?
PENTHEUS And quickly. I grudge every wasted moment.
DIONYSUS First you must put on a fine linen dress.
PENTHEUS You mean that I must turn into a woman!
DIONYSUS If they spy a man among them, they will kill you.
PENTHEUS You speak good sense, as always. I believe you.

In a mere fourteen lines, Pentheus has attained the diametric opposite of his previous position, and from this time on is Dionysus' willing slave. Although one may argue that the reversal springs from something latent in Pentheus' character – that the young king is secretly fascinated by the practice he tries to repress – this transition, in actorly terms, is unbelievably rapid, and modern actors are un-happy with it. In a number of modern revivals, directors have sought to make the transition plausible by introducing a note of supernatural command. Dionysus makes a hypnotic gesture; or a change of pos-ition or lighting reveals him as the god in his own person, and no longer as the god in man incarnate. It is doubtful whether the Greeks would have thought the transition unusual, or justification necessary. Their theatre achieved characterization by different means, and changes of mood, even in tragedy, tend to be as rapid as changes of mask.

For our final examples we return to *Antigone*, a play whose decep-tively simple action conceals some remarkable lapses in causality and logic. How has Antigone learned of Creon's edict? Who conducts the first burial of Polyneices' body? We have suggested that these features of the play defy rational explanation, but that no rational explanation is needed: they are self-sufficient, they are justified by their own dramatic importance. We may consider two other anomalies here.

The first concerns the relationship between Creon and Teiresias. When we first see Creon, it is made apparent that he has only lately come to rule. His first speech in the play is, in fact, his inaugural address. It begins with a political platitude and an appeal to the goodwill of the council of elders, who form the chorus:

> Citizens, the state has been in troubled waters
> But now the gods have set us back on course.
> My summons came to you, of all the people
> To meet here privately, because I knew
> Your constant reverence toward Laius' throne.[30]

By a brief history of the regime, Creon goes on to establish the legitimacy of his title:

> And then, when Oedipus became our king
> After his death, I saw their children
> Secure in your unswerving loyalty.
> And now this unexpected blow has taken both
> His sons in one day, each struck down by the other.
> Each with his brother's blood upon his hand,
> The throne and all its powers come to me
> As next of kin in order of succession.

He is saying, simply, this: first came Laius, and he is dead; then came Oedipus, and he is dead; then came Eteocles and Polyneices and they are dead; and now there is no one left to inherit the throne but me. Creon goes on to establish the principles by which he intends to rule. The state comes first; personal relationships or private influence cannot be permitted to intrude upon the common good; and in demonstration of this Polyneices, who outlawed himself from the commonweal, has forfeited the rights that citizens enjoy.

At this end of the play, then, we have what is obviously the speech of a new ruler, laying down the laws by which he means to govern. The speech defines Creon precisely in his social and political context. At the other end of the play, however, we are offered something different. Teiresias has just entered, with his boy to guide him, and addresses Creon and the chorus:

> TEIRESIAS Elders of Thebes, we come here side by side,
>   One pair of eyes between us; that is how
>   Blind men must go, supported by a guide.
> CREON What word have you for us, old Teiresias?
> TEIRESIAS I will tell you. Listen when the prophet speaks.
> CREON I have never yet disregarded your advice.
> TEIRESIAS And so have kept Thebes safely on her course.
> CREON I know my debt to you, and I acknowledge it.[31]

Suddenly the whole time scheme has changed, and the relationships of the characters within it. The sense of Teiresias' words is as clear as Creon's opening speech, and the two are contradictory. Creon is now set before us as a man who has been in power for some time and who has relied on the prophet for continual help and advice; this same prophet he is now about to reject.

To find a rational justification for this shift commentators have been forced to go outside the play. They point out that although Creon has come new to rule in *Antigone*, *Oedipus the King* informs us that he had been regent before, acceding to power as guardian of Oedipus' sons when their father abdicated. But is such an explanation justifiable? Each of Sophocles' Oedipus plays stands by itself; each was written at a different period of the author's life; and *Antigone* was written first. For each play, we are entitled to take only what that play tells us, and there is no mention of a regency in *Antigone*. This is one of the numerous details that Sophocles feels free to vary as he moves from one play to another.

In purely dramatic terms, the explanation of the discrepancy must surely be this. Each statement is justified by its immediate dramatic context. At the beginning, it is important that we see Creon as a new ruler because, like all those new to authority, he is afraid to be seen changing his mind. He fears that reversing his decision would be interpreted as weakness. Persuasion and opposition merely make him more stubborn, until he is driven into a corner where his only justification is the appeal to brute authority: he argues to Haemon, as Oedipus argues to Creon in almost identical words in the later play, that a king must be obeyed.

As the play winds into its closing movements, however, Sophocles wishes to focus on another aspect of Creon's character. He wants us to see how Creon has placed himself in the position of the rebel whose body he is condemning. Polyneices' offence was that he was the supreme *idiotes*, the man who set his own interests above those of the community: by declaring war on the state, he has shown his contempt for the common will. It is the central irony of the play that Creon has now placed himself in the same dilemma. We see him confronted by a series of people who try to persuade him to abandon his untenable position: the council of elders, Antigone, his own son Haemon, who clearly voices the public feeling on this issue:

> But I can hear these murmurs in the dark,
> The feeling in the city for this girl.
> When her brother died in the slaughter, she would not
> Leave him unburied, to provide a meal
> For dogs, and beasts, and carrion birds of prey.
> Is she not, then, deserving golden honours?[32]

Creon is deaf to all these appeals. It is surely fitting, then, at the cost of some wrenching of the evidence, to show him defying Teiresias, who speaks for the supreme authority, the gods, and, in order to show this defiance as misguided, to adjust the relationship so that Creon is seen as rejecting advice that has stood him in good stead for years. Once again, each scene stands dramatically by itself. The logical discontinuity between them is unimportant.

The other example from *Antigone* is a more famous one, and has long been discussed by editors and critics. It concerns the reason for Antigone's defiance of Creon. In the prologue, and in her encounter with the king after her capture, her arguments are simple, strong, and passionate. All men are equal in death; Polyneices, whatever he may have done, is as much entitled to the ultimate decency of burial as is Eteocles. This sets the tone for the exchange near the midpoint of the play:

CREON Then why be different? Are you not ashamed?
ANTIGONE Ashamed? Of paying homage to my brother?
CREON Was not the man he killed your brother too?
ANTIGONE My brother. By one mother, by one father.
CREON Then why pay honours hateful in his sight?
ANTIGONE The dead man will not say he finds them hateful.
CREON When you honour him no higher than a traitor?
ANTIGONE It was his brother died, and not his slave.
CREON Destroying Thebes! While he died to protect it.
ANTIGONE It makes no difference. Death asks these rites.[33]

The vivid cut and thrust of dialogue – tragic *stichomythia* at its best – evokes a girl who acts from an instinctive urge to protect her own; who acts without stopping to reason. Earlier in the play she has been described, in a strikingly feral image, as a bird screaming its agony over an empty nest. How ill this picture of Antigone accords with her death speech. As she is led to her tomb by Creon's guards, passion is replaced by reasoned self-justification, instinctive revulsion by a frigid logic.

Yet wisdom would approve my honouring you.
If I were a mother; if my husband's body
Were left to rot, I never would have dared
Defy the state to do as I have done.
What argument can justify such words?
Why, if my husband died, I could take another.
Someone else would give me a child, if I lost the first
But death has hidden my mother and father from me;
No brother can be born to me again.
Those are the reasons why I chose to honour
You; and for this Creon judges me guilty
Of outrage and transgression, brother mine.[34]

It is hard, perhaps impossible, to reconcile these two Antigones. The problem is compounded by the close resemblance between this speech and a passage in Herodotus, where an identical argument is placed in the mouth of a noble Persian lady whose family has been condemned to death for treason. Offered the life of any one – but only one – she chooses, she selects her brother, and justifies her choice in Antigone's terms. Some scholars have therefore been led to dismiss the speech as plagiarism by an unknown hand from Herodotus (though the reverse might equally be true; he and Sophocles were contemporaries) and excise it from the play. Even without so desperate a remedy, the difficulty remains. Antigone speaks with different voices, at different moments of the play.

We should note, first, that if we take the death speech in isolation it has a valid point to make, and one that relates powerfully to a central issue of the play. The point is that Antigone is now completely alone. Her mother and father are dead; her brothers are dead; she has never had a husband, or a child. This the speech spells out for us; and we have, only two episodes before, seen her reject her one surviving relative, her sister Ismene. Her isolation, at this moment of the play, presages that of Creon at the end. He is left, as she is left, alone. His last surviving son, Haemon, commits suicide; his wife Eurydice stabs herself; he has rejected the aid and succour of Teiresias. Coming to the central issue from opposed points of view, Creon and Antigone have reduced themselves to the same position.

The speech, then, is dramatically valid in its place; and, in the light of the other examples we have seen, the discrepancy between it and Antigone's earlier utterances should no longer concern us. Each statement is appropriate to its context. A modern sensibility, conditioned to view a dramatic character as a psychological whole, finds the discrepancy disturbing. The Greek sensibility, trained to see character as a series of disconnected appearances, would have found it merely appropriate. The tragic character, no less than the comic, adapts himself to his immediate environment.

NOTES

1   THE AUDIENCE AND THE CHORUS

1 Paul Mazon, 'La farce dans Aristophane et les origines de la comédie en Grèce', *Revue d'Histoire du Théâtre*, III, 1 (1951), pp. 7–18.
2 Aristophanes, *The Frogs*, v. 945.
3 Euripides, *Medea*, vv. 825ff.
4 Euripides, *Medea*, vv. 1,339ff.
5 Aristophanes, *The Frogs*, v. 298.
6 The story makes its first appearance in literature long after the event, in Aelian, *Varia Historia*, II, 13.
7 Aristophanes, *The Birds*, vv. 1,105ff.
8 Aristophanes, *The Clouds*, vv. 1,115ff.
9 Sophocles, *Oedipus the King*, vv. 895ff. They use the verb *choreuein*.
10 Aeschylus, *The Eumenides*, vv. 482ff.
11 Aeschylus, *The Eumenides*, vv. 566ff.
12 Herbert Blau, *The Impossible Theatre*, New York, Macmillan, 1964, p. 331.
13 William M. Calder III, 'The staging of the prologue of *Oedipus Tyrannus*,' *Phoenix*, XIII, 3 (1959), p. 121.
14 Antiphon, *On the Chorus-trainer*, 11.
15 Aeschylus, *Agamemnon*, vv. 1,346ff.
16 Aeschylus, *The Libation Bearers*, vv. 931ff.
17 Sophocles, *Oedipus the King*, vv. 1,100ff.
18 Aeschylus, *Agamemnon*, vv. 40ff.
19 Aeschylus, *Agamemnon*, vv. 60ff.
20 Aeschylus, *Agamemnon*, vv. 72ff.
21 Aeschylus, *Agamemnon*, vv. 83ff.
22 Aeschylus, *Agamemnon*, vv. 104ff.
23 Aeschylus, *Agamemnon*, vv. 227ff.
24 Aeschylus, *Agamemnon*, vv. 1,481ff.
25 Aeschylus, *Prometheus Bound*, vv. 407ff.
26 Sophocles, *Antigone*, vv. 944ff.
27 Euripides, *Medea*, vv. 1,282ff.

28 Sophocles, *Antigone*, vv. 211ff.
29 Sophocles, *Antigone*, vv. 724f.
30 Sophocles, *Antigone*, vv. 801ff.
31 Sophocles, *Oedipus the King*, vv. 483ff.

2 THE ACTOR SEEN

1 Euripides, *Alcestis*, vv. 1,143ff.
2 Euripides, *Alcestis*, v. 392.
3 Aristotle, *Rhetoric*, III, 1403b 22.
4 Aristotle, *Poetics*, 1461b 34, 1462a 9.
5 Aristotle, *Rhetoric*, III, 1403b 33.
6 Aristotle, *Poetics*, 1462a 5, 12.
7 Plutarch, *De Recta Ratione Audiendi*, 46b.
8 Euripides, *Hecuba*, vv. 342ff.
9 T.B.L. Webster, *Greek Theatre Production*, London, Methuen, 1970, p. xiv.
10 Aeschines, *Against Timarchus*, 25.
11 Quintilian, *The Art of Oratory*, XI, 3, 85ff.
12 Quintilian, *The Art of Oratory*, XI, 3, 68, 96, 166, 123.
13 Plutarch, *Quaestionum Convivalium* IX, 747A–748E.
14 Herodotus, *Histories*, VI, 129.
15 Plato, *Laws*, VII, 816a.
16 Euripides, *The Phoenician Women*, vv. 313ff.
17 Euripides, *The Trojan Women*, vv. 332ff.
18 Pollux, *Onomasticon*, IV, 103–5.
19 Athenaeus, *Deipnosophistai*, XIV, 629.
20 Aeschylus, *The Eumenides*, vv. 34ff.
21 Euripides, *Hecuba*, vv. 1,056ff.
22 Webster, *op. cit.*, p. 4.
23 Sophocles, *Oedipus at Colonus*, vv. 1,267ff.
24 Euripides, *Medea*, vv. 1,056ff.
25 Quintilian, *The Art of Oratory*, XI, 3, 83.
26 Sophocles, *The Women of Trachis*, vv. 1,181ff.
27 Euripides, *Medea*, vv. 496ff.
28 Euripides, *Hippolytus*, vv. 198ff.
29 Quintilian, *The Art of Oratory*, XI, 3, 84.
30 Xenophon, *Symposium*, 11, 16.
31 Quintilian, *The Art of Oratory*, XI, 3, 103.
32 Quintilian, *The Art of Oratory*, XI, 3, 89.
33 Euripides, *Hecuba*, vv. 59ff.

3 THE ACTOR HEARD

1 Euripides, *Hippolytus*, vv. 1,249ff.
2 Aristophanes, *The Clouds*, vv. 758ff.
3 Euripides, *Hippolytus*, vv. 601ff.
4 Aristophanes, *The Frogs*, v. 1,471.

5 Aristotle, *Rhetoric*, III, 1 passim.
6 Aristotle, *Nicomachean Ethics*, 1118a.
7 pseudo-Plutarch, *The Lives of the Ten Orators*, 848b.
8 Diogenes Laertius, *Lives and Opinions of Eminent Philosophers*, VII, 20.
9 Plato, *Laws*, 817c.
10 Vitruvius, *On Architecture*, V, 7; for other amplification devices, see V, 5.
11 Plato, *Republic*, 397.
12 Plato, *Laws*, 665–6.
13 Plutarch, *Moralia*, 737b.
14 Sophocles, *Oedipus at Colonus*, vv. 14ff.
15 Aristotle, *Politics*, 1336b 28. It is difficult to see how Theodorus accomplished this. We know that several of his roles were not the first characters to appear in the plays as written. Perhaps he altered the texts to gratify his ego; this is certainly consonant with what we know of fourth-century actors and their attitude towards their scripts.
16 Euripides, *The Madness of Heracles*, vv. 63ff.
17 Euripides, *The Madness of Heracles*, vv. 825ff.
18 Euripides, *The Bacchae*, vv. 604ff.
19 Euripides, *The Bacchae*, vv. 717ff.
20 Aeschylus, *The Libation Bearers*, vv. 560ff.
21 Sophocles, *Antigone*, vv. 155f.
22 Sophocles, *Antigone*, vv. 626f.
23 Aeschylus, *Agamemnon*, v. 493.
24 Euripides, *The Bacchae*, vv. 210ff.
25 Sophocles, *Antigone*, vv. 988ff.
26 Euripides, *Medea*, vv. 496ff.
27 Euripides, *The Bacchae*, vv. 845f.
28 Euripides, *Medea*, vv. 96ff. She interrupts several times during the scene, and it is always made clear to the audience who is speaking.
29 Euripides, *Medea*, v. 1,273.
30 Euripides, *The Bacchae*, vv. 576ff.
31 Aeschylus, *The Libation Bearers*, vv. 184ff.
32 Sophocles, *Antigone*, vv. 801ff.
33 Sophocles, *Antigone*, vv. 526ff.
34 Sophocles, *Oedipus at Colonus*, vv. 1,249ff.
35 Sophocles, *Oedipus at Colonus*, vv. 1,356ff.
36 A number of examples have already been cited to show the Greeks' perception of their theatre as a primarily oral medium. We may contrast the overwhelming testimony to the primarily *visual* appeal of the modern theatre. Here are two, at random: Elmer Rice in *The Living Theatre* (New York, Harper, 1959, p. 265) on Gordon Craig: 'While he is certainly right in his contention that most people go to the theatre to *see* plays performed . . .'; and Stark Young, *Immortal Shadows* (New York, Hill & Wang, 1948, p. 7): 'Of the two sensuous avenues by which the art of the theatre is apprehended, the eye and the ear, the eye at present is the one we travel most importantly.'
37 Euripides, *Medea*, vv. 521ff.
38 Euripides, *Hippolytus*, vv. 236ff.; vv. 1,038ff.

39 Euripides, *The Bacchae*, vv. 266ff.
40 Sophocles, *Electra*, vv. 1,033ff.
41 Sophocles, *Electra*, vv. 877ff.
42 Sophocles, *Oedipus the King*, vv. 622ff.
43 In *Aeschylus and Athens*, London, Lawrence & Wishart, 1941, pp. 189–91.
44 'The structure of *stichomythia* in Attic tragedy', *Proceedings of the British Academy*, XXXV.
45 Sophocles, *Oedipus the King*, vv. 1,152ff.
46 Sophocles, *Antigone*, vv. 681f.; 724f.
47 Aeschylus, *The Eumenides*, vv. 437ff.

4 DEBATE AND DRAMA

1 Aristophanes, *The Clouds*, vv. 1,336ff.
2 So Jean-Paul Sartre on the characters of Greek tragedy: 'they are all lawyers; and we must remember that the Greeks loved lawyers' (interview with Kenneth Tynan, *Observer*, 18 June 1961).
3 'The criticism of Greek tragedy', *Tulane Drama Review*, III, 3 (March 1959), p. 37.
4 Euripides, *Medea*, vv. 475ff.
5 Euripides, *Hippolytus*, vv. 958ff.
6 Euripides, *Hippolytus*, vv. 1,320ff.
7 Sophocles, *Antigone*, vv. 639ff.
8 Euripides, *Medea*, vv. 1,021ff.
9 Aeschylus, *Agamemnon*, vv. 1,054ff.
10 Aeschylus, *Agamemnon*, vv. 1,331ff.
11 Aeschylus, *The Libation Bearers*, vv. 299ff.
12 Euripides, *Medea*, vv. 816f.
13 Euripides, *Medea*, v. 1,396.

5 PLACE AND TIME

1 Sophocles, *Philoctetes*, vv. 1,452ff.
2 Euripides, *The Madness of Heracles*, v. 905.
3 Euripides, *The Bacchae*, vv. 585ff.
4 Aristophanes, *The Clouds*, v. 92.
5 Aristophanes, *The Clouds*, vv. 126ff.
6 Aristophanes, *The Clouds*, vv. 700ff.
7 Euripides, *Medea*, vv. 886ff.
8 Euripides, *Medea*, vv. 774ff.
9 Sophocles, *Oedipus the King*, vv. 1,511ff.
10 Aeschylus, *Agamemnon*, vv. 76ff.
11 Sophocles, *Oedipus the King*, vv. 760ff.
12 Aeschylus, *Agamemnon*, vv. 280ff.
13 Sophocles, *Antigone*, vv. 93ff.
14 Sophocles, *Antigone*, vv. 332ff.
15 Aeschylus, *Prometheus Bound*, vv. 447ff.

16 Aeschylus, *Prometheus Bound*, vv. 407ff.
17 Aeschylus, *Prometheus Bound*, vv. 723ff.
18 Aeschylus, *Prometheus Bound*, vv. 807ff.
19 Aeschylus, *Agamemnon*, vv. 1,217ff.
20 Aeschylus, *Agamemnon*, vv. 1,186ff.
21 Euripides, *The Bacchae*, vv. 976ff.
22 Euripides, *Cyclops*, vv. 212f.
23 Euripides, *Cyclops*, vv. 541ff.
24 Euripides, *The Bacchae*, vv. 199ff.
25 Aeschylus, *Prometheus Bound*, vv. 365ff.
26 Euripides, *Hecuba*, vv. 455ff.

6 CHARACTERS AND CONTINUITY

1 Aeschylus, *The Libation Bearers*, vv. 973ff.
2 Aeschylus, *The Libation Bearers*, vv. 831ff.
3 Aeschylus, *The Libation Bearers*, vv. 1,046f.
4 Euripides, *The Bacchae*, vv. 337ff.
5 Euripides, *The Bacchae*, vv. 632f.
6 Euripides, *The Bacchae*, vv. 737ff.
7 Euripides, *The Bacchae*, vv. 830–3; 836–8.
8 Euripides, *The Bacchae*, vv. 857f.
9 Euripides, *The Bacchae*, vv. 1,115ff.
10 Euripides, *The Madness of Heracles*, vv. 327ff.
11 Euripides, *The Madness of Heracles*, vv. 422ff.
12 Euripides, *The Madness of Heracles*, vv. 525–8; 562–4.
13 Euripides, *Hippolytus*, vv. 198ff.
14 Aeschylus, *Agamemnon*, vv. 944ff.
15 Aeschylus, *Agamemnon*, vv. 1,264ff.
16 Euripides, *Medea*, vv. 1,156–62; 1,185–94; 1,200–1.
17 Aeschylus, *The Persians*, vv. 832ff.
18 Aeschylus, *The Persians*, vv. 845ff.
19 Aeschylus, *The Persians*, v. 1,017.
20 Aeschylus, *The Eumenides*, vv. 1,003ff.
21 Aristophanes, *The Acharnians*, vv. 497ff.
22 Aristophanes, *The Acharnians*, v. 578.
23 Aristophanes, *The Acharnians*, vv. 593ff.
24 Aristophanes, *The Frogs*, v. 62.
25 Aristophanes, *The Frogs*, vv. 83ff.
26 Aristophanes, *The Clouds*, vv. 98f.
27 Euripides, *Medea*, vv. 844ff.
28 Euripides, *The Bacchae*, vv. 642ff.
29 Euripides, *The Bacchae*, vv. 802ff.
30 Sophocles, *Antigone*, vv. 163ff.
31 Sophocles, *Antigone*, vv. 988ff.
32 Sophocles, *Antigone*, vv. 692ff.
33 Sophocles, *Antigone*, vv. 510ff.
34 Sophocles, *Antigone*, vv. 904ff.

SELECT BIBLIOGRAPHY

In addition to the works already cited in the text, the following offer coverage of particular areas of Greek play production.

Bieber, Margarete, *The History of the Greek and Roman Theater*, 2nd edn, Princeton, NJ, Princeton University Press, 1961.

Cornford, Francis M., *The Origin of Attic Comedy*, London, Cambridge University Press, 1934.

Dearden, C.W., *The Stage of Aristophanes*, London, Athlone, 1976.

Lawler, Lillian B., *The Dance in Ancient Greece*, London, A. & C. Black, 1964.

Pickard-Cambridge, Sir Arthur, *The Dramatic Festivals of Athens*, Oxford, Clarendon, 1953.

Pickard-Cambridge, Sir Arthur, *The Theatre of Dionysus in Athens*, Oxford, Clarendon, 1946.

Taplin, Oliver, *Greek Tragedy in Action*, London, Methuen, 1978.

Taplin, Oliver, *The Stagecraft of Aeschylus*, Oxford, Clarendon, 1977.

Walton, J. Michael, *The Greek Sense of Theatre*, London, Methuen, 1984.

Walton, J. Michael, *Greek Theatre Practice*, London, Greenwood, 1980.

Webster, T. B. L. *The Greek Chorus*, London, Methuen, 1970.

Webster, T. B. L., *Monuments Illustrating Old and Middle Comedy*, London, Institute of Classical Studies, 1978.

Webster, T. B. L., *Monuments Illustrating Tragedy and Satyr Play*, I, London, Institute of Classical Studies, 1962.

Webster, T. B. L., *Monuments Illustrating Tragedy and Satyr Play*, II, London, Institute of Classical Studies, 1967.

INDEX

199